SOUTHERN EXPOSURE

CANADIAN PERSPECTIVES ON THE UNITED STATES

DATE DUE

BRODART   Cat. No. 23-221

SERIES LIST

McGraw-Hill Ryerson Series in Canadian Politics
General Editor—Paul W. Fox

POLITICS: Canada, 5th Edition
Paul W. Fox
CANADIAN FOREIGN POLICY
D.C. Thomas & R.F. Swanson
THE CONSTITUTIONAL PROCESS IN CANADA, 2nd Edition
R.I. Cheffins & R.N. Tucker
POLITICAL PARTIES AND IDEOLOGIES IN CANADA, 2nd Edition
W. Christian & C. Campbell
PRESSURE GROUP BEHAVIOUR IN CANADIAN POLITICS
A. Paul Pross
POLITICAL PARTIES IN CANADA
C. Winn & J.C. McMenemy
GOVERNMENT IN CANADA
T.A. Hockin
LOCAL GOVERNMENT IN CANADA, 2nd Edition
C.R. Tindal & S. Nobes Tindal
PUBLIC POLICY AND PROVINCIAL POLITICS
M. Chandler and W. Chandler
POLITICAL CHOICE IN CANADA (Abridged Edition)
Harold D. Clarke, Jane Jenson, Lawrence LeDuc, Jon H. Pammett
CANADIAN FOREIGN POLICY: Contemporary Issues and Themes
Michael Tucker
POLITICS AND THE MEDIA IN CANADA
Arthur Siegel
CANADA IN QUESTION: Federalism in the Eighties, 3rd Edition
D.V. Smiley
THE L-SHAPED PARTY: The Liberal Party of Canada 1958–1980
Joseph Wearing
WOMEN AND POLITICS IN CANADA
Janine Brodie
THE REVISED CANADIAN CONSTITUTION: Politics as Law
R. Cheffins and P. Johnson
SOUTHERN EXPOSURE: Canadian Perspectives on the United States
David Flaherty and William McKercher

Forthcoming

GOVERNMENT IN CANADA, 2nd Edition
T.A. Hockin
CANADA'S JUDICIAL SYSTEM
Peter H. Russell
CANADIAN PARLIAMENTARY SYSTEM
Paul G. Thomas
CANADIAN FOREIGN POLICY, 2nd Edition
Michael J. Tucker
FEDERAL CONDITION IN CANADA
D.V. Smiley

SOUTHERN EXPOSURE
CANADIAN PERSPECTIVES ON THE UNITED STATES

Edited with an Introduction by

DAVID H. FLAHERTY
WILLIAM R. McKERCHER

McGraw-Hill Ryerson Limited

Toronto   Montreal   New York   Auckland   Bogotá
Cairo   Hamburg   Johannesburg   Lisbon   London
Madrid   Mexico   Milan   New Delhi   Panama   Paris
San Juan   São Paulo   Singapore   Sydney   Tokyo

SOUTHERN EXPOSURE:

CANADIAN PERSPECTIVES ON THE UNITED STATES

ISBN: 0-07-549179-6

1 2 3 4 5 6 7 8 9 0 W 5 4 3 2 1 0 9 8 7 6

Printed and bound in Canada

Cover and book design by Dave Hader
Production editor: Hilary Kitney

Canadian Cataloguing in Publication Data

Main entry under title:

Southern exposure: Canadian Perspectives on the U.S.

(McGraw-Hill Ryerson series in Canadian politics)
Bibliography: p.
Includes index.
ISBN 0-07-549179-6

1. Canada – Relations – United States – Addresses, essays, lectures.   2. United States – Relations – Canada – Addresses, essays, lectures.   I. Flaherty, David H. II. McKercher, William Russell, date— .   III. Series

FC249.S68 1986   327.71073   C86-093817-4
F1029.5.U6S68 1986

Table of Contents

Foreword

All of the twenty books published previously in the McGraw-Hill Ryerson Series in Canadian Politics have dealt with specific aspects of Canadian government. *Southern Exposure: Canadian Perspectives on the United States* is the first book in the Series to focus on another polity.

Yet the inclusion of such a book in this Series is very appropriate, since nothing could be more Canadian than worrying about our relationship to the United States. Historically, it has been a national preoccupation. Practically, it is a matter of the greatest consequence, since a small country cannot escape the effects of living next door to a colossus.

Southern Exposure not only examines how Canadians view the United States but it also probes deeply into the nature and causes of our concerns. Nineteen eminent Canadian authorities analyze the major problems we have with the United States, ranging through politics, economics, and culture to urban affairs, and the environment and resources. Using these subdivisions, the editors have grouped the contributions together in five parts, prefacing each part with a brief summary and analysis of the contents. They also have added to the whole book a long and useful introduction which serves as an overview.

Professors Flaherty and McKercher are to be congratulated on their editorial accomplishment. They have taken a series of lectures and conference papers given at the University of Western Ontario in 1984 and 1985 and converted them into a highly readable, informative, and stimulating book with a consistent theme.

The theme is the way in which Canadians view the United States. This approach has the great merit of allowing the contributors to analyze the familiar problems that beset Canada–United States relations, while at the same time permitting them to express their own particular perspectives. The result is a refreshing and lively discussion in which some of the authors disagree not only with traditional views but with one another's opinions.

It is not every day that we are told, for instance, that "Canada . . . does not exist. What exists, in reality, is Canadians. 'Canada' is a legal fiction."

The contributors agree, however, on one point. Despite the common assumption to the contrary, Canadians have not devoted much effort to studying the United States *per se*. We have been quick to consider the impact of the United States on Canada but reluctant to study American problems objectively as scholars.

Southern Exposure: Canadian Perspectives on the United States does a good deal to remedy that deficiency. We can be grateful to the editors and the contributors for giving us a fresh and provocative look at our southern neighbour.

Erindale College,   Paul W. Fox
University of Toronto,   General Editor
15 April 1986

Preface

This volume is meant to promote an understanding of the political power and the cultural heterogeneity of the United States of America. For Canadians, such preeminent power has had an overwhelming impact that, be it benevolent or threatening, is undoubtedly one of the dominant influences upon us as a nation. We cannot ignore the domestic and international policy goals, the cultural chauvinism, the messianic pursuit of "life, liberty, and property," and the institutional and political peculiarities of the wealthiest and most powerful nation in the world. By fate and design the United States is our nearest neighbour and closest ally.

It is clear that the all-pervasive influence of the United States on Canada is a fact of life to which Canadians have often reacted with resignation, if not chagrin. The identification and analysis of Canadian perspectives on the United States should help to encourage an attitude whereby Canadians will be better able to create a future relationship, and pursue policy options that are preemptive as well as reactive.

The focus on "Canadian Perspectives on the United States" is intended to serve as the impetus for the development of a new and clearer understanding of the impact of the United States on Canada. In essence, the Canadian reaction and perspective are implicit in the greater appreciation of the bicultural and multicultural nature of the Canadian experience of nation-building. Thus, in trying to understand the United States, we tend to confirm our own national aspirations within our own cultural, linguistic, and multiracial identity.

There is a substantial literature on Canadian-American relations (mostly from the Canadian side) that has arisen from nationalistic critiques of the American presence in Canada. There is also, however, a growing literature on Canada from the American perspective promoted by Canadian studies programs at universities in the United States. This volume does not propose simply to adopt the methodology of comparative analysis in order to complement past endeavours from either side of the border. Instead we plan to engage in an interdisciplinary study. The methodological basis of the research, we hope, will be as diverse as the scholars contributing to the study.

The basic question we must ask is: what do people in Canada reflect upon when they examine the United States from their particular perspective? Within each major subject, we identify several topics of discussion that reflect some of the most pressing contemporary issues that arise in Canada's perception of, and relationship with, the United States. These topics are reflected in the various sections of the book.

This volume had its origin at the Centre for American Studies at the University of Western Ontario, specifically in a lecture series for the academic year 1984-85, and in a conference in May, 1985, entitled "Canadian Perspectives on the United States." The contributors are all distinguished Canadians with varying backgrounds in diplomacy, business, economics, literature, geography, and political science.

We are most grateful to them for the opportunity to publish their work. Articles have been revised and edited to reflect the standards of written presentations rather more than the oral form in which they were originally delivered, yet the style of these pages consciously reflects the introductory and admittedly provocative character of the enterprise.

We are also grateful to the following for their support of the Centre for American Studies and of this conference: the Faculties of Social Science and Arts, and the Academic Development Fund, the University of Western Ontario; the Social Sciences and Humanities Research Council of Canada; Northern Telecom Ltd.; and the United States Embassy, Ottawa. Two successive deans of the Faculty of Social Science at Western, B.B. Kymlicka and Denis Smith, have been instrumental in the creation, shaping, and support of the Centre for American Studies. We also wish to thank our secretaries, Penelope Lister and Frances Kyle for their contributions to the preparation of this volume. Finally, a number of our colleagues at the Centre for American Studies made timely contributions to the original conference and to the preparation of this volume.

David H. Flaherty
Director, Centre for
American Studies
Professor of History and Law
The University of Western Ontario

William R. McKercher
Department of History and
Political Science
King's College
The University of Western Ontario

London, Ontario
14 February 1986

Canadian Perspectives on the United States

David H. Flaherty
and
William R. McKercher

This book is the collaborative work of many authors, all of whom were given a seemingly simple task: to use their cumulative knowledge to provide us with a view of the United States from the perspective of their individual, practical, and academic experience. They have brought us many perspectives; not only have they given us a taste of their disciplines, but they have shown a considerable diversity of opinion. In short, they have forcefully shown us that there is no single, dominant Canadian perspective.

1. The Variety of Canadian Perspectives

This volume originated with the question: "What are the Canadian perspectives on the United States?" Its primary finding is that they are many, varied, and even contradictory. It is also evident that Canadians have only begun to refine their views in this regard.

We have a range of motives for wanting to understand the United States, beginning with our own self-interest in attempting to comprehend the motives and policies of American decision makers. But there are also benefits to Canada in having the United States understand us better, and prospective benefits for the United States of friendly criticism. Often, to criticize America in the United States is akin to engaging in an act of betrayal. On the other hand, external criticism is often viewed as blatant anti-Americanism. But criticism, like praise, must be tempered by an appreciation of its source. Canadians, neither European nor American, colony nor empire, weak nor powerful, are in an excellent position to make a contribution to the study of the United States.

It would surprise most Canadians that producing Canadian perspectives on the United States should need any kind of formal justification. The results of the process may need to be evaluated in terms of their relevance and utility, but the ability to observe and reflect is well established within the Canadian literature. The real issue, as argued by Denis Smith in this volume,

1

is why Canadian perspectives on the United States have not appeared earlier and been more sustained and diverse in their character. The fact that we have not written more to date about the United States from a Canadian perspective is a fascinating intellectual question in itself, as the Smith essay suggests.

This volume is, in every sense of the word, a first step, yet it continues a tradition that was for a time almost wholly identified with strident Canadian nationalists. Their domination of the literature has waned. The origins of this book, in public lectures and an academic conference, mean that the essays offered are not systematic nor all-encompassing. It is unfortunate, for example, that the book does not adequately reflect a francophone perspective on the United States, although William Johnson's timely observations reflect his knowledge and experience in Quebec. One could also argue that there ought to be representation from the Maritimes. At least this volume does not have a typical central-Canadian orientation, since the Western provinces of Canada are especially well represented by contributors. We believe that this book will be of benefit to those who would like to know more about the United States from a non-American point of view. We thus present a variety of regional perspectives in the process of helping to explain the United States to Canadians and to Americans.

2. The Reactions of Canadians to the United States

Perhaps the only thread of consistency weaving through Canadian-American relations is the theme of reaction. As early as 1781, Article XI of the Articles of Confederation agreed to by the American states sought to give aid and comfort to the northern English colonies by opening the door to their participation in the new union. The northern colonies were given the opportunity to be free from the tyranny of George III. But the northern colonists, together with the United Empire Loyalists, the traitors to the American revolution, and the recently conquered French, reacted with hostility or indifference. The War of 1812 with its invasion of Canadian soil by United States troops (who were repulsed) established anti-Americanism as part of the Canadian national consciousness. It has remained there ever since.

Yet many Canadians admired the American experiment with democracy and republicanism. There was a sympathetic reaction from some of the rebellious factions in British North America dissatisfied with the ruling cliques who espoused conservative values. Those who led the Upper Canadian Rebellion of 1837 were strongly influenced by the ideals of Jacksonian democracy. Louis Joseph Papineau of Lower Canada admired Jefferson and his faith in the inviolability of individual natural rights. In 1849, a group of prominent tories including John Abbott and Alexander Galt even went so far as to sign an Annexation Manifesto in Montreal. These anglophones, the latter to become a father of Confederation, the former a prime minister of Canada (1891–1892), were arguably more anti-French than pro-American. Nonetheless they believed that the prosperity of Canada lay in greater trade with the United States. About the same time, the British were decreasing military spending in the North American colonies and were denuding Canada of armed personnel. Apparently the American threat was not as great as it had been earlier in the century when it seemed obvious that Canada needed to be protected.

In 1865 the victorious northern army in the United States was over a million strong, the south lay in ruins, the republic stretched from sea to sea, and Mexico had been subdued. Only the northern colonies stood in the way of continental Manifest Destiny. Unlike Mexico, they could be easily absorbed, French inhabitants and all. Although Alaska was for sale (and bought from Russia in 1867), the British colonies were not. Annexation was an alternative, but not, according to the British, without Canadian consent.

Politicians from British North America and British statesmen reacted quickly and forcefully by adopting the British North America Act of 1867. A new nation was created, but its constitution was in clear reaction to what British North American politicians believed to be the weaknesses in the American system of government. Under the British North America Act (most of which was written in 1864 in Quebec City), Canada, the new federal state, was given a strong national government, which was to uphold "peace, order and good government." This was in direct contrast to the Constitution of the United States which had reserved non-enumerated legislative powers to the states—a problem resolved by the Civil War, and subsequent decisions by the United States Supreme Court, which decided important issues of jurisdiction predominantly in favour of the federal government. In Canada, the French-Canadians, a linguistic, cultural, and religious minority, were granted specific constitutional rights in the areas of civil law, religion, and education. Canada was created as if in fearful response to George Brown's view of 1865 that "the Americans are now a war-like people."[1]

Although they have fought no wars against one another since 1814, the two countries have a history of disputes that were more often than not seen by Canadians to be settled in favour of the United States. Such was the case with the Alaska boundary dispute of 1903, where the Americans were awarded the Alaska panhandle and Canadians saw the settlement as a British sell-out. Disputes over sea boundaries and fisheries continue to be major irritants, despite the exemplary work of our oldest bilateral institution, the International Joint Commission (IJC), established by the Boundary Waters Treaty of 1909. In 1984, the Gulf of Maine (Georges Bank) fisheries dispute was settled by the International Court of Justice (World Court) to the satisfaction of both countries. This was more than just a fish settlement, since it allowed the respective governments to lease the sea bed for future oil and mineral exploration.

Historically, as Ambassador Allan Gotlieb states in this volume, the major concern of the Canadian diplomat has been to deal with issues such as "boundary waters, fisheries questions, and territorial seas." But one might add that the relationship is far more diverse and complicated, more intricate, emotive, and regionally based than traditional diplomatic concerns would suggest. Canadians have reacted to the United States for a multitude of reasons, which as much reflect a "public mood" as they do the policy priorities of Canadian governments dominated by regional interests and the often contradictory visions of their leaders. Sir Wilfrid Laurier lost the 1911 national election over the issue of reciprocity. R.B. Bennett, Conservative prime minister from 1930 to 1935, tried to emulate President Roosevelt's New Deal with his own "Fair Deal." After the disastrous effect of the 1930 Smoot-Hawley tariff on Canadian-American trade, he campaigned in what would be his last election to reopen the borders.[2] William Lyon Mackenzie King, Canada's longest serving prime minister, also attempted to seek closer economic ties. His friendship with Roosevelt was instrumental in the establishment of the Permanent Joint Board on Defence in 1940. King's hand-picked Liberal successor, Louis St. Laurent (1948-1957), closely cooperated with the United States during the Suez Canal crisis of 1956. His Minister of External Affairs, Lester Pearson, subsequently won the Nobel Peace Prize for his efforts to establish a United Nations peacekeeping force in the Middle East. St. Laurent's government also defined and created a role for Canada in the North Atlantic Treaty Organization (NATO) by actively supporting the American drive to consolidate the military and economic power of the Western European countries.

John Diefenbaker, the populist, nationalist, Progressive Conservative prime minister from 1957 to 1963, opposed American policy on Cuba, and was not consulted on the American defence posture during the Cuban missile crisis of 1962, yet he had earlier agreed to participate in the North American Air Defence (NORAD) agreement on the understanding that it was an agreement on the "common defence" of North America. He ultimately refused nuclear warheads for Canada. He nearly destroyed the Canadian aerospace industry with the cancellation of the Avro Arrow project in 1959.[3] This helped to prolong the so-called "brain drain," as much of the Canadian research community sought opportunities south of the border. Canada has had a weaker research and development establishment ever since, although it maintains a share of defence research as a result of the Defence Production Sharing Arrangements of 1959, made by Diefenbaker.

Lester Pearson followed Diefenbaker and remained in office until 1968. He first accepted and then rid Canada of nuclear weapons. He publicly disagreed with President Johnson on Vietnam policy (to no noticeable effect) and allowed American draft dodgers to live in relatively comfortable exile while in violation of American law. The war in Vietnam introduced what was in effect a reverse movement of talented persons to Canada. Some became ardent Canadian nationalists, leading to what has been called the "Americanization of Canadian anti-Americanism."[4]

Pearson's successor, Pierre Elliott Trudeau, although a fierce opponent of nationalism, sought to strengthen the cultural and economic independence of Canada, while attempting to make the Québécois comfortable within confederation and the rest of Canada comfortable with the "French fact." His Third Option of 1972 was a proposal to reduce Canada's economic dependence upon the United States by calling for closer economic ties with Europe and Japan. This strategy became obsolete by decade's end. But the Trudeau government's creations, the Foreign Investment Review Agency (FIRA) in 1974, and the National Energy Program in 1980, led to a greater Canadianization of the economy than even most avowed nationalists could have foreseen.

Constitutional reform and the patriation of the British North America Act preoccupied Trudeau in his last years in office. On 17 April 1982, Canada "patriated" its constitution, which included a new amending formula and a national bill of rights. Trudeau's constitutional reform was achieved at the cost of great acrimony between the federal and provincial governments. Ironically, it can be argued that the Constitution Act, 1982, through the instrument of the Charter of Rights and Freedoms, will lead to the Americanization of our judicial system and will mark the beginning of a "rights culture" similar to that of the litigiously-minded Americans. Our new constitution obviously owes much to the American experience.[5]

Brian Mulroney, who came to office in September, 1984, fully intended to implement what he saw as the conservative answer to the burgeoning welfare state. His declared intention to encourage free enterprise has prompted him to attempt the reform of the social welfare system, the reduction of the federal deficit, the simplification of the tax laws, and the deregulation of gas, oil, transportation and communications. This is but another example of a Canadian prime minister attempting to copy, or take advantage of, American political initiatives and apply them to Canada. As Bennett wanted to emulate Roosevelt, so Mulroney presents Reaganomics to Canada. Ever observant of the opinion polls, however, he has not had the initial success of President Reagan, or of Britain's Prime Minister Margaret Thatcher, both of whom use their particular brands of conservative philosophy to push through untested national policies.

The issue of free trade did not die after 1911. Mackenzie King had tried secretly to negotiate a free trade agreement in 1948, only to back away at the last moment. Meanwhile, the United States market share of Canadian trade has grown from 38 per cent in 1911 to 75 per cent in 1985. Mulroney, with the support of a majority of the provincial premiers, the backing of the 1985 *Report of the Royal Commission on the Economic Union and Development Prospects for Canada* (the Macdonald Commission), some manufacturing and resource industries, and the Canadian Chamber of Commerce, began a process in 1985 seeking to guarantee Canada a secure place in the global economy by negotiating a trade agreement with the United States. Canadians, ever looking southward to create a strategy for the defence of the nation, are now about to engage in an offensive foray as a response, a reaction, to the new economic orthodoxy, whose advocates maintain that Canada requires membership in an economic trading bloc. The question is: will Canadians accept the political and cultural uncertainties of a restructured economic partnership with the United States? Free trade is a "leap of faith" like the Auto Pact of 1965. The Pact has at times been unfavourable to Canada's balance of trade. Yet, today, automobile manufacture and related industries are the backbone of the economy of Ontario and a major factor in Canada's trade surplus with the United States. Advocates of a new agreement point to the Auto Pact and state that it is time to give other regions of Canada the same opportunity.

It was contended by many a British sage in 1776 and 1789 that the Thirteen Colonies could not survive as an economic or a political entity. It is said in 1986 by, among others, Bruce Wilkinson in this volume, that Canada, like Hawaii, might not be able to resist political absorption into the United States. We have yet to live up to Laurier's forecast that the "twentieth century will belong to Canada." Our historical predilection to react to American domestic policy is likely to be a poignant feature of Canadian politics well into the twenty-first century and this may be even more important than it has been in the past century.

3. The Canadian-American Relationship

It has been said all too often that the world's longest undefended border is testament enough to the enduring and prolonged friendship between Canada and the United States. We are, after all, North Americans, and we are, unlike the Mexicans with their Spanish tradition and heritage, of a mould not dissimilar to the Americans. William Johnson, in his contribution, is certainly of this opinion.

We are both new societies, but societies which espouse disparate values. Enough has been said about Canadian deference to authority and the American obsession with individual freedom. We note the difference. Having done so, we should easily concede that the vital interests of Canada go beyond those dealing with trade, fish, boundary waters, and territorial seas, which have historically tended to dominate the literature on the bilateral relationship.[6]

Canadians of late have resisted, embraced, but rarely ignored the temptation to draw even closer to the United States. First, we as a nation have our complement of nationalists in all walks of life. Second, we seek to preserve our cultural heritage as historically derived from the early British and French settlers, and have lately recognized the multicultural dimension of our society. Third, we have an economy which is resource-based and a product of government largesse, regulation, and intervention. Finally, we have a northern environment which, as Kenneth Hare points out, has more in common geographically with Greenland, northern Europe, and the Soviet Union than any other country to the south of us. These four features, nationalism, culture, economics, and the environment are the crucial factors in determining our response to and perspectives on the United States. The government and people of Canada most often react within the confines of these rather broad categories, creating a plethora of policies, which ultimately add up to the kind of unique responses that form an important part of Canadian law and culture. It is through the process of conflict and agreement that we have come to the rather amorphous subject known as Canadian-American relations.

Although of late economic issues have tended to predominate because of the instability of the world economy, foreign debt and deficit crises, trade imbalances, currency fluctuations, and protectionist sentiments, the major irritants to the Americans are most often the result of Canadian efforts to protect national sovereignty. In order to promote Canadian ownership, the Trudeau government created barriers to the free flow of American capital to Canada through the Foreign Investment Review Agency (1974-1985). FIRA used discriminatory policies with nationalistic roots. In purely economic terms, the recent and current disputes over steel, pork, beef, lumber, fish, and wheat are the result of what one or the other country considered to be unfair trading practices. In fact these are questions of national sovereignty. The whole issue of cultural and political sovereignty is at the heart of the current free trade debate. For example, lobbyists for the American fishermen have claimed that Canadian unemployment insurance given to Newfoundland fishermen is in reality a subsidy on that export commodity. Yet such payments are a part of Canadian social welfare policy and are an effort to alleviate regional economic disparities. Culturally, as John Meisel points out, attempts by the Government of Canada to regulate the communications industry have met with retaliatory measures from the United States Congress. To Americans with an unbounded faith in the free enterprise system, government subsidy of products for export and governmental procurement policies are severe impediments to future trading agreements. These are clearly important areas of concern for business and labour and can have long-range effects on the economic stability of Canada.

In pursuing trade talks with the United States, Brian Mulroney has categorically stated that sovereignty, culture, regional equalization, social security and health care, and linguistic rights would not be sacrificed for the sake of improved economic relations with the United States. This presumably means that we shall continue to disagree with the Americans about such matters as acid rain and resource management, pollution and the extraterritorial application of American law, *Time* magazine, oil tankers on the West Coast, the management of fish stocks, the killing of seals and the pollution of boundary waters, the damming of rivers, and the extradition of criminals facing the death penalty in the United States. In his paper, Donald Munton deftly illustrates the problems Canadians face in attempting to persuade Americans to act on the issue of acid rain, when the major benefits accrue to Canadians at great cost to the American taxpayer.

Economics is an important but not the most important of Canadian priorities. There are fundamental distinctions in political culture that are entrenched in both societies. Our national health care service is a smaller part of our GNP than is the case in the American system, which has no universal scheme. We are beginning to accept our bilingual heritage, whereas some Americans, fearful of an Hispanic population that estimates say will surpass that of blacks by the year 2000, are agitating to make English the official language of the United States. Most Canadians accept the higher taxes required to sustain social welfare policies, while Ronald Reagan leads a tax revolt which has substantially reduced the tax burden of many Americans, but at a cost to the social welfare system. Judging by the size of his 1984 electoral victory, the president has successfully taken the pulse of the nation and seems to epitomize the America of the 1980s.

Despite disagreements over specific foreign policies, notably in an attempt to play the role of "middle power," Canada has staunchly supported the general goals of American foreign policy, while distancing itself from America's more volatile confrontations in Lebanon and Grenada. We are uncertain as to how we should contain the export of revolution, adapt to the new era of self-determination in Africa and Latin America, and bring a halt to nuclear proliferation. Canada has thus maintained relations with Cuba, for example. Many citizens are sympathetic to the Sandinista cause in Nicaragua, and the Canadian government has attempted to prohibit the use of Canadian nuclear technology in the production of weapons. We are a bystander in what John Kirton calls "America's hegemonic decline."

Yet our moral righteousness is complicated when we act as silent but willing partners to the American military industrial complex. So while we refuse to participate as a government in President Reagan's Strategic Defense Initiative, we are the recipients of American military contracts. The employment and profits that accrue from defence development and the Defence Production Sharing Arrangements allow Canadian industry to partake in the advanced research and technology that contributes to such advanced military operations as the space shuttle project and missile guidance systems. Canadian subsidiaries, such as Dow, Dupont, General Motors, and Litton, have produced the materials which many associate with American "imperialism." We are, nonetheless, willing partners who create the technology of war in the same manner as our allies, France and Britain. Ambassador Gotlieb observes in this volume that, " . . . Canadian foreign policy towards the United States is the obverse side of United States domestic policy affecting Canada." Canadian domestic policy often reacts to American foreign policy affecting Canada as well. The Supreme Court of Canada was forced to rule on the legality of testing American cruise missiles over Alberta in 1985. This decision, prompted by Canada's participation in joint defence agreements, changed Canadian domestic and legal culture by legitimizing the judicial interpretation of Cabinet decisions.[7]

Many have argued recently that the United States might be willing to favour Canada with preferred trading status (or more preferred) so as to show the world that protectionist policies can never lead to the economic benefits to be had from open borders. To do this the president will have to thwart the protectionist sentiments of American farmers, fisheries, forestry, steel, shoe and textile workers. Americans, as U.S. Ambassador to Canada, Thomas Niles, has stated, would like to see fewer restrictions on American banks, fewer provincial procurement policies, and a free flow in financial and communications services.[8] To U.S. Trade Representative

Clayton Yeutter there ought to be "no restrictions placed on the scope of talks with Canada about free trade."[9]

As for preferred trading status, Israel has been accorded such status by the United States, as has, to a degree, Jamaica, which is the central focus of the Caribbean Basin Initiative. What is common to both of these countries is their perceived *strategic* significance to the United States. Israel is a friend amidst the instability of the Middle East; Jamaica is meant to be the answer to the threatening socialist ideas of Michael Manley, Fidel Castro, and Daniel Ortega. Both countries are showcases, like Berlin, of strategic importance. For Canada to accept preferred status within the American trading economy, we must admit to our strategic role as an adjunct to American foreign policy. To this degree, American foreign policy could become an even more integral part of Canadian domestic policy. The cost, as is the case with all policies, could be for Canada to "pay its way," so that the foreign policy of Canadian-American relations will be the foreign policy of the United States. Many Canadians would be more than happy to abrogate such responsibilities as "defending the free world." As the citizens of Sweden and Switzerland can attest, an independent military defence policy is an expensive endeavour.

4. The Influence of the United States in Canada

One is frequently tempted to point out to Americans that they would find it hard to believe the extent of their influence, some would say dominance, in Canada. It is hard to envision them tolerating such an extraordinary "foreign" power in their own country, or such a dependent economy, as exists in Canada. Canadians have to do more to understand the United States simply in self-defence.

The extent and scope of the economic relationship between the United States and Canada are enormous. As Harold Wyatt points out, the Americans have in excess of $50 billion of direct investment in Canada, and we have at least $13 billion in the United States, the surprisingly large latter figure being a direct reminder of the self-interest argument for better understanding of the giant (or elephant) to the south. Leading Canadian businessmen, for example, feel strongly that we fail to appreciate adequately the different managerial environment that exists in the United States. Just as Canada is a natural and easy market for the expansion of any American industry, the same is now true for any large Canadian company (such as Northern Telecom) that has perhaps encountered the natural or prudent limits to its growth in Canada. As in so many other areas, a reciprocal process of direct Canadian investment in the United States is now at work. This has made Americans somewhat more sensitive about the issue of foreign ownership in a way that has been second-nature to Canadians for a long time. Yet the circumstances are hardly balanced.

Canadians still have to recognize the extraordinary extent to which their current economic prosperity depends upon the trading relationship with the Americans. Canadian nationalists, and even Quebec separatists, have had little success in persuading the general public to put the protection of cultural identity before the maintenance of their standard of living. John Meisel, in his essay, seeks to remind us of the cultural problems. Michael Goldberg goes so far as to describe Canada as having "very much a colonial economy," exporting natural resources and importing manufactured goods; the American economy, in his view, is very different, since its exports are dominated by the services sector as opposed to manufacturing. A similarly pessimistic view appears in this volume from the informed pen of Stuart Smith. In response to fundamental changes that are occurring in the world economy, he sees an increasing risk of Canadians coming to the conclusion that if our current reliance on natural resources does not maintain our high standard of living, we must inevitably join the United States.

It is clear that the process of trying to understand the United States will be an ongoing and complicated activity. The articles by Ambassador Gotlieb and David Leyton-Brown both demonstrate the importance of adequately knowing how the American political process works, which is something we ignore at our peril, as we saw in the Georges Bank fishing treaty. In this instance federal officials negotiated a treaty with the Carter administration, only to have it ignored by the Senate. It was never ratified.

The prospective benefits of building Canadian expertise in the American political process are great, especially outside of the federal and provincial governments, because the U.S. Congress thrives on pressure from private, special interest groups. The record of the federal government lobbying in such areas as acid rain and steel quotas does not promote total confidence in a process that would allow our foreign relations with the United States to be completely under the dominance and control of the Department of External Affairs. Neither business nor the public will benefit by the continuation of such traditional approaches. Provinces, as well as special interest groups, should continue to take their own initiatives in the United States where circumstance and self-interest warrant.

It must be admitted that much of the American influence in Canada is predictable, and a good deal of it is even desirable. As Constance Hunt shows, the development of Canadian resources law and practice owes a debt to American experience and solutions. The advent of the Canadian Charter of Rights and Freedoms, it can be argued, further necessitates close study of the American constitutional process.[10] This is especially true in the areas of judicial review and, increasingly so, in the creation and operation of powerful special interest groups, who seek to challenge Canadian law and traditions.

But at the same time, John Meisel, who until 1983 was chairman of the Canadian Radio-Television and Telecommunications Commission (CRTC), has performed a valuable service in this volume by indicating, in a way that may surprise some Americans, the extent to which the American cultural influences in Canada are detrimental. This criticism may be levelled by almost any observer in the Western community of nations, because of the penetration of American ideas through the media, but

Canada is particularly vulnerable owing to the immediacy of our exposure. Most Canadians have access to all of the major American television networks, facilitated, ironically, by our success in telecommunications, which has made us the most "wired" nation in the world. American newspapers, such as *The New York Times*, and *The Wall Street Journal* and *U.S.A. Today*, are available on many urban newstands each morning. Many of us read them with great benefit and indeed expect them to be available.

The United States is a dominant presence in the life of every Canadian in a way that would be inconceivable in reverse. Thus Meisel can describe American popular culture as an "immense Trojan horse enabling foreign concerns and priorities to infiltrate our very minds and beings." Yet this provocative statement illustrates the very mass/elite dichotomy that his article describes; on the one hand, there is cultural vulnerability and, on the other hand, an avid thirst for things American. That the United States is a ubiquitous and inescapable presence in Canada is a fact that is also unlikely to change. Hence Meisel is not simply being ironic when he concludes that "inside every Canadian, . . . there is, in fact, an American." The Canadian problem comes from the fact that the phrase would be ludicrous in reverse.

There is some useful tension in the following pages from the fact that a number of the authors, notably William Johnson, were able to write their essays with the texts of other contributors before them. Johnson was the national correspondent for *The Globe and Mail* in Quebec during the time in the 1970s when the separatist challenge was threatening to change the face of Canada. He is currently the national correspondent in Washington for the same newspaper. It is a time of intense Canadian interest in Canadian-American affairs because of the apparent ideological and personal kinship between President Reagan and Prime Minister Mulroney. Johnson's article not only illustrates the variety of Canadian perspectives on ourselves and the United States but also launches a strong attack on positions taken in this volume by John Meisel, Bruce Wilkinson, Harold Wyatt, and Peter Buitenhuis. Meisel's rejoinder appears after Johnson's article.

In particular, Johnson is very critical of Meisel's concern about the extinction of Canadian culture, a position that is at the very least provocative. Johnson regards Canada as having a strong culture, but argues that it is only marginally distinctive from American culture. He will raise nationalistic hackles by his judgment that we are "largely a single society," thus confirming the view of many Americans who cannot imagine why we should be worried about issues of cultural identity. With regard to transborder travel, Johnson states that "this permeability of our border has given Canadians a great enrichment to their cultural life," while at the same time he argues the need to protect our culture. This position may not be much different, in the end, from Meisel's. The problem with either view is that, to date, as Meisel notes in his discussion of the border broadcasting dispute, the United States has been extremely sensitive about Canadian cultural protectionist measures. The contrasting insensitivity of many protectionist measures against foreign countries being proposed in Congress in 1986 is instructive. Yet one still is left with Johnson's persuasive view that Canada and the United States (but not Mexico) share a North American culture when viewed from any kind of global perspective.

One of the fundamental problems in dealing with the preponderance of American influence in Canada is to try to make Americans understand the Canadian dilemma and the differences that do exist. Some informed observers think that the real problem is to persuade Americans to understand *anything* about Canada. Jeffrey Simpson, the editorial-page columnist for *The Globe and Mail*, concluded after a recent trip south that "in short, the friendly ignorance of Americans about Canada remains as boundless as ever."[11] Those of us who aspire to specialized knowledge of both countries make the mistake of thinking that we know more than we actually do about the other country. There are formidable problems confronting any Canadian or American wanting to become very familiar with the other country. Even experts understand relatively little about existing differences and similarities below the level of the activities of the respective federal governments. If, as Wyatt argues in his essay, Americans ought to change their attitude to Canada, an appreciation of basic differences would be a significant step in the right direction.

These basic differences are discussed in various essays. For example, Canadians have accepted a larger role for government, as opposed to reliance on market forces, in the development of society. Stuart Smith, who combines a medical background with experience as leader of the Ontario Liberal party, is the chairman of the Science Council of Canada. In reaction to the demonstrated ability of the United States to adapt to an "information society" and changing technology, Smith insists that the effort to promote such adaptive activity in Canada must be done with the help of governments. Of course, given the critical role of the U.S. Department of Defense in promoting technological developments, the difference in the role of government in the two societies may be more rhetorical than real.

Harold Wyatt, who has had a distinguished career with the Royal Bank of Canada since the end of World War II, wants to improve Canadian-American relations. He begins with the premise that we are not the same. Even allowing for any deficiencies in his analogy relying on the elephant and the flea, it is evident that there are considerable differences in scale between the two countries. This, he argues, prohibits the automatic export to Canada of American solutions to various problems.

David Leyton-Brown discusses the dramatic differences between the prime minister and the president in their ability to obtain legislative results. As mentioned earlier this lesson was brought home to Canadians in the Georges Bank dispute, when our government was apparently surprised by the politics of the American treaty-making process.

In his fascinating discussion of the myth of the North American city, Michael Goldberg, himself an American immigrant, describes numerous instances in which the two countries are institutionally and socially different. He deals with patterns of assimilation, the treatment of property rights, levels of economic development, and the handling of urban issues. Goldberg argues that cities in the two countries are so different that the transfer of urban policies from one country to another is not likely to be successful. Indeed, he claims that the American urban model is not only unique, but probably inappropriate for adoption elsewhere in the world.

In emphasizing that Canada is indeed different in demonstrable ways, and in trying to indicate to Americans the enormous sway they already exercise in this country, Canadians should be prepared to be perceived as challenging some basic aspects of the American way of life. This, of course, is to be expected. Certain American readers may even feel uncomfortable reading some of the articles in these pages on the grounds that they appear to be unfriendly to American interests. This condition partly explains why Peter Buitenhuis, one of the main advocates of American studies in Canada, draws attention to the paradox at the heart of the Canadian-American relationship. "That the personal encounter can be so warm and friendly, while the national one can appear to be so hostile and threatening" is indeed a dilemma. In fact, Americans should be no more surprised by Canadian nationalism than they are by their own—which is taken for granted. However, nationalism in the United States does not have an equivalent to the anti-American component that has long been a staple of Canadian nationalism, except perhaps for anti-communism.

It is often awkward to criticize or resist Americans, even within the limited sphere of admittedly self-serving relations between the two countries, without producing the volatile relations that Wyatt has deftly identified as bad for Canadian business. Although Americans can perceive enhanced trade between the two countries as of primary benefit, an economist like Bruce Wilkinson, whose nationalistic stance is admittedly not the via media among the majority of his colleagues, emphasizes the large risks of a free trade agreement to Canadian sovereignty. Wilkinson represents well the important nationalist tradition in his discussion of the negative aspects of the further expansion of American ownership in Canada. He discusses the commitment to free trade as being de facto irreversible for Canada's manufacturing interests but not for those in the United States. He may even be perceived as unfriendly to any warm American entreaties with his suggestion that Canadian interests might continue to be better protected under the umbrella of negotiation in the General Agreement on Tariffs and Trade (GATT).

5. The Centrality of the United States in Canada's External Relations

Canada and the United States enjoy the largest bilateral economic relationship in the world. As a country that wants increasingly to be viewed as a trading nation rather than an exporter of natural resources, our economic relations with the United States are of vital importance. We trade in an amount equivalent to 30 per cent of our GNP versus only 10 per cent for the United States, Japan, or the European Economic Community. Even though the United States needs constant reminding of the central and indeed primary importance of the trading relationship with Canada as compared to its other trading relationships, it is also true that this trade with the United States is even more important to Canada today than it was after World War II. At the same time it is less important today for the United States than it was then. John Whalley points out that 75 per cent of Canadian trade is now with the United States.

The scale of trading activity of the United States is enormous with respect to any single country, including Canada. With regard to domestic activities, David Leyton-Brown notes in passing that more money was spent on the hotly-contested North Carolina senate race in 1984 than in the critically important Canadian federal election of the same year. Canada is indeed a small country in terms of population, with all of the attendant fears about dominance by a large one, a point that needs to be understood in our relations with the United States. Canadian fears are further fuelled by America's dominant role in the world as a whole.

Thus it is important that we invest in the Canadian studies movement in the United States. However, it would be viewed with suspicion if the American government committed comparable resources to an American studies movement in Canada. Canadians might point out the preponderance of centres for Mexican-American or Japanese-American studies in the United States, over those that focus on Canada, yet English Canada itself did not have a university-based research institute dedicated to the study of the United States until 1984.

With the benefit of hindsight, it is hard to understand our failure to recognize the need for Canadians to study the United States. Ambassador Gotlieb notes the critical extent to which Canadian interests are intertwined with domestic political issues in the United States. The impact of American domestic decisions on Canada is inevitable, given the nature and scope of the relationship, yet until recently Canada has not been well represented in Washington, even with respect to the interests of the private sector, which saw no need to lobby in Washington. For example, Canadian steel companies belonged to the American Iron and Steel Institute and, not having one of their own, counted on the American industry group to represent their interests in Washington. Hence their surprise at protectionist moves against the Canadian steel industry in 1983-1984.

The complexity of the American political process demands that a Canadian perspective on that country include the development of some depth of expertise on American regulatory commissions and administrative agencies. For example, the United States International Trade Commission supports a cadre of specialists on Canadian trade that does not appear to be matched by Canadian expertise on the United States.

The essays in this volume by John Kirton and John Whalley point out that Canadian-American relations have to function in a global environment. In fact, one of the major reasons for the American failure to recognize the importance of the Canadian connection is that it is taken for granted in economic terms but is otherwise of little consequence for American foreign policy. Whalley draws the important conclusion that for a large country, trade policy is intertwined with foreign policy; for a smaller country, like Canada, the economic dimensions of foreign policy come to dominate, because we are so much more dependent on foreign trade.

Canadians have to live with the fact that the United States is economically much more important to us than we are to them. Thus Russell Boyer, in his article on the contributions of Canadian economists (a notable number of whom work in the United States) to understanding American fiscal policy, illustrates how Canadians are constantly and necessarily reacting to all aspects of American financial policies through the media. Some observers question whether it is possible, or at least practical, for Canada to have a monetary policy truly separate from that of the United States.

It also seems inevitable that the major concerns of Canadians will rarely come to the attention of the American media. The 1985 voyage of the United States icebreaker, *Polar Sea*, through Arctic waters claimed by Canada was controversial news in Canada, but not in the United States. When Prime Minister Mulroney announced his intention to enter into comprehensive trade negotiations with the United States, not one of the three commercial American networks reported it on the evening news. Thus a heated debate over closer trade ties with the United States is occurring mainly on one side of the border. Canadians became excited about the risks of acid rain long before it attracted any attention, and certainly any decisive action, in the United States. Americans have similar trouble being concerned about the extra-territorial application of their own laws, preferring to view this as part of a critical fight against drug-trafficking or the Soviet Union, as the case may be.

6. The Intrinsic Interest of Canadian Perspectives on the United States

Canadians will write about the United States, because it is intrinsically interesting and valuable to do so. There are notable examples of books on American history, written by Canadians, which do not overtly manifest a Canadian perspective of any sort.[12] One might even want to test whether the *Canadian Review of American Studies*, for example, truly reflects a Canadian perspective, as opposed to being an outlet for scholarship on the United States primarily written by Canadians.

The pursuit of intrinsic interest is illustrated in the pages of this book. John Kirton presents a bold, critical analysis of the United States' declining hegemonic position since World War II. Similarly, David Leyton-Brown explains the complex role of independent regulatory agencies in trade matters. James Lemon, an American-trained historical geographer, presents a provocative set of reflections on the American urban experience. American readers may have especially negative reactions to the articles by Lemon and Kirton, because both writers are critical of certain American claims and pretensions. Such a friendly scepticism is likely to be a central component of Canadian perspectives on the United States.

Constance Hunt's informed article about natural resources law in the two countries is indicative of the strength of comparative analysis. She notes first the general paucity of Canadian scholarship about American law, best explained by the infancy of legal research and writing on Canadian topics. Hunt then charts the intertwining of Canada–United States natural gas interests with respect to sources, prices, volume of exports, regulatory approaches, and private ordering. Despite the cyclical character of what has transpired since World War II, she observes, "a noticeable shift away from Canadian efforts to be independent of American law and policy in the energy field," and asks whether a common North American energy policy is inevitable. However informed the observations, and however much they may strike an American reader as "the natural order of things," they arouse fears and concerns for Canadians sensitive to issues of economic independence.

Beyond intrinsic interest, therefore, it is in the national interest for Canadians to write about the United States. Peter Buitenhuis further argues that it is necessary for Canadian writers to understand the United States in order to understand Canada better, in his words, "to plunge into the American funhouse and find their way out." It is also vitally important for such writing to help make Americans more aware and understanding of Canada and its interests, in addition to the contribution of Canadians in defining and criticizing the American literary tradition.

It is probably inappropriate for Canadians to argue that our writing about the United States will be of benefit to that country. On the other hand, John Whalley makes the point that an understanding of the importance of the global trading system and how it works can contribute as much to Americans as Canadians, especially given the former's preoccupation in the 1980s with the Japanese export challenge. Russell Boyer criticizes the current loose fiscal policies of the Reagan administration, using a model developed from Canadian insights into international finance. It is a matter of considerable interest whether an article such as Boyer's could be duplicated for other fields in the arts and social sciences.

Canadian research and writing about the United States will also be of potential benefit to both countries, because it will inevitably be comparative. Since Americans are less likely to write about Canadian topics, it remains for authors and researchers to demonstrate the relevance of their work to American problems. The Canadian system of health-care delivery to the general public, for example, is one area where progress has been achieved north of the border. Canadians are also in a position to counter certain American traits, such as isolationism and self-centredness, which can lead to relative myopia about the rest of the world. Canadians should be capable of less self-interested analysis of American topics; the reverse benefit is of course true for an American analysis of Canadian issues. Moreover, the peculiarities of the American constitutional system of government also reduce the capacity of the United States to assimilate and apply foreign experience.

7. The Characteristics of Canadian Perspectives on the United States

One of the dominant characteristics of any Canadian perspective on the United States is that it will be cyclical, in part because it will be political. The cycles that Leyton-Brown notes in presidential-congressional relations are also true for Canadian-American relations. They are never permanently fixed and are thus always in flux, as perhaps befits relations between two independent nations. Ambassador Gotlieb's identification of the "public mood" in the United States as a critical variable in Canadian-American relations is a factor on both sides of the border and also changes over time. Thus Harold Wyatt is wise to advocate taking the longer-term view in Canadian-American relations, which is hard to do in practice.

The political character of Canadian perspectives on the United States has been well illustrated during the last generation. As prime minister for most of this period (1968-1984), Pierre Elliott Trudeau was determined to lead Canada on an independent course in the world, not least with respect to the United States. In part, this reflected the more confident and assertive posture that the country has adopted since celebrating its centenary in 1967. The Trudeau stance also reflected the attitudes of an independent leader towards his counterparts in the American presidency during his term of office. Trudeau's often unpredictable performance on the world stage reflected the best and worst of Canadians' ambivalence about themselves. In terms of domestic policies, Trudeau's Liberals followed a variety of nationalistic programs, such as establishing FIRA and the National Energy Program, that met their criteria for being in the national interest and had the added advantage of twitting the Americans where it hurt.

Prime Minister Mulroney came to power in September 1984 primarily because of public disenchantment with the Liberal's lengthy rule and poor economic record. He is committed to improving our working relations with the Americans. Nationalists and others, however, may well be very wary about the character of his performance with respect to the United States. He can be perceived as a "branch-plant" prime minister. Such nationalism is particularly evident among members of the New Democratic Party (NDP), the labour unions, and those who are trying to make job creation and job protection a national priority. The New Democrats, along with many Liberals, are very sensitive to the risks of closer economic ties with the United States.

Another significant trait of Canadian perspectives on the United States is that they are, at least to some extent, regional in character. Because of the nature of population distribution along the Canadian side of the border, all Canadians are well aware of the nearby American presence, yet perspectives change from the western provinces of British Columbia and Alberta, concerned about promoting exports of natural resources and petroleum products, to the manufacturing centre of the nation in Ontario, concerned about the risk of the loss of jobs in freer trade with the United States. The Atlantic provinces have had a traditional affinity with the New England states, illustrated by substantial exchanges of population during the nineteenth and early twentieth centuries. Fish exports to the United States are a crucial part of their economy. The variety of Canadian perspectives from a regional point of view was displayed during discussions of trade issues at the conference held by the provincial premiers in August 1985, nine out of ten of whom agreed that preliminary trade talks were necessary. The regional theme has its counterpart in the difficulty of knowing with certainty what Canadians mean by the United States, because of our regional and variable exposure to that country. We have much more experience with the east coast than with the south (except Florida), the southwest, and California; in American terms, central Canada (Ontario and Quebec) perceives itself as eastern rather than mid-western, although an American might draw the opposite conclusion. One of the goals of developing Canadian expertise on the United States has to be an informed appreciation of regional differences.

Canadian perspectives on the United States are further diversified on the basis of age, experience, exposure, education, interests, and occupation. They may differ depending on whether they originate with journalists, francophones or anglophones, ordinary citizens, business men and women, or academics. The latter may have widely differing views of the United States depending on whether they were trained at the graduate level in Canada, the United States, the United Kingdom, or France. The contributors to the present volume include persons who were born and/or educated in Canada, the United States, the United Kingdom and Europe. Although the level of understanding of the United States of those educated there may be much greater than for others, there is no assurance that their attitudes will reflect the fascination/aversion so typical of the general public.

Thus Canadian perspectives on the United States can also be contradictory and cynical. None of us may in fact have enough experience of living in the United States to understand it properly; on the other hand, perhaps Buitenhuis and Denis Smith are right in advancing the view that we are too close to the United States to have a good perspective on it. The Canadian ambivalence and dilemma are well illustrated by the current debate over free trade. How can we really anticipate American intentions in a free trade agreement? Would an agreement on freer trade be irreversible for Canada? Could we withhold our natural resources from the United States at a later date if our major manufacturing operations were to move south of the border?

What do Canadians really want in their relations with the Americans? It is superficial to suggest that we simply want to be left alone. Canada is a physically large and, indeed, accomplished country; its inhabitants want to be noticed and liked in the United States. We become very excited about baseball games featuring American players, wearing the uniforms of the Toronto Blue Jays or Montreal Expos, but playing the American national game. Perceived slights against Canada during a critical game in New York can arouse national ire.[13]

In fact, it is widely recognized that the "special relationship" that Canada has with the United States has historical roots that are both positive and negative. Government observers on both sides claim that the relationship is very well managed, given the volume of trade between the two countries. Kenneth Hare's article in this volume illustrates the large amount of unfinished business in our transboundary environmental linkages and the need for strong mechanisms for dispute settlement, perhaps along the lines of the International Joint Commission.

In the current volume, persons as diverse as Stuart Smith and Harold Wyatt, the politician-public servant and the banker, want "family-style relations" with the United States; it appears to reflect as well as any other approach the realities of sharing the North American continent. The desire for "family-style relations" is a reflection of our southern exposure.

Canadian perspectives on the United States are now entering a period of extraordinary ferment. The Macdonald Commission and the Mulroney government are proponents of enhanced trading agreements, perhaps even free trade, with the Americans.[14] Most provinces are in general agreement about the need to negotiate, but three of the most important, Quebec, Ontario, and Alberta, have new premiers. Opposition parties, in particular, have every incentive to take more nationalistic positions in this situation. The United Auto Workers of Canada, newly independent from their American counterparts, are another straw in the wind. As the debate over our relationships with the United States continues, Canadians only seem sure about their desire to remain a sovereign nation, and even that very sovereignty is challenged by the debate over the future of Canada–United States relations. Politicians on both sides of the border will have to make (or avoid) some critical decisions.

Notes

1. P.B. Waite, ed., *The Confederation Debates in the Province of Canada/1865* (Toronto: McClelland & Stewart, 1963), p. 73.
2. This tariff was passed by Congress June, 1930, and placed high duties on agricultural and industrial goods. This in effect intensified the economic war between Canada and the United States.
3. At the time of its cancellation in February, 1959, the Avro Arrow project was producing prototypes of a world class jet bomber with Canadian expertise and technology. By 1961, Canada was relying upon U.S.-made Voodoo interceptors and Bomarc missiles for air defence.
4. As quoted by Peyton Lyon, "The Canadian Perspective," in H. Edward English, ed., *Canada–*

United States Relations, Proceedings of the Academy of Political Science, Vol. 2, No. 2. New York, 1976, p. 20.

5. See: Alan Westin, "The United States Bill of Rights and the Canadian Charter: A Socio-Political Analysis," in William R. McKercher, ed., *The U.S. Bill of Rights and the Canadian Charter of Rights and Freedoms* (Toronto: Ontario Economic Council, 1983), pp. 27-44.

6. For those who would like a broad historical view of Canadian-American relations in these and other years see E.E. Mahant and G.S. Mount, *An Introduction to Canadian-American Relations* (Toronto: Methuen, 1984). For a more political and provocative view see Richard Gwyn, *The 49th Paradox: Canada in North America* (Toronto: McClelland & Stewart, 1985).

7. On 9 May 1985, the Supreme Court of Canada, ruling on an injunction filed by Operation Dismantle ruled that the testing of cruise missiles did not violate the Charter of Rights. However it also ruled that it had the right to judge the constitutionality of cabinet decisions, a new, and some would say, a unique limitation placed upon the executive power of the Canadian government. See, *Operation Dismantle Inc. et al* v. *Canada et al.* (1985) 59 N.R. 1 (S.C.C.).

8. "Social Programs Not at Risk, U.S. Envoy Says," *The Globe and Mail*, 30 September 1985, p. 3.

9. Christopher Waddell, "U.S. wants 'everything' Open in Trade Talks with Canada," *The Globe and Mail*, 19 December 1985, p. 1.

10. For more detail see William R. McKercher "The U.S. Bill of Rights: Implications for Canada" in William R. McKercher, ed., *op cit*, pp. 7-26.

11. Jeffrey Simpson, "Issues and Non-Issues," *The Globe and Mail*, 27 August 1985, p. 6.

12. See, for example, James T. Lemon, *The Best Poor Man's Country: A Geographical Study of Early Southeastern Pennsylvania* (Baltimore: Johns Hopkins University Press, 1972); Robert D. Cuff, *The War Industries Board; Business Government Relations during World War I* (Baltimore: Johns Hopkins University Press, 1973); and Stephen J. Randall, *The Diplomacy of Modernization: Columbian-American Politics* (Toronto: University of Toronto Press, 1977).

13. See Douglas Martin, "Canadians Find No Yankee Hospitality," *The New York Times*, 17 September 1985, p. 24.

14. *Report of the Royal Commission on the Economic Union and Development Prospects for Canada*, (Ottawa: Minister of Supply and Services Canada, 1985).

PART I

The American
Political Process

The United States, founded in revolution, has the world's oldest written
constitution still forming the basis of a system of government. It is a brief
document with but twenty-six amendments that has been made into a subtly
workable whole. This document truncated the power of government through
the separation of powers, divided the power of government by creating a
federal state, and limited the power of government through the Bill of Rights.
The constitution was the basic law of the republic that set in motion a process
of government that had to contend with the demands of the sovereign people.

The political process continually responds to special interests and pluralist
alliances. To many observers, the question of how to deal with the constantly
changing institutions, their nuances and complexities, is almost beyond com-
prehension. The politics of the nation is even more perplexing to foreigners.
Nowhere is the process more misunderstood than in the interaction among
the institutions that vie for prominence under the doctrine of the separation
of powers, which provides for the president, the Congress, and the Supreme
Court sharing authority.

It is no accident then that the first two chapters of this book focus on the
problems associated with the separation of powers. In Chapter 1, Allan Gotlieb
shares with us the frustrations of a foreign diplomat coming to terms with
the pitfalls which face policymakers who, used to dealing with executive
branches of government, are compelled to contend with a powerful bicameral

legislature. How does a foreign government ascertain the chances of success in dealing with such a body? This chapter examines how American domestic legislation is of import to Canada. Such legislation has foreign policy implications for other nations which should not be ignored.

In Chapter 2, David Leyton-Brown focuses on relations between the president and Congress, but also discusses in more detail the particular impact of lobbyists (the pluralistic voice of the people) on the congressional system. When bills, after subjection to intense constituency pressure, are passed into law, the process of implementation begins. The discussion at this point turns to the regulatory agencies, which are supposed "to be relatively immune to political and discretionary decisions on the part of the United States government." Leyton-Brown contends that they are but another point of access for special interest groups. These agencies, such as the International Trade Commission, must be properly identified within the political process if lobbyists intend to affect the decision makers.

In Chapter 3, John Kirton moves us from the national/domestic front to the international/foreign policy field as it has developed since 1968. "The primary academic question is the prospect and path for international cooperation after an American hegemony that all assert once existed, but has now clearly gone." This comprehensive piece of work deals with the concept of hegemony, the case for American preeminence and the cause of its decline beginning in the 1970s. In dealing with the Reagan record, Kirton claims that "outside of oil, signs of any Reagan revival, let alone hegemonic restoration, are nowhere to be seen." He concludes that "there is little evidence of an American restoration." Although "the American public's commitment must not be confused with its self-confidence," it is clear that "American citizens face the twenty-first century with a high degree of optimism."

CHAPTER 1

The Canada–United States Relationship

Allan E. Gotlieb

Clearly, no one needs to be reminded of the classic Canadian complaint about how much less our American neighbours know about us, than we about them. The Canadian government, with the active support of the academic community in our country, has, for several years now, been making a deliberate and not unsuccessful effort to promote Canadian studies programs at the university level on campuses throughout the United States. In the American context, this kind of institutionalized approach was felt to be necessary as a vehicle for instilling the desired awareness of America's northern neighbour as a field of academic endeavour.

Here in Canada the situation has, of course, been somewhat different, although it has been the judgment of the University of Western Ontario, one which I share entirely, that we in Canada have not done all that we could or should in our scholarly scrutiny of our neighbour to the south.

For all the obvious geographic, historic, linguistic, and economic reasons, Canada's perspective on the United States is unique. Relations with the United States, be they good or bad, are not for us a matter of choice—we have them whether we want them or not. The length of our common border, the nature of our economic systems, the openness and the pluralism of our political systems, all combine to create an unequalled mass of contact and movement between our two societies that scholars must try to analyze and I, as ambassador, must help in part to manage. I am not sure who has the more impossible task. I have now been Ambassador to the United States for four years and have had an opportunity to form some impressions about the nature of the Canada–United States relationship.

I first started to deal with Canada–United States relations as a very junior officer in the Department of External Affairs twenty-nine years ago. At that time the United States Division consisted of two officers, if I recall correctly, while the Legal Division, in which I worked, was a trifle larger. The issues that concerned both divisions and myself were related to boundary waters, fisheries questions, and territorial seas. A decade later, when I was a good deal more senior, as an Assistant Under-Secretary and Legal Adviser in Ex-ternal Affairs, I found that when I dealt with Canada–United States issues—and I did so much of the time—boundary waters and fish and territorial seas and baselines took up a great deal of my time. And a decade later, when I was still more senior—as Under-Secretary of State for External Affairs—my experience was not entirely different.

In the late 1970s during my tenure as Under-Secretary, our two govern-ments decided that they were going to make a grand effort, a supreme effort of unprecedented proportions, as a matter of the highest national priority, to settle a whole range of issues that were seen by both sides as interrelated and requiring definitive resolution. The Canadian prime minister and the United States president—Messrs. Trudeau and Carter—personally approved special negotiators directly responsible to themselves or their cabinets to try to reach accommodation and formal agreement on the whole range of outstanding coastal waters issues, fisheries problems, and the increasingly important oil and gas jurisdictional disputes on the continental shelf. This embraced the boundaries on the continental shelf in the Gulf of Maine, the Straits of Juan de Fuca, Hecate Strait, Dixon Entrance, and the Beaufort Sea. It also embraced a whole range of fisheries issues on both coasts relating to shares and conservation of such important species as scallops, salmon, cod, and every kind of groundfish that was edible (and maybe a few that were not).

In Canada, a special cabinet committee was set up to monitor the work of our negotiator, Marcel Cadieux, a former Under-Secretary and Ambas-sador to Washington. The United States negotiator, Lloyd Cutler, was White House counsel to the president and likewise worked under the highest direction. Their results were impressive in scope, exceedingly comprehen-sive, ambitious, innovative and far-reaching, although limited to the east coast issues only. No agreement seemed to be attainable on west coast issues.

There were in fact two resulting agreements: the Fisheries Treaty, creating a new bilateral body to allocate quotas and manage all the eastern coastal fisheries resources; and an Arbitration Treaty, in which the two sides agreed to submit their differences on the dividing line of the continental shelf on Georges Bank to a special Chamber of the International Court of Justice. The two agreements, said by the negotiators to be indivisible, were signed by the United States Secretary of State and the Canadian Ambassador to Washington at the time and submitted—in keeping with American consti-tutional doctrine—to the Senate, for approval or advice and consent. The Arbitration Treaty emerged from the Senate, but the Fisheries Treaty never received the requested Senate ratification and was allowed to die by the Reagan administration shortly after it took office in 1981. Although the International Court handed down its decision on the Gulf of Maine boundary in October 1984, there was and is no comprehensive Fisheries Treaty in effect between our two states.

I have related this history to you in order to set the stage for telling you what happened in Canada when it became clear in 1980 that the Senate would not approve the Fisheries Treaty. The reaction in industry, as well as in both the federal and provincial governments, was one of surprise, disappointment, and consternation. How was it possible for the United States government to proceed through the laborious negotiation of this agreement, with all of the consultations and trade-offs involved, the seemingly endless sessions, debates and compromises, and not bring the treaty into force? How could President Carter fail to press the treaty through the ratification process? How could he fail to move the Congress? How could this Democratic president fail to move the Democratic senators who were the source of the problem? How could the Senate fail to see the benefit to the United States of the complex architecture and innovative undertakings of the treaty? How could the Senate, with its historic responsibilities with respect to the ratification of treaties, yield to the opposition of one or two senators who were unhappy about certain provisions of the treaty as they related to one species— scallops?[1] Where was their view of the larger interests of the United States?

There was a strong belief in Ottawa that the administration let us down. In response to our public and private criticisms, a number of different comments were heard from time to time, south of the border, although not from the administration. It was said that Canada bargained too hard, or we should have known the deal was too rich to go through, that we should not have relied entirely on the administration to give us a reading of the Senate's attitude or that of the United States industry and that, most disturbing of all, we should have directly lobbied the Senate, or at least kept in constant direct touch with the key senators throughout, so as to assess better whether the administration was negotiating realistically. After the treaty floundered, similar voices were suggesting that it would be possible to revise the agreement, if we were to allow the Senate to bring forward revisions and test them for negotiability.

Most disconcerting in all of this discussion were the following implications:

(1) that we could not rely on the administration to provide us with a definitive assessment of the prospects of Senate action;

(2) that we should directly deal with the Senate itself;

(3) that the United States should, so to speak, be able to have two negotiating positions—one, that of the administration, the second, at a later date, that of the Senate, whereas, we, the other party, should have only one.

There was, I should add, a tendency in Canada at that time, to seek to understand the situation in the light of the American domestic post-Vietnam, post-Watergate situation. The decline in the prestige of the presidency, the accompanying rise of congressional power in foreign relations, the lack of political discipline, the emergence of a more fractious legislature, could all be understood as anomalies in the American system. The United States system was not working, so to speak, and it should be only a matter of time and electoral fortunes before it worked again.

But I believe, in retrospect, that the Canadian experience with the Fisheries Treaty was a historic turning-point in a better understanding of the complexities of the American political process and what Canada must do, as a foreign player, to promote and protect its interests in the country. We came to understand that, in many ways, what we witnessed was not so much an anomalous characteristic of American politics, as a fundamental and unique quality of its Constitution, that is, the separation of powers between the executive and the Congress. What we had witnessed in a broad perspective was the American political system working as it had been designed by the founding fathers.

After my several years in Washington, I remain convinced that it is exceptionally difficult for almost all foreign interests to grasp the true significance of the doctrine of the separation of powers. Even in the case of Canadians, so many of whom were, like myself, educated in the United States, there has been the seemingly incurable tendency to try to see or understand the United States Constitution through the prism of a parliamentary system. And since none of the European continental democratic systems parallel that of the United States, the European vision is equally, indeed more, clouded.

At the very heart of the American experience is the fact that in respect of any number of key issues, there are two co-equal decision-making centres. (I leave aside for this purpose the third, the Supreme Court of the United States.) Accordingly, when the laws are passed, it must be a result of a deal or agreement that is negotiated or hammered out between these two bodies. In no area is this more true than in the vital sphere of economic interests. Since the great economic downturn at the end of 1981, and through the recession and recovery years that followed, Canadians, in a wide variety of fields, have learned the realities of American political life, and we have learned them the hard way, in the school of practical economic experience.

What clearly emerges is the realization, over these past few years, that the problems that affect Canadians in the United States are not, for the most part, problems with the Reagan administration. They are problems with the workings of the American domestic political process. So many of the issues we have recently had, as I will shortly demonstrate, arise either through initiatives originating in the Congress or in the United States domestic regulatory bodies.

No country becomes so much engaged in the domestic processes of another as Canada does in that of the United States. The reason, of course, is that we have by far the largest trading and investment relationship in the world, and the deepest, densest, most intertwined reciprocal involvement of any two nations. When over three quarters of your exports are being sent to a single country, and if you value that access, which gives you about 25 per cent of your GNP, then it behooves you to understand that country. It behooves you to understand all of its processes and understand them very well. If you fail to do so, you act at your peril. Most importantly, you must know how to assess threats to your access to that economy and how best to try to protect that access from harm in the most complicated legislative system in the world.

Thus a great deal of United States foreign policy towards Canada is not really its foreign policy at all but its domestic policy. Put another way, United States foreign policy towards Canada is largely an aggregation of domestic political and economic thrusts. The result is that Canadian foreign policy towards the United States is the obverse side of United States domestic policy affecting Canada. And so inevitably, we are drawn into the American domestic process, whether we like it or not.

So, looking at the United States domestic scene, and recognizing its unique importance for Canada, what is the situation? What do we see? We find ourselves gazing into a kaleidoscope of constantly changing images composed of seemingly infinite variables. But we can recognize that there are probably three primary variables at play. In many respects they determine the context or general pattern of the environment in which our interests must be dealt with in the United States.

The first of these variables is what might best be described as the public mood in the United States. It is in turn reflected in the kinds of impulses which manifest themselves today in American political institutions. The public mood is not a constant. But there is detectable today a newly developed spirit of nationalism and patriotism which is a product of many things. It stands as a marked contrast to the public mood of only a few years ago, which was confused and confounded by the traumas of Watergate, the Vietnam War, and the oil crises of the 1970s. What it means, in a broad sense, is that Americans feel they are not going to be pushed around any more, by foe or by friend.

There is also the belief that, in a world economic climate of shrinking expectations, United States interests have not always been dealt with fairly, that other countries, allies and third world countries alike, are well advised to play by the same rules as the United States or else face criticisms or retaliation or be in some other form of trouble. Of course, this is an oversimplification but this describes the broad public mood today in the United States. We sensed it during the recent Olympics. We see it in the phrase, "not free trade but fair trade." We see it in trade union concern about the export of jobs. We have seen it in foreign policy, most recently in the great popularity of the Grenada affair. We see it in the shaping of trade policy, in the clamour for reciprocity. And we saw it as an important factor in the tremendous personal popularity and landslide electoral victory of President Reagan.

These are not necessarily the dominant sentiments or views of the Reagan administration, and certainly not as applied to the economic relationship which it is meant to manage with Canada. The administration itself remains committed to an outward-looking trade and economic policy with the rest of the world. It is extremely positive about its relationship with Canada and the new Progressive Conservative government. But most of our problems are not with the administration but with Congress, which more specifically reflects the public mood.

That brings me to the second variable representing an area of difference: the institutional. The result of the unique system of checks and balances which divides power among the three branches of government is that, unlike our system, the legislature has an independent responsibility for involving itself directly or indirectly in United States relations with other countries. This it does on a grand scale. Even more important than the celebrated prerogative to advise and consent in the Senate is the extent to which Congress, in the *normal* course of its business, independently takes specific decisions which affect our interests, sometimes unintentionally as far as Canada is concerned, but at considerable potential costs to those interests.

Then there is the third variable—the difference in the regulatory systems of our respective countries. Our different geography, demography, climate, linguistic and ethnic mix and cultural heritage, and a whole lot of other features, have required our respective governments to deal over the years with specific development problems in ways suiting our respective national circumstances.

The United States is now on a course of massive deregulation. We are not on this path at this time, although our new government is clearly seeking a more competitive environment in Canada for various basic services. Indeed, our Minister of Finance has recently declared that "we must reduce the regulatory burden."[2] But the fact is that we have had different national experiences, and different needs, and in consequence we have and will continue to have a different regulatory concept in many areas, whether in the industrial, transport, communications, financial services, or broadcasting fields. Examples are the issuance of licences to cut timber on public lands, or to explore for oil and gas on such lands, or the adoption of policies to encourage vital air transport to communities. One country's regulatory system is not necessarily better than another, but there are significant differences in the systems. We have seen that in times of economic difficulty, these differences can be misdiagnosed in public political moods as representing threats. The institutions can translate these threats into retaliatory action. Thus we had the recent trucking "war" between our two countries and our large-scale softwood lumber dispute.[3]

These remain times of economic uncertainty, as we well know. Even as economic recovery takes hold, it does not do so evenly across the United States. Clearly some areas are more affected than others, and growth will continue to be uneven. The United States may also be on the verge of an economic down-turn.

There has been an important and continuing movement of people out of the older north-eastern and mid-western industrial areas toward the south-western and western sunbelt. This is part of a highly significant process of economic restructuring. It involves moving away from traditional "smoke-stack industries" into both high-tech industries and low-tech, service-related industries, bringing with it some dislocation and some uncertainty. This in turn leads to demands for assistance, intervention, or protection. Union jobs are perceived to be leaving for non-union areas. The effect is largely one of regional competition for industries and for jobs. It is important for Canadians to recognize that those parts of the United States which are feeling most defensive about the exodus have traditionally been the most outward-looking. They are, significantly, also those which are contiguous to Canada.

All of these factors have an impact on the Congress. But the Congress of today is a very different one from twenty years ago. The most important difference is that it is *decentralized*. Up until some fifteen years ago the Congressional leadership, through the seniority system, could much more easily control the chambers and, particularly, block legislative initiatives which were not deemed convenient or desirable. The administration could put together deals and rely on Congress to respond, on most issues of national interest, to the administration's lead. Foreign governments were therefore in a position where they could more or less consider that the executive to which they are accredited would take care of their interests in Congress.

Perhaps Woodrow Wilson, with his experiences with the Treaty of Versailles, would not agree that I am describing novel events, but I think it is generally recognized that, since the Vietnam War and Watergate, there is indeed a greater degree of independence from the administration experienced by Congress as an institution. And since the time of the basic reforms of the early 1970s within Congress, which by and large did away with the seniority system, there is much greater decentralization within the power structure of Congress itself.

The legislative committees and subcommittees of the Congress are in many respects the new power centres of that institution. There are more than 100 in the Senate and more than 150 in the House of Representatives. The individuals who lead these committees or subcommittees represent a basically independent power base. This has led to a situation which some observers see as atomization or fragmentation in Congress. Sometimes as many as a half-dozen committees can be dealing with the same issue at the same time. And the political anatomy of each committee can differ profoundly, requiring a micro-strategy for each micro-issue.

Among other developments that have reinforced these trends are the diminished discipline of political parties, the emergence of political action committees, and the surge in single interest constituencies, bringing pressure—often in a highly sophisticated manner—on legislators. Further, the impact of television on political campaigns has encouraged greater self-reliance and independence among members. Many seem to run on their own ticket. In the 1984 election, it was common among Democrats, running against a popular president, for political affiliations to be played down or ignored. The end result is an institution which responds more directly and immediately to regional and local pressures from its specific electorates. These are the same electorates which were earlier described as nationalistic and among whom protectionist sentiment is strong. We should reemphasize that these feelings are not directed against Canada; Canada is indeed popular in the United States as opinion polls consistently show. But these phenomena do not necessarily help our case.

A congressman who has no specific economic interest in the matter is not likely to oppose legislation which hurts Canada, if a colleague considers such legislation to be in the great and pressing interest of his constituents. To think he would oppose it on the grounds of being unfair to a country he likes is to place too much faith on rather fragile sentiments, when the issue boils down to the politics of hard regional trade-offs. Canadian interests will prevail, in such a situation, only if they are *consonant* with American interests that can prevail.

To cite an obvious example, when there was acid rain falling only in Ontario, or so it seemed, there was sympathy and understanding among many in the United States national and state legislatures. But it was not until it was known that there was acid rain falling on the lakes in Maine, New Hampshire, New York and Vermont, that there were actually going to be some votes in the same direction.

What kind of legislative impulses can affect Canada?

(1) Legislation specifically directed against Canadian interests can emerge, such as the recent uranium dispute, or our trucking "war," or the congressional proposals affecting the import of natural gas, or the regulation of border broadcasting. In the closely related semi-judicial area, there have been the important cases on softwood lumber and subway cars.

(2) Legislation can be generalized in its attempt to protect Americans against trade practices of quite different countries, often the Europeans or the Japanese, or a third-world exporter, but sideswipe Canada in the process. Examples are the proposed steel import quota legislation, or the Surface Transportation Assistance Act with its impact on steel and cement, or the auto domestic content legislation in Congress, which, mysteriously, keeps being brought forward, notwithstanding the strong performance of the United States auto industry.[4]

(3) Legislation can be domestic in direction and not intended to deal with other countries at all, such as the Clean Air Act and its innumerable amendments, which are the legislative focus in the debate over acid rain control.

(4) Legislation can also be aimed at general trade reform, introducing such novel concepts as reciprocity, downstream dumping, and upstream subsidy. A few key players in both the House of Representatives and the Senate have spearheaded these thrusts. Again, they are not, generally speaking, aimed at Canada, but they have the potential to affect the United States' principal trading partner *more* than any other partner.

(5) Then there is the type of legislation that seems to come from somewhere in Congress, but no one is quite sure where, how, or why, such as the law passed by Congress in 1984 that requires engraved markings on steel tubes and pipes.[5] It can have a large negative effect on some

$350 million of two-way trade, yet its origins seem to lie in a local thrust to protect a manufacturer of man-hole covers in the southern United States.

All of these initiatives and ideas were originated or surfaced in the Congress or in regulatory bodies. We have come to accept, with some regret, that they do not reflect an anomalous situation or even, alas, a temporary one. They are to be seen as a prominent feature of the normal workings of the American system.

The fact of the matter is that the overall foreign policy of the United States toward Canada is, in a certain measure, an aggregate of all of these various types of action. Our relations with the administration can be very good; indeed they are truly excellent. The administration is our close ally in dealing with almost all of these issues. Yet these Congressional initiatives can still leave us with a lot of continuing and new problems.

The administration remains and has to remain our principal interlocutor, and it is vitally important to have it on our side. The administration is, generally speaking, the single most important source of influence within the United States sphere as a whole and will surely remain so. But we must recognize, realistically, that a great deal of work must be done ourselves. In fact, the administration expects that, as a matter of course, we and other foreign governments should be actively defending our interests in the Congress. Often the administration has too many of its own problems to devote the needed time and effort to representing the interests of foreigners. An active and public diplomacy, which is the only possible antidote, is meant quite simply to impress legislators, or their constituents, or other players, with the wisdom of not taking action against Canadian interests. This must be explained not on grounds of being nice to Canada, but on grounds that such action can hurt specific American interests. Accordingly, we must engage those American domestic interests that share a similar outlook to our own. We must seek allies among those who could be hurt by proposed legislation.

The private sector has a key role in this type of diplomacy. It is up to those who sell the product or service in the United States, and who are vulnerable to adverse action, to make sure that the purchaser, the beneficiary, is communicating just that point. There are risks in this type of diplomacy. We may be perceived as interfering in United States domestic affairs. But I think fears of this type of criticism can be overdone.

It is true that years ago, the "Hill" was considered off-limits. It was thought that the administration's leverage on Congress was far stronger than ours, so why bother to try. If they cannot succeed, how can we? Today, no foreign power fails to seek to influence the outcome of a debate in the United States on a vital issue affecting its interests. It is also most important to bear in mind that in Canada's case we are, in most instances, acting in concert with the administration and with its active support or encouragement.

We have just scratched the surface of the Canada–United States relationship but we have scratched deeply enough to explain how subject Canada is to the workings of the United States domestic system. We need to continue to look for ways to live with unpredictability and to reduce the potential damage it causes us. A dozen or so years ago, a policy called the Third Option was designed, which was believed to be suitable for Canadian circumstances then.[6] It is a fact that a lot has happened since.

I believe that Canadians sense that their institutions are strengthened in some key areas of economic and cultural life, and that their nationhood and identity are not fragile. We can, perhaps, judge that this strengthening of our institutions over many years was required, because of what is sometimes seen as the "inadvertent power" of the magnetic forces of the United States over so many aspects of Canadian life. But the country is changing and is understandably a more self-confident one.

Today, with the emergence of our new Progressive Conservative government, policy approaches more in tune with the needs of the next decade are bound to be studied. What better conclusion can be offered than to cite the words of the Speech from the Throne on 5 November 1984: "There are many areas where the national interests or the national policies of the two countries diverge or compete. There are, as well, numerous and as yet untapped possibilities for fruitful cooperation between our two countries. Restoring a climate of goodwill between our governments (was) an essential step towards the resolution of our conflicts and the realization of our opportunities. My government views this initiative as a confirmation of our national strength and maturity."

Notes

1. Agreement between the Government of Canada and the Government of the United States of America on East Coast Fishery Resources, signed at Washington D.C., 29 March 1979; withdrawn from the Senate by the president after opposition in the Senate Foreign Relations Committee in 1981. Senators Pell (D.–R.I.) and Kennedy (D.–Mass.) led the opposition in Congress to this treaty.
2. Minister of Finance, Hon. Michael H. Wilson, "Economic and Fiscal Statement" delivered in the House of Commons, 8 November 1984.
3. In 1980, Congress deregulated the trucking sector (The Motor Carrier Act, Public Law 96-296 of 1 July 1980) and for the first time Canadian truckers were able to enter the U.S. market in considerable numbers. U.S. truckers protested, claiming they were being discriminated against by Canadian regulations. The Interstate Commerce Commission (ICC), feeling the pressure, imposed an administrative moratorium on new Canadian truckers (ICC Docket Number MC-109294 [Sub. No. 28] Commercial Truck Co., Limited extension—general commodities, not printed. Served 17 February 1982). Congress subsequently legislated a two-year moratorium on Canadian truckers entering the United States (Bus Regulatory Reform Act, Public Law 97-261 of 20 September 1982). After two years of litigation and intense bilateral negotiation, the two governments managed to resolve the issue.
    On 24 May 1983, the U.S. Department of Commerce's final determination in the softwood lumber countervail investigation ruled that provincial stumpage practices were not subsidies 48 Fed. Reg. 24-159 (1983).
4. Bill HR 5081 introduced by Rep. Gaydos (D.–Pa.)—Fair Trade in Steel Act of 1984—a bill to reduce unfair practices and provide for orderly trade in certain alloy and stainless steel mill

products, to reduce unemployment, and for other purposes (Bill had 222 co-sponsors). The bill died in the House Ways and Means Committee at the end of the 98th Congress.

Bill HR 3103 introduced by Rep. Anderson (D.–Ca.)—Surface Transportation Technical Corrections Act of 1983. Senate passed HR 3103 with an amendment to roll back partially the "Buy America" restrictions imposed under section 165 of the Surface Transportation Act of 1982 (Public Law 97-424). The Bill died in House/Senate conference at the end of the 98th Congress.

Bill HR 1234 introduced by Rep. Ottinger (D.–N.Y.)—Fair Practices and Procedures in Automotive Products Act of 1983—a bill to establish domestic content requirements for motor vehicles sold or distributed in interstate commerce in the United States. The bill passed the House with amendments (3 November 1983; vote 219 to 199). It was then sent to the Senate and was referred to the Senate Committee on Commerce, Science and Transportation. There the bill died at the end of the 98th Congress, along with the similar Senate Bill S707 introduced by Sen. Reigle (D.–Mich.).

5. Section 207 of Public Law 98-573 of 30 October 1984, Trade and Tariff Act of 1984.

6. In 1970, the Canadian Government published a comprehensive foreign policy review entitled "Foreign Policy for Canadians." A subsequent publication by Hon. Mitchell Sharp, Secretary of State for External Affairs, "Canada-U.S. Relations: Options for the Future" (a special issue of *International Perspectives*, Autumn, 1972), elaborated on the alternatives for the general thrust of Canada's external relations. Of the three options proposed, it was the Third Option—strengthening the Canadian economy through diversification of foreign markets and the resulting lessening of vulnerability vis-à-vis the United States—which was highlighted. The options of maintaining the (1972) status quo or moving toward closer integration with the United States were considered as inadequate responses to the rapid economic transformations taking place and the perceived threats to Canada's national identity.

CHAPTER 2

The Domestic Policy-Making Process in the United States

David Leyton-Brown

On both sides of the border, we are deluded by the similarity of language, the similarity of terms, and the apparent structural similarities of political institutions, into imagining that there is a greater comparability between the Canadian and United States political processes than in fact exists. It behooves us not only as scholars, but also as citizens of an interdependent neighbouring country, to have a closer appreciation of the nature of the policy-making process in the United States. This essay focuses upon four particular aspects: the workings of the executive branch of government in the American political process; the relationship between the executive branch and the legislative branch; the responsiveness of both of these branches of government, and especially the legislature, to pressures from the American public; and the regulatory apparatus which deals with the legislative products that emerge from the political process.

First, though the United States has a cabinet and an administrative structure broadly familiar and comparable to what we have in Canada, it is, of course, constructed on the basis of an entirely different set of fundamental political assumptions. Canadians are accustomed to a system of responsible government in which the executive serves only so long as it is responsible to, and enjoys the full confidence of, the legislature; that is not the case in the United States. This does not mean the American system of government is an "irresponsible" method of governance, though one may feel that way at times. Rather it means that the independence of and, indeed, competition between the two branches is the starting point for an understanding of the entire system. The executive remains in office until the next scheduled election (barring death or impeachment), regardless of legislative support for, or opposition to, its policies and legislation.

Conduct within the executive branch itself is further distinguished from the parliamentary notion of cabinet solidarity and collective responsibility. In Canada, once a government decides upon a policy, all members of the cabinet are individually and collectively responsible for it, and defending that policy in parliament and in public is the price of remaining in the cabinet. Since any differences of opinion prior to the decision are shielded from public view by the doctrine of cabinet secrecy, the executive (cabinet) presents a unified front. By contrast, public disagreement between members of an American cabinet, both before and after the introduction of legislation, is commonplace. Cabinet officers freely advocate and promote particular policy objectives in their overlapping areas of responsibility without regard for the parliamentary ideals of cabinet solidarity. There are many examples of a cabinet officer working hard, and sometimes successfully, to overturn policies advocated and even initiated by cabinet colleagues.[1] The notion of cabinet secrecy is surely not a powerful one in a political culture which so values and cultivates leaks to the press as a standard part of the policy-making process.

Thus there is a very different role for the chief political actors in the United States than in a parliamentary system. The president is both the central figure, in a way that the prime minister in a parliamentary system is not, and also more limited in his ability to achieve the policy objectives he pursues.

To shift from the general to the particular, consider the operating style of Ronald Reagan's administration. This president in particular sees his role as the enunciator of a political vision. He defines the broad direction of policy which his administration will pursue, while delegating to subordinates (cabinet secretaries and the White House staff) the detailed implementation of that broad vision. The process within the executive branch of the present government is one of fairly uncritical acceptance of recommendations that emerge from the subordinate executive structure. This works effectively so long as the senior staff agree and achieve consensus, but flounders when there is division and disagreement among those advisers. A second feature of the Reagan administration is the fact that the process of policy formulation appears to be less a matter of rational policy analysis, or the determination of a particular course of policy on its merits, than a struggle to win the mind of the president—a struggle to legitimize preferred policy options in terms of his broad vision and previously indicated philosophy.

A recent policy example concerns the condition of America's highways.[2] Studies by the United States Department of Transportation discovered serious structural degradation in the federally financed interstate highway system. Without massive repairs, portions of the highway system would become unsuitable for the heavy volume of traffic. The then Secretary of Transportation, Drew Lewis, called for a major federally-funded program to reconstruct the surface transportation system, and to that end proposed a 5¢ per gallon increase in the federal gasoline tax to finance the program. However, at a press conference in September 1982, Ronald Reagan, who had run for president in 1980 on a platform of tax reduction rather than tax increases, opposed the 5¢ per gallon tax and colourfully said that only a "palace coup" would make him support it. This appeared to be a definitive statement, but nothing could be further from the truth. Secretary Lewis knew better than to take no for an answer. He argued to the president that the 5¢ per gallon charge should not be considered a tax increase, but rather a user fee designed to make those who drive on the nation's highways pay for their upkeep. User fees were entirely compatible with Ronald Reagan's political philosophy, and he appeared about to support the proposal.

David Stockman, then Director of the Office of Management and Budget, who had been the chief opponent of the proposal because of his primary objective of reducing the federal deficit, also returned to the fray. Having been outflanked on the question of terminology, he countered that whether it was called a tax or a user fee, using federal money to finance repair work done by states and local authorities would violate another of Ronald Reagan's campaign platform commitments—the New Federalism concept of transferring expenditure programs under state jurisdiction from the federal government back to the states. This argument, too, appeared persuasive.

However, Secretary Lewis again approached the president to remind him that, when governor of California, he had agreed to an increase in the state gasoline tax which was rebated to localities. If it did not contradict his basic principles then, surely it would not do so now. That argument carried the day. Less than two months after his definitive statement of opposition, and even without a palace coup, Ronald Reagan publicly endorsed the 5¢ per gallon tax surcharge. A month later the United States Surface Transportation Act was passed into law.[3]

This illustration demonstrates that once the issue was raised, it ceased to be discussed in terms of the need for highway repairs and for raising the funds to pay for them. The policy issue was no longer addressed on its merits, but developed into a theological citation of opposing gospels. It became an attempt to use Ronald Reagan's previous policy utterances to legitimize the opposing points of view among his senior staff. Far from being unique, this illustration is quite representative of the current executive policy-making process in Washington.

Second, turning from the executive branch to the relations between the executive and the legislature, surely no reader needs to be reminded of the doctrine of the separation of powers and the checks and balances between Congress and the presidency. However, one should be aware of the cyclical and secular trends in the relationship between these two branches. Since decades before World War II, there has been oscillation between the ascendancy of one branch or the other. Periods in which either the president or Congress has achieved relative ascendancy have been explained as responsive to conditions of war and peace, or to the strength or weakness of particular executives.[4] Many have argued that the recent period of congressional assertion in the 1970s is merely another stage in this cyclical evolution in the post-Watergate and post-Vietnam era. This view maintains that, as do all cyclical phenomena, the circle will complete itself, and will move again to a relaxation of congressional rule and a further ascendancy of the executive.[5] Though, indeed, such cycles can be expected to continue, they must be understood as taking place within a context.

There is a secular trend in which the role of Congress in the American domestic political process is undergoing irrevocable change, because of a number of internal transformations within the legislative branch itself. The most outstanding of these has been an unprecedented and qualitative change in staff expertise available to individual congressmen and senators and to their committees. For the first time in American political history, it has become possible for the legislative branch to contain its own independent sources of information and policy analysis rather than merely relying upon testimony from administration officials and outside witnesses brought before committees.[6] This is perhaps most evident in the budget process, in which a separate, large, and coherent budget planning staff exists within the Congress, which, in effect, conducts a parallel budget planning exercise while the executive branch is preparing budget proposals.[7] The current clash over budget priorities goes far beyond what would have been the level of congressional involvement in these financial areas twenty or more years ago.

At the same time that the staff resources presently available to the legislative branch have transformed its capacity to be involved in the policy-making process in an independent way, internal rule changes within the legislative branch have led to a decentralization of power. This diffusion of the power structure within the legislative branch has reached the point at which it is probably wrong to think of a single legislative branch checking and balancing the president. Perhaps one should think more and more of 535 autonomous legislative branches, each of them elected to the House of Representatives or the Senate. Some of these internal changes have had to do with the modification of the seniority system, the democratization of the selection of committee chairs, and the change in the bottle-neck control that the rules committees, or their equivalent, used to have in terms of the assignment of legislation to particular committees for consideration.[8] It has now become possible for the same item of legislation to be considered simultaneously in several committees, rather than only in a single committee preferred by the congressional leadership.

In short, it was always the case in previous cycles of congressional ascendancy that there was a struggle between its leadership and the president. Now that the power of the congressional leadership has been weakened within Congress itself, struggles are between individuals or ad hoc clusters of congressmen and the president, and there has ceased to be a single point of contact for the executive branch in negotiations which attempt to reach some mutually acceptable compromise. As power has become diffused and expertise has increased, Congress will never again occupy the same position in the American domestic political process that it did prior to the 1970s.

Third, this change within the legislative branch, and hence in the relationship between the legislative and executive branches, has taken place at the same time as there has been a striking transformation in the social or popular context within which that process takes place. This is a transformation in the number and effectiveness of special interest groups. Here it is important not to overstate the case. The American political process, from its origins, has been pluralistic, and dependent upon inputs from competing special interests. To observe that there are special interests involved in the process is to say nothing new. Rather the argument is that the number, coherence, organization, and impact of those interests has been transformed for two principal reasons.

The first of these is internal to interest groups themselves. It has become possible within the last ten or fifteen years, for interest groups to develop a professionalism and hence an effective impact that was not accessible to them in the past. Through such modern techniques as computerized mailing lists, direct mail solicitations, issue polling, and the hiring of skilled political professionals, it has become possible for an enormous variety of special interests to identify their constituencies and to get action from members of those constituencies. That action can range from financial contributions and letter-writing campaigns to turning out at nominating meetings, or voting. Accordingly, it has become possible for these single issue, highly-focussed groups to have a far greater impact than has been the case before, especially as legislators are particularly sensitive to pressures from the electorate.

This internal transformation of interest groups has taken place at the same time as Congress has invited such groups, by means of amendments to the Federal Election Campaign Act, to play a greater role. Beginning in 1974, election campaign laws in the United States created what is now a ubiquitous phenomenon, the political action committee (PAC).[9] Since 1974, the number of legally constituted political action committees, which are created as a channel for campaign contributions and election financing, have prolif-erated from 608 in the first year to 1 146 in 1976, to 1 653 in 1978, to 2 551 in 1980, to 3 371 in 1982, and to 4 009 in 1984.[10]

More striking than the sheer numbers of political action committees is the amount of money at their disposal. Expenditures began modestly in 1974 with some $12.5 million being channelled through political action committees. That amount grew to $22.6 million in 1976, $35.2 million in 1978, $55.3 million in 1980, and approximately $90 million in 1982. Po-litical action committees have replaced the political party as the major funding vehicle of election campaigns in the United States. The party has not vanished as a funding vehicle, but it has fallen to second place. Inter-estingly, the Republican party in particular has been rebuilding with many of the same fund-raising and organizational techniques.[11]

To give one further example, in the November 1984 election, more money was spent in the single senatorial election contest in North Carolina, largely by political action committees though not directly by the candidates, than was spent in the entire Canadian federal election in September, 1984. The scale of financial capabilities that the political action committees employ is a transformation of the American electoral process.

When political action committees first began having such influence, mem-bers of Congress quite deliberately created an incentive in federal election laws for them to concentrate their funding on congressional and senatorial races rather than on the presidential race. The means of doing so was somewhat simple. They put a low ceiling on the contributions that could be given to a presidential candidate by any particular individual or organizational donor in order to be matched by public funding, which is the main source of money for presidential campaigns. There is no such matching funding in congressional and senatorial races, and the maximum contribution limits were substantially higher. There is no limit on spending to oppose a candidate or on independent expenditures in support. Not surprisingly, political action committees recognized that their leverage would be greater in legislative races, where they concentrated their funding to great effect. On 18 March 1985, the United States Supreme Court determined that the $1 000 restriction on contributions to presidential campaign funding was a violation of the freedom of speech provisions in the first amendment to the United States Constitution and struck down that aspect of the law.[12] This decision will not have the effect of reducing the impact of political action committees. If anything, it will encourage them to be more involved in presidential campaigns than they were in the past, without necessarily diverting them from the other kinds of campaigns upon which they have also concentrated.

Such developments suggest that at the same time as Congress has become more unpredictably and autonomously involved in the policy-making process, it has become more responsive to the domestic pressures of constituents and campaign contributors. The transformation in patterns of campaign funding suggests that the long-standing efforts to pull together voter coalitions are under serious threat from incentives to campaigners to appeal in a fragmented way to small but well-organized and well-financed single issue pressure groups.

Finally, one should consider the regulatory process for the executive implementation of laws and the quasi-judicial interpretation of the products of the American political process. Characteristically, the desire has been to reduce administrative discretion in the implementation of legislation and to make legal remedies widely accessible.

The structures existing under United States trade laws offer a useful illustration. A process has been created for the application of countervailing duties, anti-dumping duties, and contingent safeguards in conformity with international trade agreements negotiated under the General Agreement on Tariffs and Trade (GATT). The process is intended to be relatively immune to political and discretionary decisions on the part of the United States government. Rather the criteria of judgment are specified in law. Quasi-judicial investigative and regulatory agencies are established under legal authority, and any interested American individual company or association of companies feeling injured by imports from abroad is free to raise a complaint against those imports.

For example, in the case of a complaint calling for countervailing duties to offset a "bounty or grant" paid to foreign exporters, the regulatory process is complex, following a strict, prescribed schedule and involving a variety of government and independent actors. Once a proper petition has been filed, two parallel investigations are initiated. The International Trade Administration (ITA) of the Department of Commerce determines in a preliminary way, and then finally, whether subsidies as defined in the United States trade law exist (above a *de minimis*, or inconsequential, level of 0.5 per cent of the value of the product), and sets the amount of countervailing duty, if one is justified. The International Trade Commission (ITC), an independent regulatory agency, determines in a preliminary way, and then finally, whether there is or may be material injury to an American industry. The ITC must make a determination of material injury before the ITA can assess a countervailing duty, and the investigation is terminated if the preliminary or final determination of material injury by the ITC is negative, or if the final determination of the existence of subsidies by the ITA is negative. Any factual findings, legal conclusions, or decisions may be contested by any party to an investigation in the United States Court of International Trade.

In this area, and in a number of other policy areas that are more domestic than international, the role of the independent regulatory agency should also be seen as a part of the political process.[13] Neither the president nor any other branch or part of the United States government can directly influence the outcome of a regulatory process, or even exercise discretion as to whether to entertain a case, without thereby laying the grounds for a legal challenge. Not only should the independent regulatory agency be recognized as a quasi-independent actor in the American policy process, but the ability of an individual or interest group to create the agenda of those independent agencies should be recognized as a means of access to that process.

In summary, though the similarities between Canada and the United States are pronounced, the American policy-making process differs quite markedly from that in Canada. Both political systems are representative democracies, but they have different structures, rest on different fundamental assumptions, and exist in different social contexts. The presidential system functions differently than the prime ministerial one, and the decision-making style of the current Reagan administration has several unique and important features. The secular trend toward greater expertise with more diffused power within Congress is transforming the pattern of legislative/executive relations. At the same time, the growing number, effectiveness, and financial impact of special interest groups is building upon the existing responsiveness of elected legislators to constituents and contributors in a fashion that may alter the process of coalition formation that underlies the pluralistic American political system. The autonomy of, and private access to, independent regulatory agencies provides another important dimension to the American policy process. The American policy-making process is worthy of study by Canadians, not only because of its inherent fascination, but because the outputs of that process matter so much to America's nearest and most interdependent neighbour.

Notes

1. Personalized accounts of feuding between White House staff and cabinet secretaries, or among members of the cabinet, are common. A good example is Alexander M. Haig, Jr., *Caveat: Realism, Reagan and Foreign Policy* (New York: MacMillan, 1984).

2. This case was first drawn to my attention in George J. Church, "How Reagan Decides," *Time*, 13 December 1982, pp. 10–15.

3. This act should not be confused with the earlier Surface Transportation Assistance Act of 1978, which was of particular interest to Canada because of its provision that forbade states and municipalities from using federal funds for buying foreign-produced mass transit equipment or steel for highway construction unless it was more than 10 per cent cheaper than corresponding American products.

4. See John Mueller, *War, Presidents and Public Opinion* (New York: John Wiley, 1973), or Frans R. Bax, "The Legislative-Executive Relationship in Foreign Policy: New Partnership or New Competition?" *Orbis* 20 (Winter 1977).

5. Contrasting arguments on this question of legislative-executive relations are reviewed in David Leyton-Brown, "The Role of Congress in the Making of Foreign Policy," *International Journal* Vol. xxxvii, No. 1, Winter 1982-3.

6. Personal and committee staffs have more than tripled since 1954, and now exceed 17 000 persons. A further 6 000 are found in congressional research agencies (e.g., General Accounting Office, Congressional Research Service, Office of Technology Assessment, Congressional Budget Office). See Thomas M. Franck and Edward Weisband, *Foreign Policy by Congress* (New York: Oxford University Press, 1979), ch. 10, especially p. 228 and fn7, p. 377.

7. The Congressional Budget Office was created in 1974 under the authority of the Congressional Budget and Impoundment Control Act (1974). See: James P. Pfiffner, *The President, the Budget and Congress: Impoundment and the 1974 Budget Act* (Boulder, Co.: Westview, 1979), ch. 3.

8. See: Thomas E. Mann and Norman J. Ornstein, eds., *The New Congress* (Washington, D.C.: American Enterprise Institute, 1981).

9. Under the Federal Election Campaign Act of 1974, corporations, trade associations and allied special interest groups are allowed to form political action committees, defined as "separate, segregated funds to be utilized for political purposes." The law further limits contributions to a presidential candidate receiving federal campaign funding to $1 000, and to a congressional or senatorial candidate in each primary or general election to a maximum of $1 000 from individuals or $5 000 from organizations (including PAC's). There are no limits on general spending to oppose a candidate, or on "independent political expenditures," defined as expenditures made without the cooperation or consultation of the candidate, or his representative.

10. "FEC Says PAC's Top 4 000 for 1984," Federal Election Commission press release, 28 January 1985.

11. Gary C. Jacobson. "The Republican Advantage in Campaign Finance," in John E. Chubb and Paul E. Peterson, eds., *The New Direction in American Politics* (Washington, D.C.: The Brookings Institution, 1985).

12. The decision was in a case brought by the Federal Election Commission and the Democratic Party against the National Conservative Political Action Committee and the Fund for a Conservative Majority, for allegedly planning to violate the spending limit in 1984.

13. The constellation of such actors includes about fifty-five independent agencies and government corporations, five quasi-official agencies, and seventy-five boards, commissions, and committees. See: Randal Ripley and Grace Franklin, *Congress, the Bureaucracy and Public Policy*, rev. ed. (Homewood, Ill.: Dorsey Paperback, 1983).

CHAPTER 3

America's Hegemonic Decline and the Reagan Revival

John J. Kirton

In the analysis of international politics and American foreign policy during the post-1968 era, there are few points accorded such widespread acceptance and central significance as the loss of America's global hegemony.[1] The consensus on the accuracy and importance of this phenomenon embraces those from both the policy and scholarly communities and from the interpretive traditions of realism and interdependence alike. For the leading modern realist, Henry Kissinger, what was fundamental to his international vision and his conduct of American foreign policy within this system was the following trend:

> The late 1960's had marked the end of the period of American predominance based on overwhelming nuclear and economic supremacy. The Soviet nuclear stockpile was inevitably approaching parity . . . . The percentage of the world's Gross National Product represented by our economy was sinking by 10 percent with every decade: from 52 percent in 1950 to 40 percent in 1960, to some 30 percent in 1970 (it is [in 1982] 22 percent) . . . . Still the strongest nation but no longer pre-eminent, we would have to take seriously the world balance of power . . . .[2]

And for students of interdependence, the primary academic question is the prospect and path for international cooperation after an American hegemony that all assert once existed, but has now clearly gone.[3]

This profound intellectual conviction, triggered by the self-imposed defeat of the United States in the Tet offensive in Vietnam in the spring of 1968, prevailed without serious challenge through the frustrations of the Vietnam withdrawal, Watergate and the Carter presidency.[4] Yet while the conviction has persisted to this day, it has, since 1980, grown increasingly at odds with the rhetoric of the American leadership and the mood of its people. Indeed, the entry of Ronald Reagan into the White House at least coincided with, and perhaps helped inspire, a sharp shift in the dominant popular perception in America from one of "eagle entangled" to one of "eagle defiant."[5] Supporting this perception have been several visible and arguably vital developments. A major rearmament program begun in the late 1970s quickly acquired an unusual intensity and has been sustained for an exceptionally long period of time. Joining this trend after the trough of the American recession in 1982 was a booming economy and a sustained soaring exchange rate for the United States dollar. The proclamation of the Strategic Defense Initiative in 1983 and the invasion of Grenada in the same year signalled, respectively, American determination to reclaim the high frontier of advanced technology and its willingness and ability to employ military force abroad. Underscoring the drama of these developments was the decline in the record of America's non-communist rivals, as economic stagnation in Europe, declining real prices for oil, and the debt crisis amongst the newly industrializing third world countries emerged as durable features of the international landscape.

Is the revival of the United States under President Reagan real? While few have argued that recent American performance has restored the United States to a position of international hegemony, or even rendered such a possibility likely, the record of the past half decade has destroyed any complacency about assuming the United States to be a long-term loser in the international system.[6] Moreover, in contrast to presumptions that international decline is a unidirectional, ever continuing process, it is possible that America's very freedom from hegemonic responsibilities has enabled it to reconcentrate its energies and restore its national power.[7] And while most regard hegemony as a condition that comes once and is gone forever, there is at least one widely accepted historical example of a country that bounced back rapidly to enjoy a second era of predominance.[8]

This essay makes no attempt to specify the precise category in the international status order in which the United States currently resides, to chart America's long-term fortunes as a future or fast-fading hegemon, or to enrich the competing theories of hegemonic emergence and decline.[9] The far more limited objective is to assess whether the Reagan revival in America has challenged or qualified the intellectual convictions of the previous decade about America's downward descent.[10] Thus, the essay first deals with the competing conceptions of hegemony, to see precisely what the United States is supposed to have once had, then lost, and now wants to regain. It next assesses the evidence to see whether the common view of the post–World War II record is correct. And finally, it assesses the record of the 1980s to see if past convictions are appropriate now. The conclusion offers some speculative interpretations for the apparently confused empirical pattern which the 1980s provide.

1. The Concept of Hegemony

The distinguished American scholar of the international economy, William Diebold, Jr., wrote in 1983 that from the pens of American statesmen there are "no memoirs called 'my days as a happy hegemon.'"[11] And others, in-cluding those who participated in the construction and early management of the post–World War II international order, are quick to caution those who assume America's predominance—particularly its capacity to "make and enforce the rules" —as an easily recognized, widely accepted reality of those difficult years.[12] These cautions betray an uncertainty not only about American capability and power, but also about the concept of hegemony itself. It is a term of the scholars rather than the practitioners, and the former have varied considerably over its meaning. The most simple conception, provided by Martin Wight under the label of "dominant power," is "a power that can measure strength against all its rivals combined."[13] Echoing this maximalist conception is George Modelski, who equates hegemony with the dominance of a "world power," formally defined as a unit "monopolizing (that is, controlling more than one half of) the market for (or the supply of) order-keeping in the global layer of interdependence."[14]

Despite this simplicity, the Wight-Modelski conception raises important ambiguities concerning the capabilities ("strength") to be measured, the balance between producing ("supply") and consuming ("market") capa-bilities, the extension of dominant capabilities into predominant outcomes, and the scope of the system over which dominance is to apply. The question of *which* capabilities begins with such perennial issues in international politics as the balance between military and nonmilitary resources, which capabilities in each category are truly critical, and whether such critical capabilities are constant over time (e.g., steel production) or ever-changing according to developments in technology or shifts in the international sys-tem. It extends to most of the remaining issues in capability analysis, in-cluding the vital technical problems of how one aggregates diverse capability measures into a single standard, treats as comparable varying cross-national statistical series and economic structures, and deals with the inevitable fluctuations in the exchange rates that render such overall comparisons possible.[15]

A second major issue is how to deal with consumption at home and production abroad, once the proper national capabilities are defined. One's national consumption is alternatively a drain on the national production (or surplus capability) available for foreign policy (hegemony maintenance) purposes, a source of leverage over actors at home or abroad who supply this market (when the home government can suppress or divert this con-sumption), or a source of vulnerability (when other actors can control supply and the home government cannot control demand). Finally, when and how does one credit to a home government the capabilities or pro-duction located abroad, which it or its nationals own, control or to which they can gain access?[16]

A third issue concerns the lengthy and complex process of translating capability into control over outcomes, and where along this spectrum analyses should centre. Three processes are involved. The physical pro-cess involves moving from potential resources, to resources that can be mobilized, to "in place" capability, to effectively deployed and employed instruments of statecraft. The cognitive process involves moving from one's recognition of capabilities, through the will to assert them, and their recognition by others, to their ultimate deference to them. And the third is the process of moving from short-term to long-term victories and from desired outcomes on key issues to the creation of a desired system that other states want, benefit from, and for which they pay the price.[17]

The final major issue concerns the scope of the system in question. Does one focus on the Eurocentric (central, land-based) system, or the global (peripheral, maritime) system? Does one compare a leader's capability and control against all other actors combined or just against its closest rival? And can one multiply a state's control over core groups into control over the full system by arguing, for example, that the United States dominates the seven countries of the western summit, the seven dominate the Organization for Economic Co-operation and Development (OECD) countries, the OECD countries dominate the north-south exchange system, and this system dominates the world economy?[18]

Many of these ambiguities are resolved or reduced in the less ambitious conception of hegemony offered by Robert Keohane and Joseph Nye, Jr.[19] For these authors, hegemony exists "when one state is powerful enough to maintain the essential rules governing interstate relations, and willing to do so."[20] In the "overall structure" version of this model, the key capability is military power with its supporting economic basis as a secondary item. Capability is restricted to national production, power extends to the ability and willingness to discard, veto, and create rules, and the scope of the system is "the world structure of military and economic power." Within this framework, the stronger prevail.[21]

Apart from such reductions in ambiguity, the Keohane-Nye conception offers two advantages. Firstly, it adds the national actor's choice of a foreign policy role with an emphasis on leadership and "systematic" orientation. Here, a hegemon must: (a) identify its interests with those of the system it manages (and avoid nationalism, bilateralism and autarchy); (b) see itself as the consumer of long-term benefits produced by the regime; and (c) thus be willing to give up short-term gains in bargaining in order to preserve the regime.[22]

Secondly, Nye and Keohane provide an extensive list of signs to suggest whether hegemony exists or is in decline. Briefly, hegemony exists when there is military preponderance and general prosperity in the system, and when other states benefit and can even grow more rapidly than the hegemon. Hegemony is in decline when there is an abundance of crises, ad hoc policy measures, dissenters, arguments over burden sharing, and secondary governments demanding status and autonomy.

Despite these conceptual advances, two major problems remain. First, the focus on military and supporting economic capabilities is too general and elusive a set of variables for easy empirical analysis. And compounding this problem is the development of a co-existing "issue structure" model, whose very existence suggests that there are no core military and economic resources which control everything else, and no single, integrated, comprehensive system in which hegemony (which implies a single actor dominating a single system) can prevail.

The second, and related, problem concerns the emphasis on the essential rules of the system. As students of international regimes have discovered, it is very difficult to define the rules and decide which ones are essential, even when the identity and boundary of the system are known. It becomes virtually impossible to do so when it is not known if there is one system, or several, existing at varying if subordinate levels of generality below, with an unspecified relationship to one another and to whatever overall system might exist.[23] One is thus left with the challenge of conducting empirical analysis without really knowing what capabilities to look for at the start, and what outcomes to consider at the end.

These two problems are reduced in the most recent, and precise definition, provided by Robert Keohane in *After Hegemony*.[24] In his work hegemony is defined as "preponderance of material resources." Preponderance means "stronger on [four] dimensions, taken as a whole, than any other country."[25] The four dimensions are:

(1) control over, or access to, crucial raw materials such as oil;

(2) control over, or guaranteed access to, major sources of capital, especially the national possession of well-functioning capital markets so the government can borrow cheaply, provide credit to friends, and deny it to adversaries;

(3) control over markets, or the maintenance of a large market for imports, where the government has great discretion in opening it up or closing it off;

(4) comparative advantages or competitive superiority in the production of highly valued, or high-value-added goods, with a premium on goods using complex or new technology, not labour intensive, not produced with well-known production techniques, the most profitable products, and those providing the basis for producing even more advanced goods and services in the future. The basis for this is technological superiority and political control over valuable resources yielding significant rents.[26]

Despite its advantages, this formulation presents three difficulties. The first is its exclusively economic emphasis (with an unspecified relationship to the military sphere). The second is the ease with which it slides along the spectrum of national production, control, guaranteed access, and merely access, without indicating if these are each full substitutes on a scale of hegemonic decline. For example, did the United States lose hegemony when it became a major oil importer in the 1950s, or regain it with the end of the Arab oil embargo in 1974? The third problem consists of the internal contradictions of requiring a hegemon to have, simultaneously, an economic structure with a strong primary (raw material), secondary (technology-intensive goods, capital goods) and tertiary (capital markets, trade) sector, and of being, over time, both relatively autarkic (control over its market) and having the global reach that hegemony implies.

Finally, it is useful to consider the signs of hegemonic decline offered by Robert Gilpin, as elaborated and applied to recent American foreign policy by Kenneth Oye.[27] Here the focus is on "external burdens of leadership, internal secular tendencies toward using consumption, and the international diffusion of technology."[28] External burdens comprise disproportionate alliance defence costs, military consumption, and financial, security, and trade assistance to maintain allegiances and the strength of allies. Consumption deals with the shares of GNP devoted to consumption and investment. And the international diffusion of technology focuses on "margins of technological superiority on which economic and military advantage may be based."[29]

From these partly competing and overlapping conceptions of hegemony, this essay constructs and employs a two-stage formulation, centred on the distinction between simple and complex hegemony. Simple hegemony, based on the Wight-Modelski formulation, exists when a single state possesses, within national boundaries, over 50 per cent of the military and economic product of the entire system, its controlling subsystem, or the group composed of a state and its major rivals, actual and potential. In a condition of simple hegemony, the hegemon's willingness to lead the system is largely irrelevant since its very overarching presence offers such leadership regardless of the choices of its citizenry or state. Complex hegemony in contrast, based on the essential features of the Nye, Keohane, and Gilpin formulations, exists when a state has a secure leading position over rivals, and the ability and willingness to lead the system.

Simple hegemony is an easily understood, but empirically rare, phenomenon. Complex hegemony, on the other hand, is conceptually richer, empirically more common, more relevant to an understanding of America's contemporary fate, and more closely related to those political processes of bargaining and system management whose explanation induces us to focus on hegemony in the first place. It has two major dimensions, the first concerned with *capability*, the second concerned with *role*. In the realm of capability, one looks for a state in a first place position, with a stable and substantial lead over its nearest rival, sufficient to withstand short-term surprises or disruptions in the international system and to sustain short-term losses. Secondly, one looks more precisely for a state's surplus capability, or the resources it has beyond those required for basic security and economic needs at home and abroad, and hence freely disposable by the leadership on order maintenance tasks abroad. And thirdly, one looks for a state's deep capability of reinforcement, in the form of its control over access to critical capital, natural resources, and technology abroad.

The second dimension of complex hegemony provides its fourth characteristic—the choice of a role of leadership. Here emphasis is on the willingness of a country's government to exercise leadership in the international system, and the willingness of its own citizens and other major states to accept this as legitimate, i.e., to follow that lead. This element of choice becomes vital for a state which does not automatically provide leadership by its overwhelming presence, and which can see close rivals, some of then compatible, with sufficient capability to assume the burdens of leadership and thus avoid systemic anarchy and collapse.

2. American Hegemony—the Golden Age?

Having established what hegemony might be, one can turn to the empirical question of whether the United States once had it at the outset of the post–World War II period. Despite the variability of the concept and deficiencies in the data, it is clear that it did. It was in such measure as to lend substance to widespread perceptions of American preeminence and subsequent decline. Only the actual degrees of predominance and the date of the transition to a subsequent state remain in dispute.

Even by the most stringent standards of simple hegemony—the 50 per cent of global productive capacity underscoring the Wight-Modelski formulation—it is clear that American hegemony once existed. In 1960 American military spending represented 51 per cent of world military spending. As Henry Kissinger reminded us, in 1950 the United States GNP represented 52 per cent of the global total.[30] And in the more limited range of United States Gross Domestic Product as a percentage of the United States and its major economic rivals, the European Economic Community and Japan, three different statistical surveys gave the United States as high as 69 per cent, and never lower than 54 per cent, during the period from 1950 to 1970.[31]

To sustain this exceptionally strong conception, it is of course necessary to accept a few devices. One must pair 1960 military expenditure with 1950 GNP, thus pairing Korean War and Sputnik induced rearmament with American preeminence in a war-shattered world a decade earlier. One must measure military expenditure, in strong United States dollars, rather than armed forces personnel, where the United States provided only 13 per cent of the global total in 1960 and only 14 per cent, after a decade in Vietnam, in 1970.[32] One must accept certain foreign statistical series and cross-national dollar conversion formulae, while noting that other, non-Kissingerian calculations give the United States at best only 39 per cent of Gross World Product from 1950 and beyond.[33] And one must exclude, as economic rivals of the United States, the Soviet bloc, major third world states, and Canada and the fellow dominions.

As one moves toward less stringent conceptions of hegemony, the case for United States preeminence becomes almost incontrovertible, despite the vastly overestimated Soviet challenge in an allegedly bipolar system, and the vastly underestimated endurance of the global reach and responsibility of William Fox's third superpower—the United Kingdom.[34] The Americans were in first place, with a substantial lead and substantial surplus capacity, in virtually all relevant categories. To be sure, the United States provided only 18.4 per cent of world trade in 1950 (compared to 24 per cent for Britain in 1870), and only 33.3 per cent of the U.S.A.-EEC-Japan total in

1950.[35] Yet elsewhere there is little doubt. Figures on currency reserves, investment abroad, and aid, all point strongly to American preeminence.[36] Resources tell a similar story, unless one adds consumption figures as a sign of vulnerability (rather than of market control) and subtracts them from national production.[37] In technology the issue is in doubt only if one values highly the actual detonation of a nuclear device, or the ability to launch a satellite into earth orbit. While such ambiguities are genuine, taking them seriously leads to the conclusion that the countries preventing America from a hegemonic position were the United Kingdom and Canada as much as the Soviet Union.[38]

All three veto powers can be readily dismissed when one examines their capacity to influence or be influenced by the United States, and, far more importantly, the exercise of world leadership. After America's decision to fight in Korea, there was no doubt about the American attachment to a global role. No other country came close to the crusading messianism of John Kennedy's Inaugural Address in January, 1961. It is indicative of the identity of the United States with global interests, and probably American leadership in defining the latter, that from 1947 to 1965 the United States each year voted with the majority in the United Nations General Assembly never less than 50 per cent, and often as high as 66 per cent, of the time.[39]

3. The Decline of American Hegemony

Even more apparent is America's loss of this preeminence by the decade of the 1970s. United States military spending as a share of global spending had fallen to 42 per cent by 1970 (despite the concentrated, stimulative impact of the Vietnam War), and to 28 per cent by 1980 (with Vietnam gone)—a decline of 33 per cent in a single decade.[40] During the 1970s most students of comparative national power placed Soviet military capability well ahead of America's.[41] And U.S. armed forces personnel as a share of world personnel declined from 14 per cent to 8.3 per cent, an impressive 40 per cent decline in a decade.[42] Indeed, from 1960 to 1979 the U.S.S.R. was investing on average almost twice as much of its GDP into military spending as was the United States.[43]

Signs of economic erosion abound as well. The statistics with the least grandiose conception of American immediate postwar primacy—those of the Central Intelligence Agency—show America's share of gross world product falling from 25.9 per cent in 1960 to 21.5 per cent in 1980.[44] America's GDP share of the U.S.A.-EEC-Japan total dropped even more impressively from about ten points above the 50 per cent threshold (depending on the statistical series) to about ten points below.[45] From 1960 to 1979, the United States was consistently beaten, by healthy margins, by the Federal Republic of Germany, Japan, and the Soviet Union, in annual growth rate and the share of GDP devoted to fixed capital formation. And a comparison of growth rates in the manufacturing sector saw the United States beaten substantially

Table A

Summit Seven GNP, 1979

	U.S. $ (billions)	% of total
U.S.A.	2 614	41.5
Japan	1 153	18.3
Germany, Federal Republic	848	13.4
France	634	10.1
United Kingdom	445	7.1
Italy	368	5.8
Canada	243	3.9
	6 305	
EEC 4 combined	2 295	36.4
Japan-Federal Republic of Germany-France combined	2 635	41.8

Source: Based on Walter Jones, *The Logic of International Relations* (Toronto: Little, Brown, 1985), p. 253.

by the Federal Republic of Germany, Canada and France in 1960–70 and the latter two in 1970–81.[46]

One must recognize that in 1979 the United States still ranked first in the world with a GNP of $2 614 billion, surpassing the second-ranked Soviets by almost 100 per cent ($1 424 billion) and the third-ranked Japanese by over 100 per cent ($1 153 billion).[47] Yet in that year, the last before Reagan's electoral victory, America's share of GNP among the seven western summit powers was only 41.5 per cent of the group, a share rivalled by the 36.4 per cent combined share of the four EEC members.

The question of markets presents a less obvious pattern. America's proportion of world trade has declined only marginally, from 18.4 per cent in 1950, to 15.3 per cent in 1960, to 14.4 per cent in 1970, to 13.4 per cent in 1977.[48] Yet the decline has been rather more dramatic when one considers the American share of trade by the core GATT group of the U.S.A.-EEC-Japan, where the American figure has fallen from 33.3 per cent in 1950, to 27 per cent in 1960, to 23.5 per cent in 1970, and to 22.1 per cent in 1980.[49] The reason for the slow rate of American decline, particularly in the 1970s has been the rapid and massive shift of the United States during that decade toward the position of an open economy. Both exports and imports as a percentage of GNP doubled for the United States, from around 6 to 12 per cent from 1970 to 1980, with imports showing the sharper increase.[50] Such a shift has sustained United States market power, while, simultaneously, sharply increasing its sensitivity and vulnerability to forces abroad.

This increase in openness and decline in surplus capacity is vividly seen in the issue area of capital. In official development assistance, where the United States long provided over one half of the world's share, its 1971–81 average annual contribution of 0.2 per cent of GNP (compared with France at 0.6, Canada at 0.5, the Federal Republic of Germany and the United Kingdom at 0.4, Japan at 0.2 and Italy at 0.1) placed it second last among its summit partners in its ability and willingness to give.[51] Moreover, the sustained generosity of the Scandinavians and Dutch during this period, and the emergence of the oil-rich Arab states as major donors, has increasingly confined the United States to a minor position. In national currency reserves, the United States in both 1970 and 1976 possessed less than 50 per cent of each of France, Canada, Japan and the Federal Republic of Germany. Indeed in 1976 the United States had only one third the currency reserves of Kuwait, one sixth those of the United Arab Emirates, one tenth those of Canada, and smaller proportions of those of France, Venezuela, Iran, Japan, Saudi Arabia and the Federal Republic of Germany.[52] Commensurate with this lack of liquid funds was a shift in the pattern of direct investment overseas. In 1970, direct foreign investment in the United States represented 17.6 per cent of the value of American direct investment abroad. This figure rose to 22.5 per cent by 1976, 26 per cent by 1978, and 30 per cent by 1980.[53]

In the area of national resources, the portrait of American decline depends heavily on the patterns in, and significance of, oil. For minerals as a whole, in 1975 the United States retained its number one position as a principal producer, even if the Soviet Union was a very close second, and Canada a rather close third.[54] Yet in oil, the shift of the United States from being an export capable power, as in the 1967 mid-east embargo, to an import dependent power, as in the 1973 embargo, was dramatic. In 1967 American net oil imports represented 19 per cent of American oil consumption and 9 per cent of total energy demand. By 1979 they represented 48 per cent and 22 per cent respectively. From another vantage point, in 1970 oil constituted 7.3 per cent of the value of American imports. By 1980, oil imports constituted 31.7 per cent.[55]

Finally, it was in the realm of leadership commitment that the American decline was most pronounced. United States voting with the majority in the United Nations General Assembly fell from 50 per cent in 1965 to 25 per cent in the 1970s.[56] From 1973 to 1978, over 41 per cent of the American people thought the United States was spending too little on domestic programs, while about 44 per cent thought they were spending about the right amount on defence.[57] During the mid-1970s only a *minority* of Americans wanted the United States to defend Europe or Japan if the U.S.S.R. attacked them, over 70 per cent wanted to think less in international terms and more on building domestic strength and prosperity (up from 55 per cent in 1964), and unprecedentedly high numbers favoured not worrying about other countries agreeing, letting other countries get along by themselves, and not taking into account the opinions of allies in deciding on world affairs.[58]

4. The Reagan Revival: Rhetorical or Real

President Reagan entered office in January, 1981, with a simple and single-minded goal of restoring American power to the international prominence it once enjoyed. After half a decade of sustained and focused commitment to this task, it is reasonable to inquire, at least in a preliminary fashion, how successful the effort has been.

The most striking success, and one with enormous visibility and multiplier effects, has been in the exchange rate of the United States dollar. From 1973 to 1979, the trade weighted exchange rate of the United States dollar declined by 10 per cent. Yet in the half decade from 1979 to 1984, there was a 50 per cent increase in the dollar's real purchasing power abroad, with virtually all the gain coming from 1981 onward.[59]

This one change has had, not surprisingly, a significant, widespread effect in restoring American relative power in all areas where the comparison is made in United States dollars. Yet in no area has it carried America back anywhere near the 50 per cent threshold reached in the 1950s. And to take comfort in its restorative effects, one must accept that this rapid exchange rate appreciation represents or reflects a real increase in capability rather than a statistical artifact, will continue at the same rate, or at least not be followed by a substantial depreciation, and has generated positive effects (e.g., a lesser foreign aid burden) which outweigh possible negative ones (e.g., the United States trade deficit).

In the military realm, there is little doubt that the Reagan administration has made a concentrated effort to rebuild relative American might. Since 1978 defence spending in the United States has increased twice as fast as non-defence spending (to 1984).[60] Defence spending as a share of national output rose from 4.6 per cent in 1978 to 6 per cent in 1984.[61] And defence spending, which represented 23 per cent of American government spending in 1978, rose to almost 30 per cent in 1984.[62] Yet the impact to date on the world military balance has been marginal when measured in noncurrency items. For example, in 1983, countries with forces permanently stationed on land abroad ranked as follows:[63]

1. U.S.S.R.	700 880
2. U.S.A.	461 130
3. Vietnam	215 000
4. United Kingdom	93 860

Even if the 284 000 United States service personnel afloat are included, there is no case here for United States hegemony and no comparison with the late 1960s when over half a million American troops were stationed in Vietnam. Similar if less stark conclusions emerge if one ranks countries in 1983 by the number of countries in which their troops are permanently stationed abroad.[64]

1. U.S.A.   40
2. U.S.S.R.   24
3. United Kingdom   14
4. France   12
5. German Democratic Republic   12

Finally, any effort to develop a case for restored American military hegemony, actual or prospective, must deal with the shift since the 1960s, when the United States had three invulnerable legs of its strategic nuclear triad and the Soviets had none, to the current condition of two for the Soviets and one or two for the United States; the continuing political unacceptability of conscription in the United States and the attendant higher expenses and lower skill levels and mobilization reserves of all volunteer armed forces; and the particular uses of the new American defence systems (e.g., heavy battleships on hulls of World War II vintage).

In the economic sphere, apart from exchange-rate sensitive items, the case for American renewal is less clear, especially as the early Reagan recession cut into much of the more recent strong real growth. American national currency reserves recovered strongly from $0.3 billion in 1976 to $8.8 billion in 1981, but in that year France had $20 billion, Japan $24.7 billion, Saudi Arabia $28 billion and the Federal Republic of Germany $39.6 billion.[65]

Of equal interest, given the debt crisis of the 1980s, are the principal national suppliers of public and publicly guaranteed external capital for the third world.[66] In 1981, Saudi Arabia and the United States tied for first with $5.8 billion each, followed by France with $4.8 billion, the Federal Republic of Germany and Japan with $3.2 billion each, and the United Kingdom, the Netherlands, and Canada with over $1 billion each. There is clearly no case for United States hegemony here, regardless of whether this is a measure of a strength or a vulnerability.

Sorting out that issue is, however, important in considering the American trade balance and the net direct investment position. A $2.2 billion trade surplus in 1975 slipped into a deficit in 1976, reached a deficit of about $40 billion in 1979 and 1980, and has since risen steadily toward an estimated $140–160 billion in 1985.[67] Foreign direct investment in the United States climbed from 30 per cent of American direct investment abroad to 46 per cent in 1982 alone.[68] In 1985 the United States became a net debtor for the first time in seventy-one years.[69] It was estimated that this inflow of foreign capital offset 50 per cent of United States government borrowing and prevented a one-third cut in American investment.[70] And it was also estimated that only one-third of such capital inflows were going into productive investments in the United States.[71]

This enormous trade deficit and capital inflow represent, at first glance, a strong sign of United States control over others' access to its market for goods and services and over its access to the capital of others. Yet these superficial indicators of hegemony quickly lead to deeper questions about the longer-term vulnerability that these patterns represent. Despite recent United States government success with import restrictions on Japanese automobiles (since lifted), the Reagan administration's strong emphasis on government non-interference in the economy and the rising protectionist pressure in the Congress both compromise the capacity of the United States government to alter access to its market in a controlled fashion. Moreover, the foreign supply of low-cost capital to the United States is hardly inexhaustible, particularly as the United States growth rate slackens, that of other countries rises, and the paying capacity of a debt-ridden third world diminishes. Yet, the inflow carries the burden of future dividend repayment from a productive base, which it seems, on the whole, the United States is doing little to rebuild outside of the service sector.

In the field of resources, judgments about restored American hegemony depend critically upon the centrality accorded to the single commodity of oil. Here the United States has done much to reduce its vulnerability of the 1970s, even if it is far from restoring its hegemony of more distant decades.[72] American oil imports as a percentage of its total imports peaked at 31.7 per cent in 1980 and declined to 21 per cent in 1983, thus reducing substantially this drain on the United States balance of payments.[73] And by 1981 an admittedly recession-ridden America was importing one-half as much oil as in 1977 from a weakened OPEC, with a considerable part of the imports going into the United States Strategic Petroleum Reserve.

Outside of oil, signs of any Reagan revival, let alone hegemonic restoration, are nowhere to be seen. In 1984, in the militarily strategic mineral of uranium, the United States lost its status as the world's largest producer, being replaced by Canada, which supplied one-third of the world's needs (compared to just over one-sixth for the United States).[74] And in 1982, in the economically strategic mineral of gold, the United States ranked only fifth as a producer, led by South Africa (21.38 million ounces), the U.S.S.R. (9.86), Canada (1.84), China (1.77), and the United States (1.42).[75]

Equally damaging to President Reagan's crusade is the pattern in technology, an area particularly vital to the case and strategy the administration produced. A simple sense of the trend comes from figures on the third quarter of 1984, when 43 per cent of American capital spending in high technology areas was on imported goods, compared to 23 per cent in 1982.[76] Yet technology is enormously difficult to measure, especially if one focuses upon the kind of innovative, advanced technologies in which the United States is thought to have a leading edge. In the view of technological optimists, it is precisely this American lead that will render other standard factors of national power irrelevant, and with them the United States inferiority in these categories.

Some of these difficulties can be avoided by a focus on "hegemonic technologies"—those involving big project science (with a high ratio of inputs to outputs), usually pioneered and produced by those states which lead the globe in other dimensions (given their high surplus capability), and closely related to the national security functions of the state (which places a premium on national production rather than access abroad). Five

Table B

Hegemonic Technology by Country, 1981–85 (% of Global Total)

Technology	Country Rank			
	1	2	3	4
1. Spacecraft (1985)	U.S.A. (37%)	Japan (17%)	U.S.S.R. (15%)	European Space Agency (15%)
2. Reactors (1983)	U.S.A. (27%)	France (12%)	U.S.S.R. (8%)	United Kingdom (8%)
3. Computers (1981)	U.S.A. (42%)	Japan (11%)	Germany, Federal Republic (7%)	U.S.S.R. (6%)
4. Super-computers (1984)	U.S.A. (60%)	United Kingdom (8%)	n.a.*	n.a.
5. Robots (1983)	Japan (30 000)	U.S.A. (6 000)	n.a.	n.a.

Source: See respectively: *Aviation Week and Space Technology*, 12 March 1984, pp. 131-2; Brian Milner, "Nuclear Industry is Stalled Despite Economic Gains," *The Globe and Mail*, 16 January 1984, p. B8; Andrew Pollack, "The Far-flung Wards of Mighty I.B.M.," *The New York Times*, 19 September 1982, p. F26; Jonathan Chevreau, "U. of Calgary to Install Supercomputer," *The Globe and Mail*, 20 July 1984, p. B18; and Stephen Strauss, "Finding Niches, Canada's Aim in Robotics Sector," *The Globe and Mail*, 13 May 1983, p. B13.
* not available

indicators, listed in order of their fidelity to the definition are: operational spacecraft types, operating nuclear power reactors, mainframe computer capacity, installed supercomputers, and industrial robots. Table B lists the global leaders in these categories in recent years.

In only one of the five areas, supercomputers, does the American share entitle it to the status of simple hegemony. Yet in only one area, robotics, the one which most poorly meets the definition, is the United States not in first place. In the remaining three areas, computers, reactors, and spacecraft, its share of the global total is well under 50 per cent, although the United States ranks first in all, and everywhere has twice as much as its nearest rival. It is clear that there is a single emerging challenging state, Japan, which ranks first in one category and second in two others. However, the strong showings of the European states mean that the United States faces a diffuse and divided set of challenges, even though these competitors are close allies of the United States and most are still dependent upon it, especially in the security field. In short, the United States, even with its low numbers, is in

Table C

Launch Vehicles, Research Rockets, and Spacecraft Types, 1985

Launch Vehicles		Spacecraft Types		Research Rockets	
U.S.A.	22	U.S.A.	57	U.S.A.	33
Japan	4	Japan	25	Japan	9
U.S.S.R.	3	U.S.S.R.	16	Canada	8
European Space		European Space		United Kingdom	6
Agency	3	Agency	15	Brazil	3
China	2	China	5	Poland	3
India	1	Canada	4	U.S.S.R.	2
		France	4	France	1
		Intelsat	4		
		Federal Republic of			
		Germany	2		
		Sweden	2		
		NATO	2		
		United Kingdom	1		
		Arabsat	1		
		Australia	1		
		Brazil	1		
		Mexico	1		

Source: Based on *Aviation Week and Space Technology*, 18 March 1985, pp. 170-175.

a leadership position far more secure than it would be if the U.S.S.R. and China occupied the second and third places on the list.

On the dimension of capability then, the American claim to continued preeminence lies not in the ethereal realm of culture but in the hard, central core of national security technologies. But even here the challenge of the Europeans and Japanese is clear. A more refined look at the spacecraft category (see Table C) indicates that American hegemony is secure only in the rarefied realm of spacecraft launch vehicles and supercomputers. The restoration of American hegemony could thus seem to rest critically on the fate of its Strategic Defence Initiative and the commitment and skill of the United States in managing the western alliance.

An examination of the dimension of leadership potential suggests that the requisite investment in alliance management may well be lacking. For despite the defiant rhetoric of the administration, profound isolationist sentiments seem to be at work. In 1980, 56 per cent of Americans, including presidential candidate Reagan, thought the United States was spending too little on defence.[77] Yet by 1982 this number had dropped back to a figure, normal for the second half of the 1970s, of 29 per cent. In 1982, 30 per cent of Americans thought too much was being spent on defence, while 45 per cent wanted more spending on domestic programs. While suggesting a tenuous satisfaction with Reagan's initial great leap forward in rearmament, these figures indicate that the enthusiasm was neither open-ended nor recession-proof. Unless one believes that the public favours greater federal government spending across the board (for *both* defence and domestic programs), it is clear that the willingness to invest in the restoration of America's previous military primacy had quickly run its course.

The American public's commitment must not be confused with its self-confidence, for in the latter realm the Reagan administration has marked a decisive change from the previous decade of despair. A 1984 poll of ten countries revealed that American citizens faced the twenty-first century with a high degree of optimism.[78] Perhaps more significantly, citizens of all ten countries in the survey saw the United States as becoming even more important internationally. Yet while Americans, and others, had clearly caught the sunny self-confidence President Reagan exuded about America's prospects, the country was by no means alone in this respect. Australians and South Koreans were comparably optimistic about their national futures, while across the ten countries, all saw the U.S.S.R., Japan and China as also being countries of greater consequence in the future.

The resulting condition of miserly self-confidence in the American citizenry provides appropriate sustenance for a self-absorbed administration unwilling, as a matter of ideological principle, to take the lead in shaping the emerging world order and in supporting the international institutions on which that order depends. The United States withdrawal from UNESCO is the most visible instalment of a systematic assault that has succeeded in crippling the great accomplishment of a United Nations Law of the Sea Treaty, and which threatens to destroy the entire structure of United-Nations-based multilateralism. Symptomatic of the severity of the attack is a recent United States threat to withhold its financial contributions from the GATT unless that institution does America's bidding in structuring its agenda.[79] Equally important, the progression of the seven annual western summits since 1975 in agenda formation, diplomatic initiatives, and results, suggests a diminished capacity, and subsequently a willingness, on the part of the United States, to secure a consensus for its priorities or any consensus from that group.[80]

This erosion in the instinct for and results of American leadership is particularly and most paradoxically pronounced in the military realm. Here the picture of success provided by the United States invasion of Grenada is highly misleading. It is curious that an invasion of a proximate island ministate of 100 000 souls by the armed forces of a superpower of 225 million should be seen as a sign of the effective power, rather than the diplomatic and political desperation of the latter. More broadly, a review of American history demonstrates that its military intervention in the western hemisphere in a southward direction, from its nineteenth century absorption of northern Mexico, to its Central American struggles today, is a far better indicator of United States isolationism than of American international hegemony or primacy. The latter is better measured by the capacity to generate successes, or sustain involvements, in distant theatres such as Indochina, or more pivotal areas like Lebanon. In Lebanon, the experience of the United States in 1984 stands in stark and humiliating contrast to its record in 1958.

5. Conclusion

This survey of America's fortunes in the globe suggests that what many had long assumed to be true on the basis of simple calculations is indeed a durable reality with enormous consequences for the international system and the world order of the future. American hegemony, both simple and complex, did exist and formed the defining empirical feature of the post–World War II international order. Subsequently, that hegemony in both forms slowly slid away, as a result, not of America's failure to retain its 1945 allies, the Soviet Union and China, but of its success in restoring its adversaries, Japan, Germany, and Italy, and its failure to cope with the long-term legacy of a defeated but ever defiant France.

The record of America's proclaimed revival in the 1980s provides only a fragile foundation for the expansive optimism that Americans feel. Whether one examines the military or economic fundamentals of national power, or moves from the capacity, through the willingness, to the results of the United States in its global leadership role, there is little evidence of an American restoration. Yet there is some. For in those particular areas, notably oil, where a pronounced clear and present danger and government determination has persisted for over a decade, the American political system has demonstrated its capacity to respond effectively. On the whole, the areas of decline appear to be too numerous, and too entrenched, to permit the appropriate governmental reaction. Those devoted to a revival of American hegemony can only hope that a theory of long-term leadership based on a soaring superdollar, the success of the Strategic Defense Initiative, and the sunny self-confidence of the citizenry, is far less fragile than it appears to be.

Notes

1. See, for example, Stanley Hoffman, *Primacy or World Order: American Foreign Policy Since the Cold War* (New York: McGraw-Hill, 1978); Robert Keohane and Joseph Nye, Jr., *Power and Interdependence: World Politics in Transition* (Toronto: Little, Brown, 1977); Robert Keohane, *After Hegemony: Cooperation and Discord in the World Political Economy* (Prince-

ton: Princeton University Press, 1984); and, for a partially competing view, Peter F. Cowhey and Edward Long, "Testing Theories of Regime Change: Hegemonic Decline or Surplus Capacity?" *International Organization* 37 (Spring, 1983), pp. 157-188.

2. Henry Kissinger, *Years of Upheaval* (Toronto: Little, Brown, 1982), p. 238.

3. See Keohane, *After Hegemony*.

4. The changing consensus is well-reflected in the shift in the title of two major books. George Liska, *Imperial America: The International Politics of Primacy* (Baltimore: The Johns Hopkins Press, 1967); and Richard Rosecrance, ed., *America as an Ordinary Country* (Ithaca: Cornell University Press, 1976).

5. These themes form the titles of two books: Kenneth Oye *et al.*, eds., *Eagle Entangled: U.S. Foreign Policy in a Complex World* (New York: Longman, 1979), and Kenneth Oye *et al.*, eds., *Eagle Defiant: United States Foreign Policy in the 1980's* (Boston: Little, Brown, 1983).

6. There are, however, some who dispute the fact of American decline in the first place, led by Bruce Russett, "The Mysterious Case of Vanishing Hegemony; or, Is Mark Twain Really Dead?" *International Organization* 39 (Spring, 1985), pp. 207-231.

7. The possibility of such a process is noted by, *inter alia*, Charles Doran, *Economic Interdependence, Autonomy, and Canadian/American Relations* (Montreal: Institute for Research on Public Policy, 1983).

8. The example is that of the United Kingdom from the eighteenth to the nineteenth century.

9. See, for example, George Modelski, "The Long Cycle of Global Politics and the Nation State," *Comparative Studies in Society and History* 20 (April, 1978) pp. 214-238; Robert Gilpin, *War and Change in World Politics* (Cambridge: Cambridge University Press, 1981); Mancur Olson, *The Rise and Decline of Nations: Economic Growth, Stagflation and Social Rigidities* (New Haven: Yale University Press, 1982).

10. While space constraints preclude the use of multiple measures of most dimensions and a direct focus on many important measures, the data presented here can be supported from these other realms.

11. William Diebold, Jr., "The United States in the World Economy: A Fifty Year View," *Council on Foreign Relations*, New York, 16 May 1983.

12. See, for example, John Holmes, *The Shaping of Peace: Canada and the Search for World Order 1943–1957* (Toronto: University of Toronto Press, 1979 and 1982).

13. Martin Wight, *Power Politics* (Harmondsworth, England: Penguin, 1979), p. 34.

14. George Modelski, "The Long Cycle," p. 216.

15. For a treatment of some of these issues see Klaus Knorr, *The Power of Nations: The Political Economy of International Relations* (New York: Basic Books, 1975).

16. On the concept of "surplus capability" see David Dewitt and John Kirton, *Canada as a Principal Power* (Toronto: John Wiley, 1983). See also Charles Kindleberger, "Dominance and Leadership in the International Economy," *International Studies Quarterly* 25 (June 1981), p. 245.

17. It is thus inadequate to deal with the question of outcomes by arbitrarily specifying the objectives of American foreign policy circa 1945, and declaring continued American success in containment (despite Indochina and Afghanistan) and in preventing Japan, Germany, and Italy from declaring war on other major powers, as advanced by Bruce Russett in "The Mysterious Case of Vanishing Hegemony; or, Is Mark Twain Really Dead?" *op cit.*, n. 6.

18. A comparable argument from a military-centric viewpoint would have the United States dominating the Soviet Union (and perhaps China) in the central security system and thus dominating the globe. A variant would have the era of detente representing a Soviet-American condominium exercising hegemony over all below.

19. Robert Keohane and Joseph Nye, Jr., *Power and Interdependence*.

20. *Ibid.*, p. 44.

21. *Ibid.*, pp. 42-44.

22. *Ibid.*, pp. 44-46.

23. Stephen Krasner, ed., *International Regimes* (Ithaca: Cornell University Press, 1983).

24. Robert Keohane, *After Hegemony*.

25. *Ibid.*, pp. 33-34.
26. *Ibid.*, pp. 32-33.
27. Robert Gilpin, *op. cit.*, and Kenneth Oye, "International Systems Structure and American Foreign Policy," in Kenneth Oye *et al.*, eds., *Eagle Defiant*, pp. 3-32.
28. Kenneth Oye, "International Systems Structure and American Foreign Policy," p. 10.
29. *Ibid.*, p. 12.
30. See note 2.
31. Computed from Oye, p. 8.
32. *Ibid.*, p. 9.
33. *Ibid.*, p. 8.
34. William J.R. Fox, *The Superpowers: The United States, Britain, and the Soviet Union — Their Responsibility for Peace* (New York: Harcourt, Brace, 1944).
35. Keohane, *After Hegemony*, pp. 36, 199.
36. For an overview, see John Kirton, "Canadian Foreign Policy in the 1980's," *Current History* 83 (May 1984), pp. 1-2.
37. Keohane, *After Hegemony*, p. 199.
38. While the Soviet Union ranks second in the nuclear and first in the space category, Canada and the United Kingdom rank third and fourth as the globe's nuclear-weapons capable and spacefaring powers. If one accepts the more stringent criteria of actual detonation, indigenous launch capability, and the ability to detonate or launch first, the Soviet Union alone prevents American hegemony.
39. Walter Jones, *The Logic of International Relations* (Toronto: Little, Brown, 1985), p. 556.
40. Oye, "International Systems Structure," p. 9.
41. See, for example, Peyton Lyon and Brian Tomlin, *Canada as an International Actor* (Toronto: Macmillan, 1979), p. 62; and Ray Cline, *World Power Assessment, 1975* (Boulder, Col.: Westview Press, 1977).
42. Oye, "International Systems Structure," p. 9.
43. *Ibid.*, p. 10.
44. *Ibid.*, p. 8.
45. *Ibid.*, p. 8, and Keohane, p. 197.
46. *Ibid.*, p. 10 and Walter Jones, *The Logic of International Relations* (Toronto: Little, Brown, 1985), p. 93.
47. Jones, p. 253.
48. Keohane, p. 36.
49. Keohane, p. 199.
50. Oye, "International Systems Structure," p. 25.
51. Walter Jones, *The Logic of International Relations* p. 192; see also p. 191.
52. As cited in Jones, p. 480.
53. As cited in Jones, p. 473.
54. Harald von Riekhoff, "The Natural Resource Element in Global Power Relationships," *International Perspectives* (September/October 1974), pp. 63-76.
55. Keohane, p. 199 and Jones, p. 459.
56. Jones, p. 556.
57. William Schneider, "Conservation, Not Interventionism: Trends in Foreign Policy Opinion, 1974–1982," in Oye *et al.*, eds., *Eagle Defiant* p. 36.
58. *Ibid.*, pp. 50-51.
59. Based on figures from the Board of Governors, Federal Reserve System. See also Dallas Batten and Michael Belongia, "Farmers' Ills: Not the Dollar's Fault," *The New York Times*, 14 April 1985.
60. As cited in Jack McArthur, "Does Defence Spending Aid Growth?," *Toronto Star*, 18 April 1985, p. E2.
61. *Ibid.*
62. *Ibid.*
63. Ruth Leger Sivard, *World Military and Social Expenditures 1983: An Annual Report on World Priorities* (World Priorities: Washington, D.C., 1983), p. 9.

64. *Ibid.*

65. Jones, p. 480.

66. *Ibid.*, p. 191.

67. *Ibid.*, p. 459.

68. *Ibid.*, p. 473.

69. "Figures Point to U.S. as Net Debtor, Official Says," *Toronto Star*, 18 June 1985, p. 1.

70. Martin Feldstein, " The Future According to Feldstein," *The Globe and Mail*, 7 January 1985, p. B11.

71. John Williamson, as cited in "Economists Fear Havoc if U.S. Debt Spree Goes Unchecked," *The Globe and Mail*, 28 March 1985, p. B22.

72. It remains unclear how permanent this achievement will be. See "Oil Consumption in U.S. Rises Following 5 Years of Decline," *The Globe and Mail*, 19 February 1985, p. B21.

73. Walter Jones, p. 459.

74. "Canada in First Place in Uranium Production," *The Globe and Mail*, 20 January 1983, p. B2.

75. John King, "Canada Third in Gold Output," *The Globe and Mail*, 20 January 1983, p. B2.

76. These figures come from a Morgan Stanley and Co. study, as cited in Fred Harrison, "Booming U.S. Economy has Losers," *The Financial Post*, 2 March 1985.

77. William Schneider, p. 37.

78. Ann Duncan, "Poll Finds Canadians Prepared to Sacrifice," *The Globe and Mail*, 3 April 1984, p. 1.

79. "GATT's Survival Questioned as U.S. Proposal Defeated," *The Globe and Mail*, 23 July 1985, p. B14.

80. Robert Putnam and Nicholas Bayne, *Hanging Together: The Seven-Power Summits* (Cambridge, Mass.: Harvard University Press, 1984).

American Economic Power

Ever since the innovative American business community took to heart the message in Adam Smith's *Wealth of Nations* and married it to the belief that government was instituted to protect life, liberty, and property, the United States has become, in total assets, the richest nation on earth. The earnestness with which the nation sought to protect individual rights brought forth a vigorous combination of talent which was to make America the champion and chief architect of capitalist enterprise. It is the case recently, however, that the United States as an *economic* unit has not had the highest per capita Gross National Product in the industrialized world. In 1984, the per capita Gross National Product of the ten nations of the European Economic Community surpassed that of the United States. In 1985, the United States became a debtor nation for the first time since World War I, and partially because of the strength of the dollar, has amassed the greatest trade deficit in its history. Record budget deficits under President Reagan have become the norm. But the United States has taken up the challenge as was aptly expressed in the president's 1986 State of the Union Address to Congress.

True to the spirit of competition, the United States has begun to react to its falling share of world markets by calling for, among other things, freer trade through a renegotiation of the General Agreement on Tariffs and Trade (GATT), threatening to enact protectionist barriers against uncooperative trading partners, helping to force a devaluation of the dollar, asking for voluntary export restraints, and agreeing to enter into free trade negotiations with its largest trading partner, Canada.

The three economists and the businessman who have contributed to this section write in this context and thus touch on these and many more issues in discussing the overwhelming world presence of American economic might. They disagree on the problems as well as the solutions. But the complexity of the issues guarantees that there can be no comprehensive solutions, especially given the improbability that we could agree on the goals to be pursued at the dawn of the "Information Age."

The premise of Russell Boyer in Chapter 4 revolves around a fundamental truth: Canada's economy is effectively integrated with that of the United States and the financial policies which originate in the United States. "To ignore those events, or to remain silent on their consequences would mean to surrender whatever modest influence we do have on American policies." This chapter reveals the extent to which Canadian economists have contributed to the theories and models, which, "in the field of international finance, was dominated by Johnson, McKinnon, and Mundell." Boyer pays great attention to the role of the current account, fiscal policy, and monetary and capital mobility as they are applied to the United States. In doing so he shows that the Canadian "Mundell-Fleming model, which emphasized the role of the exchange rate in a world of close economic integration," was consistent with "the painful adjustment of the American economy" over the past decade. Boyer's research is a forthright example of his belief that Canadian perspectives on the United States lead to significant outcomes.

In Chapter 5, John Whalley takes a global view of the trading partnership between the United States and Canada. He analyzes how this is affected, and to some degree determined by the global trading system which currently exists. The partnership could, as we are reminded, be very different depending upon the success of the next round of the GATT negotiations which are about to begin. Whalley asserts that "trade policies towards the developing world are going to be again the key issue facing the global economy during the next generation." He examines the increasing importance of non-tariff barriers as traditional tariffs have been lowered, and the role of the International Monetary Fund, the World Bank, and, what he views as the most important, the GATT. In reviewing the Canada–United States trade relationship in some detail, he explains how the global economic system will be a major factor in developing and defining that relationship in the future.

In Chapter 6, Bruce Wilkinson pays particular attention to what is involved for Canada should it pursue a policy of bilateral free trade with the United States. Initially he provides a brief review as to the consequences of a new trading relationship. He gives two examples which show that such arrangements have ultimately led to the political absorption of the smaller economy by the dominant economy. In reviewing the current state of affairs between the two countries, Wilkinson discusses in detail "buy domestic" policies, the trade in services, industrial development, and natural resource policies. He concludes, among other things, that "there will be no 'free lunch' for Canada in any bilateral free trade agreement" because "for every gain Canada receives, the Americans are going to expect something in return." He recommends "working through the GATT system" as "bilateral free trade is only a reasonable way to proceed, if we are not too concerned about possible, eventual political union with the United States."

Harold Wyatt does not see the United States in such a threatening manner. In Chapter 7, his business perspective shows his concern for making Canada a competitive nation in the international marketplace. He advises Canadians "to take a longer-term view in a dispassionate manner" so as not to undermine the special relationship between the two countries. The premise of his essay is that "*We are not the same.*" He discusses the irritants between the two nations in a wide number of areas, from protectionism, investment, and cultural sovereignty, to transborder data flows. Wyatt's position as a vice-chairman of the Royal Bank of Canada, and a member of a number of associations, committees, and boards which deal daily with such problems, makes his contribution especially valuable, since it is derived from first-hand experience. In conclusion, Wyatt challenges Canadian governments and the Canadian business community to prepare for continuous negotiation by exerting "new and imaginative efforts at all levels of the American policy process." It is a call to action.

Recent U.S. Financial Policies: Canadian Contributions and Perspectives

Russell S. Boyer

1. Introduction

The Canadian perspective on all aspects of United States financial policies is aired in the media everyday. The proximity, size, and integration of that economy with ours makes essential an awareness of developments there. To ignore those events or to remain silent on their consequences for us would mean to surrender whatever modest influence we do have on American policies, and to give up the opportunity for timely adjustment and response. There is no danger that the Canadian perspective, in the sense of representing our own self-interest, will fade away. This is evidenced by the fact that conferences on Canadian-American relations are becoming more frequent events.

What has not received sufficient coverage is the fact that there have been substantial contributions by Canadians to American economic policy-making in the last three decades, especially in the macroeconomics arena. These contributors have drawn upon a perspective that is Canadian, in the sense of being derived from experiences which they had living in Canada. The uniqueness of the Canadian experience can be attributed to the openness of its economy, in particular, to its long-standing freedom of capital movements, and the episode of exchange rate flexibility during the 1950s.[1] Insights gained from this experience were directly applicable to the United States economy, as it became more integrated with its trading partners.

Unfortunately, one of the most important lessons of the Canadian model has been forgotten under the Reagan administration, namely, that with close financial integration and a flexible exchange rate regime, policy actions tend to have a more rapid, more decisive impact than otherwise. In the present context, this means that the loose fiscal policy in the United States has quickly created enormous economic imbalances, in which some sectors are thriving and others are depressed. The attempt at resolving these problems has caused substantial conflict among the policy-making bodies in Washington.

The failure of a small economy to heed this lesson would not have important consequences for trading partners. But recent policy actions in the United States do have far-reaching implications for the rest of the world, because of its size and the roles that it plays: as a protagonist for free trade and as the world central bank. Unless the government deficits in the United States are quickly ended, it is unlikely that the present period of financial uncertainty can be resolved without the United States behaving irresponsibly in one of these two roles.

2. Economic Integration and the American Economy

Canada has lived with the quandary of being an open economy for more than a century. Its economy has maintained its high level of trade with the rest of the world, with imports and exports valued at roughly one quarter of Gross National Product, during the entire twentieth century. During this time, the major development for Canada has been the move away from the United Kingdom as a major trading partner, and the movement towards greater interdependence with the United States. Obviously other countries have had as great openness to trade in goods and services, many with lower tariffs (although they lacked Canada's proximity to the United States). What differentiates the Canadian experience is the extraordinary degree of freedom permitted agents in capital markets.[2] In addition, Canada had a flexible exchange rate regime for the years 1950–62, long before it became the fashionable thing to do in 1973. This experiment was unique at the time in that it showed a currency could maintain its value based on its own intrinsic merits, rather than because of its convertibility into another currency.[3]

In contrast with Canada, the American economy was relatively closed until after World War II. Imports and exports amounted to around 5 per cent of GNP. Transactions on capital account were minimal, since capital controls in Europe and the sterling bloc had been in effect continuously since 1914. This situation for financial transactions ended abruptly in 1944, because the nature of the agreement at Bretton Woods implied an important new role for the United States capital account. The International Monetary Fund (IMF) was set up at that time, but on such a modest scale that it was clear that the American dollar would be a major component in the postwar international monetary system. The dollar played an ever larger part, with the gold standard based upon IMF quotas quickly being replaced by a gold-exchange standard and the dollar shortage making it clear that the United States dollar was the most sought after form of reserve asset. The role which the dollar has played in providing liquidity has mushroomed beyond all expectations, such that it is no exaggeration to call the Federal Reserve System (the central bank in the United States) the "world central bank."

The openness of the United States to trade flows began to increase substantially in the mid-1960s during the Vietnam War build-up. Its trade account surplus (the difference between the value of goods exported and the value of goods imported) evaporated rapidly during that decade. The surplus on service account (the value of services exported minus that of services imported) being larger than the trade account deficit, sustained a favourable current account balance until into the 1970s. But in 1984 the current account deficit was a record $120 billion, approximately 3 per cent of GNP. Early in the 1960s imports or exports amounted to around 5 per cent of GNP. Now these are equal to around 15 per cent of GNP. In this regard, the United States continues to look more like Canada.

3. The Role of the Current Account

The increasing integration of the world economy, and the greater openness which this implied for the American economy, led to a number of problems which the United States had not been forced to face before. Those which attracted the most attention in the 1950s and 1960s were intimately related: the undervaluation of gold and the increasing United States balance of payments deficit.

To deal with the problems of the open economy, a number of models were developed and analyzed. Most of these models are named after the economists who developed them or the countries to which they are directly relevant. The Salter-Swann model is named after Australians; the Scandinavian model and the Dutch disease models were constructed to describe these economies.[4] The most famous such model is named after a Canadian economist and a British economist: the Mundell-Fleming model. Because of the model's applicability to the high capital mobility, flexible exchange rate context describing the Canadian economy, this model is called the Canadian model in this essay. This term is appropriate for another related reason: without exaggeration it can be stated that during the first two decades of the postwar era, the field of international finance was dominated by Canadians. Johnson, McKinnon, and Mundell were the most prominent contributors, but the names of Chipman, Penner, and Viner should also be mentioned.[5] This is not surprising, since Canadian economists had a comparative advantage in thinking about the central concepts of international finance, gained from the experiences of their native country.[6]

The balance of payments accounts measure transactions between residents of one country and those of the rest of the world. The focus of much analysis of these accounts is on the state of their current account portion, which, as noted above, measures the difference between the value of goods and services exported and the value of those imported. The capital account has an analogous definition with respect to transactions in financial capital (such as stocks and bonds). The current account assumes critical importance because of the central role it plays under all exchange rate regimes and all levels of capital market integration. Before describing this role, we should outline some of the basic consequences of an imbalance in the current account.

Three basic observations are important in this context. The first relates to the fact that if balance of payment accounting is done on a consistent basis, then the value of any country's current account must equal that of the rest of the world, but with the sign reversed. That is, if Canada runs a current account surplus, the rest of the world has a current account deficit. In other words, a country which deliberately attains current account imbalance is forcing the necessity of adjustment on the rest of the world. This raises relevant questions concerning the appropriate distribution internationally of the burden of adjustment.

The second observation is that the current account is equal to the difference between domestic income and expenditure.[7] Thus a country with a deficit is necessarily spending more than its income and building up debts to the rest of the world. Of course, this means that at least one other country must have income in excess of its spending and is thereby becoming more of a creditor.

The final observation is that on average, over any long period of time, the current account for any country must balance at least approximately, because any borrowing undertaken during one time period must eventually be repaid, so that there is lending (reverse borrowing) at a later date.[8] This implies that one generation, in running a current account imbalance, is forcing adjustment upon a future generation. As a result, questions concerning intergenerational (or intertemporal) equity naturally arise.

In the early postwar period, analytic models of an open economy were simple variants of those developed for the closed economy, in which weak linkages with the rest of the world were appended as afterthoughts.[9] The general nature of these linkages and their consequences is easily stated: domestic policies undertaken within such a construct tend to have diminished impact on domestic magnitudes, because some of their effect is dissipated via flows through the foreign sector. In addition, these linkages guarantee that shocks occurring in the rest of the world have effects on the domestic economy.

In these models, often the only linkage was via trade in goods and services. The integration of financial markets was assumed to be so limited that international transactions in financial assets could safely be ignored. The expression used to describe this state is zero capital mobility. With trade in financial assets curtailed, the only way the domestic economy can have an impact on (or be influenced by) the rest of the world is through an imbalance in the current account. Any policy action which has no impact on the state of the current account has the same consequences as it has in a closed economy. In those circumstances the economy, although open, is insulated from international influences.

One way to accomplish such insulation is to have a floating exchange rate regime, because without capital flows or intervention by the monetary authorities, the role of the exchange rate is to maintain balance in the current account. In this situation, the floating exchange rate creates what amounts to a state of barter trade in which the value of exports and imports must be equal. With low and in the limit zero capital mobility, if the exchange rate is free to move, it insulates the domestic economy from events in the rest of the world. We shall see below that, in contrast, when there is high capital mobility, as arises from the close financial integration that the Canadian (Mundell-Fleming) model assumes, the exchange rate no longer plays this role.

4. Fiscal Policy and Capital Mobility

The discussion above ended with the suggestion that the degree of financial integration among open economies determines the role which the exchange rate plays. In turn, the response of the exchange rate influences the impact of any policy shocks on the domestic economy and on the rest of the world. It is worthwhile expanding on these observations by analyzing the consequences of an increase in government expenditure under a flexible exchange rate regime. Such an analysis is germane to recent United States financial policy-making, since a loose fiscal policy is the hallmark of the Reagan administration.

Let us consider two polar cases: zero capital mobility and perfect capital mobility.[10] The zero capital mobility case is one in which there are no international financial transactions among private agents. With perfect capital mobility, investors are so attracted by even marginally higher rates of interest (and repelled by marginally lower ones) that rates of return throughout the world can be viewed as equal. Though it is clearly an exaggeration to identify the zero capital mobility case with the American situation in the pre–World War II setting and the other case with the present American situation, it is certainly true that economic integration has proceeded over time, so that the results derived here portray, through their stark contrast, the changing set of outcomes which American policy-makers should have expected during this period.

Most discussions of open economy macroeconomics use a distinction made popular by trade theorists analyzing small open economies. This distinction is between traded (non-sheltered, import-competing) goods and non-traded (sheltered) goods. It is assumed that there is a class of goods (typically services, especially government services) which have a secure market within the economy. Another class of goods for sale both at home (where they substitute for imports) and abroad (where they must be exported) faces competition from the rest of the world. The two classes should not be viewed as entirely separate, nor are they unchanging over time. (In this essay the impact of increasing integration of markets for goods and services, which we have witnessed recently, is ignored.) This distinction enables the analysis to portray the differential impact of government policies on various sectors. Increased government expenditures are viewed as falling upon the sheltered goods sector, and this analysis follows through the consequences that these expenditures have and, in particular, how the effects depend upon the degree of capital mobility.

(a) Zero Capital Mobility

The response to increased domestic government expenditures on sheltered goods can be easily traced. These expenditures increase the output of such goods and, before intersectoral flows of labour and capital occur, have limited impact on the output of goods in the traded goods sector. Therefore aggregate output (and income) in the economy rises. It is likely that some of this increased income is spent upon imports, which, previously, domestic residents could not afford. This effect guarantees that the current account worsens.

But this is not the end of the story. In a zero capital mobility world, the role of the exchange rate is to balance the current account, as noted above. The impact of the policy shock is to worsen that account, which implies that the domestic currency depreciates. This depreciation makes domestic goods look cheaper to foreigners; it makes foreign goods more expensive on the domestic market. As a result, exports expand and imports decline, pushing the current account towards balance.

This exchange rate movement has a number of important consequences. It restores the current account to balance and, therefore, spillover effects of fiscal policy to trading partners, even close ones, are limited. This is an example of the insulation property of the flexible exchange rate regime mentioned above. In addition, the exchange rate causes the relative prices of non-sheltered goods in terms of sheltered goods to be restored. The initial influence of the policy shock was to expand output (and likely raise the prices) of sheltered goods. The exchange rate movement raises the price (and raises the output) of import competing goods. This description shows that government expenditures in the zero capital mobility case have expansionary consequences in both sectors of the economy. Since both sectors join in the expansion, we find that the expansion of output is larger than it would have been if the exchange rate were fixed. This is another facet of the insulating properties of a flexible exchange rate regime with low capital mobility: domestic policies have greater impact than otherwise, because foreign sector flows are reduced.

Finally, it has been implicit in this discussion that monetary policy is set so as to keep interest rates at fixed levels. The increased output raises money demand, which could be choked off by a rise in interest rates. In resisting this tendency, the central bank raises the money supply passively, in step with the increase in demand.

(b) Perfect Capital Mobility

Let us now turn to the other extreme assumption about capital mobility: namely, that it is perfect. This assumption is certainly the more relevant to current policy problems, as integration of financial markets has continued at a rapid pace. In this case the central bank can no longer control rates of interest, so we assume here that it conducts monetary policy by setting the money supply at a specific level. With large potential capital flows, clearly there is no necessity for the current account to balance. The exchange rate therefore takes on a different role: its value is now determined by the need for the demand for money to equal the autonomously given supply.

If we enquire as to the consequences of increased government expenditures in the United States in this setting, it would be convenient to begin by assuming, as before, that these expenditures fall on the sheltered goods, generating an excess demand there. The initial response is an increase in their output (and output in general) and a worsening of the current account as before. This situation is sustainable if the authorities increase the supply of money sufficiently to maintain this higher output, as they would do to fix the exchange rate.

With perfect capital mobility, the relevant consideration for the exchange rate is not the worsening of the current account but rather the increase in output, which boosts demand for money above the level supplied by the central bank. This calls for an appreciation of the United States dollar, which has three consequences. It dampens any increase in output so the effects on the domestic economy in aggregate, both as to output and to inflation, are minimized. But it also worsens the state of the current account, since import-competing goods are put at a disadvantage. This guarantees that the consequences for other countries are significant. Finally, the appreciation accomplishes these effects via a change in the relative price of goods produced in the two sectors. Output and (to some extent) prices increase in the sheltered sector because of the authorities' augmented demand for such goods. In contrast, the appreciation of the United States dollar reduces demand for American produced import-competing goods. This is true both for American-source demand and foreign-source demand. In the United States, domestically produced goods become relatively expensive (as the appreciation has reduced the United States dollar price of foreign produced goods) while foreigners see American produced goods as expensive when prices are expressed in local currency. This reduced demand causes the import-competing sector in the United States to be depressed.

This analysis highlights a noteworthy consequence of fiscal policy in an open economy, namely the differential impact which it has on the structure of output: the sheltered-goods sector expands, and the import-competing sector contracts. As a result, there emerges a two-tier economy in which certain sectors thrive and others are depressed. An important accompanying effect is that wage rates and returns to capital move accordingly. Labour and capital in the sheltered sectors receive abnormally high returns; whereas those in the import-competing sector receive below-average returns. These alterations in factor rewards are, in part, essential to the purpose of the fiscal policy: they increase the amount of labour and capital in the industries which the authorities wish to expand, and they reduce it in the industries which become uncompetitive as a result. However, what needs to be emphasized here is that because of the rapid adjustment in the value of the exchange rate, these effects occur quickly and in an exaggerated fashion.[11]

This discussion has emphasized fiscal policy actions and ignored monetary policy changes. The justification for this emphasis must be found in a closer look at the details of recent American financial policy. With that done we will assess the relevance of the Canadian model to recent economic developments in the United States.

5. Recent United States Experience

Before providing a Canadian perspective on recent American financial policy, we must pinpoint the salient characteristics of that policy. This turns out to be a simple task, since there is one obvious feature of the "Reagan revolution": the tremendous increase in federal government deficits. Other aspects of policy are of less consequence, as the following review demonstrates.

(a) Fiscal Policy

The federal deficit as a percentage of GNP has increased enormously during the Reagan years. During the last Carter fiscal year the deficit was approximately 2 per cent of GNP: expenditures were 22 per cent and taxes were 20 per cent. For fiscal year 1985, the deficit is likely to be 6 per cent of GNP. Expenditures have increased to a peacetime record of 24 per cent, while taxes have been reduced to 18 per cent.

The Reagan revolution emphasized the slashing of tax rates over a three-year period, at the end of which they were 25 per cent lower than before. Official forecasts using supply-side tools (such as the Laffer curve) claimed optimistically that the economy would provide a growth dividend such that any short-run deficiency of taxes would be made up over a three-to-five-year period. Others, impressed by the fervour of the tax revolt, raised their voices in support on the following reasoning: if the Laffer-curve mechanism provided a free lunch, one would be foolish not to accept it. If that mechanism did not work, then the resulting deficit would increase pressure to reduce government spending.[12] In the event, neither of these outcomes occurred. Total tax revenue appears to have been reduced on a long-term (structural) basis. And the president, through his increased defence spending, has raised government expenditures to a record high level. Some domestic programs have been eliminated, but there has not been sufficient paring in these to offset the military build up, which is now about 30 per cent of the federal budget.

There are two aspects of the Reagan fiscal policy which should be distinguished. First, government expenditures in total have increased and this fact alone generates a need for adjustment within the American economy. This is, however, not as dramatic as the second fact—the massive increase in budget deficits. Some have argued that these deficits are not important because individuals will take account of the future tax liabilities which servicing the debt implies.[13] The argument is that any reduction of taxes which is made up by deficit financing (leaving government expenditures unchanged), causes individual taxpayers to increase their saving sufficiently to pay for future, increased tax burdens. To avoid discussion of this issue, we focus here on the recent rise in government expenditures, rather than upon the way in which it is financed.

(b) Monetary Policy

The conventional view of recent monetary policy is as follows: in contrast with fiscal policy, monetary policy has been very tight since October, 1979, when the Federal Reserve System embarked on its current monetarist path. This policy has been discredited in the eyes of most economists, and yet the central bank continues with its tight money policy.

But, in truth, Federal Reserve policy has been far more varied than this conventional view acknowledges. Federal Reserve pronouncements since 1979 have been fairly monetarist, promising strict adherence to target levels for various monetary aggregates. However, its actions have been somewhat different. In particular, the credit control program in place from March to July, 1980 distorted the meaning of monetary aggregates at the time. As a result most economists would assert that the monetarist experiment cannot be viewed as starting until after that episode.[14] During the next year (July, 1981–August, 1982) money was tight, it is generally agreed, with M1 (the narrowest of monetary aggregates) growing very slowly. However, since that time M1 has been growing consistently at the upper end of the target band, at around 9 per cent or above. Recently this growth has been well into the double digit range, which will undoubtedly be inflationary if sustained for another year. In summary, given this varied experience it is not accurate to describe Federal Reserve policy as either tight or monetarist.[15]

(c) Domestic Consequences of U.S. Fiscal Policy

Loose fiscal policy is the hallmark of the Reagan revolution in financial policy-making. Before employing the analysis laid out in the previous sections, we must identify what aspects of recent American policy can be captured in a simple macroeconomic model. Expansionary fiscal policy has many interpretations, and it is far from clear that the increased expenditures in the sheltered sector on which the model focuses are the most relevant in the U.S. case.

As noted above, there are two aspects to the Reagan policy, using the crudest of distinctions: taxes have been reduced, and government expenditures have been increased. For reasons given above, taxes are not a central concern here; rather we focus on the size of expenditure increases and their sectoral distribution.

In the sheltered sector, there has been an overall increase in expenditures. The reason is that social programs of various sorts where spending has been cut have been more than matched by increases in defence spending on such items as large armed services. In addition, in so far as a reduction in taxes increases expenditure in the private sector, some of this increase as well will occur on sheltered goods.

The tradable goods sector too has had increased sales domestically, and for similar reasons. But the sales from this sector to the authorities are on newly emerging markets, such as high technology industries and munitions. There have been reductions in expenditures for the output of traditional, basic industries such as agriculture, automobiles, and steel.

An increase in expenditures on the tradable goods sector has a clear but perhaps exaggerated outcome in our model. Namely, such expenditures cause an equal worsening of the current account with no effects on other variables: the exchange rate, domestic output, and relative prices in the two sectors.[16] The reason for this result is that the economy in question was viewed as small; this is hardly an appropriate characterization of the American economy. Nonetheless, the thrust of the conclusion seems correct: the impact of American policies in the traded goods sector should fall upon the world market. As a result, there should be major impacts on quantities such as income and expenditure, and these variables are measured in the state of the current account. There may be influences on world-wide variables such as interest rates and price levels. But there should be limited impacts on international relative prices from expansionary policies directed towards the traded goods sector. In order to bring about changes in relative prices it is necessary to change the state of the market for sheltered goods. It is for these reasons that the increased expenditures on defence, without an equal reduction in expenditures in other government programs, are highlighted in this discussion.

The Canadian model predicts that this policy should cause the United States dollar to appreciate. This, of course, has occurred, with a total appreciation of the U.S. dollar on a trade-weighted basis of between 25 and 50 per cent since 1980. The model also indicates that it is likely that inflation is minimally affected by fiscal policy alone, and this conclusion too is consistent with recent American experience in which inflation rates have been in the 3 to 5 per cent range. As a result the appreciation of the exchange rate involves an increase in the real exchange rate, the price of American goods in terms of foreign goods, when converted at the existing exchange rate.

The model's conclusion with respect to the influence of fiscal policy on output is also roughly consistent with the facts. Output in the United States has grown rapidly at times, but the average growth rate from 1980 to 1985 is somewhat less than 3 per cent per year. This is the historical average growth rate for output during the postwar period.

The minimal impact on the aggregate growth rates is due to the expansion of the sheltered goods sector (especially defence, and the high technology and other industries supplying them) and a contraction of industries which face international competition. Such industries are often called basic ones: steel, automobiles, and farming have been identified as those hardest hit by changes in real exchange rates. The depression in these industries from the change in relative prices would have been far greater had various forms of protection for them (notably Voluntary Export Restraints) not been enacted. If the basic industries are more capital intensive than the service (sheltered)

sector, then the reallocation of production can cause changes in employment which appear to be large as compared with output changes.

Finally, the movement of the exchange rate tends to worsen the current
account by an amount roughly equal to the increased government expenditures. This is true of the United States where the current account and the
federal budget have both worsened over the last five years by around
$120 billion per annum.

(d) Conclusions

Early models of the open economy assumed that capital mobility was low
and showed that a floating exchange rate regime had insulating properties.
Such models do not capture the mechanisms that are at work in the world
at present. Instead, what I have called the Canadian model, which views
capital mobility as very high, seems to explain recent American experience.
The main lesson of that model is that a flexible exchange rate regime does
not insulate an economy from all shocks. On the contrary, the appreciation
of the United States dollar in response to a fiscal policy shock creates
imbalances within the economy that cause more rapid but more painful
adjustment than would occur if capital mobility were low, or if the
exchange rate were fixed.

6. Canada's Self-Interest

So far attention has been given to the consequences of a floating exchange
rate for the American economy. One of them is that expansionary fiscal
policy causes a worsening of the current account of an amount approximately equal to the increase in government expenditures. This implies that
there are spillovers to the rest of the world, and especially to Canada, her
most important trading partner. The worsening of the United States current
account implies an equal improvement in the accounts of other countries
with increased exports and reduced imports, which represent a boon in
that their domestic traded-goods sectors should run at higher capacity than
otherwise. This effect raises factor rewards in the economies of trading
partners so that their welfare increases. Improvement in the performance
of basic industries in Canada, Europe, and Japan has clearly taken place
lately.[17]

In addition, the United States surplus on capital account provides foreigners with a number of benefits. Since World War II the United States
dollar has been a very liquid asset for the rest of the world, as a result of
its role as a reserve currency. Now that a high yield is available on dollar-
denominated assets, they are even more attractive to foreigners as a vehicle
for accumulating their savings. Therefore both the current account deficit
and the capital account surplus for the United States can be seen as providing
substantial benefits to the rest of the world. There seems to be little justification for discomfort among her trading partners in the current situation.

However, they *are* uncomfortable, and this can be attributed to nervousness about the likely outcome of the policy gamble which the Americans have undertaken. There are many uncertainties about the longer-term consequences of current policy actions, and further policy actions are likely to be undertaken as a result of the current economic imbalances. Perhaps we can attribute some of the discomfort to differences in degrees of risk aversion. Canadians appear to be more risk averse (as evidenced by their higher saving rates and life insurance coverage) and therefore they are made more uncomfortable than other nationals by a rise in the general degree of uncertainty.

Although such differing responses to a rise in the general level of uncertainty may be part of the story, there is a more potent mechanism at work. Namely, other countries perceive that the United States has created economic imbalances at home between the various sectors of the economy and in foreign trade, through her enormous current account deficit. To eliminate these imbalances, further policy actions must eventually be undertaken. These policies probably will be such as to place major burdens on foreign countries, in order to minimize costs at home.

The policy action which created these problems was an expenditure-increasing one, and the most efficient resolution of it involves an elimination of the budget deficit through an expenditure-reducing policy. Such a process, while efficient from an economic point of view, is very costly politically, as current observers of the American scene have noted. A more likely policy response is an expenditure-switching action which places burdens of adjustment on other countries.[18] More specifically, the actions are likely to be a more expansionary monetary policy to eliminate the overvaluation of the dollar and/or protectionist legislation in order to counter the effects of the overvaluation.[19] In the case of protectionism, a distinction needs to be made between comprehensive policies and policies aimed at specific industries. Either policy action is irresponsible relative to the roles the United States plays as "world central bank" and world's largest free trade area.

The effects of expansionary monetary policy are intuitively clear. The overvaluation of the dollar is due to the fact that monetary policy, although quite variable, has not changed markedly in the last five years, while there has been a substantial loosening of fiscal policy. As we argued above, some of the economic imbalances would be diminished if monetary policy were more stimulative. Recently the Federal Reserve System seems intent on such a change in policy, in spite of the inflationary pressures that are likely to ensue.

From the American perspective comprehensive protectionist legislation is self-defeating under a floating exchange rate regime. If enacted by the United States, its sole effect would be to raise the value of the dollar. Indeed, a persuasive argument can be made that some of the overvaluation of the dollar is due to market participants anticipating the effect of the enactment of protectionist legislation. The consequences of such protectionism once enacted are negligible on variables like the current account, the relative prices between sectors, and the level of output and inflation as compared with the initial situation in 1980.

What is true for the economy as a whole, however, is not true for any specific industry. Comprehensive protectionist legislation is self-defeating because it would be offset by the strengthening of the foreign exchange value of the currency. In contrast, any specific industry that is favoured with such legislation does not have to worry about these exchange market effects. As a result, incentives for seeking industry-specific protectionist legislation are not influenced by the exchange rate regime.

Canada, being on the receiving end of these policies, has a different perspective of their consequences. The view of producers is that monetary policy and comprehensive protectionist legislation have similar effects in reducing access to and revenues from American markets. Demand, expressed in Canadian dollar terms, is reduced in either case: in the one, through a cheaper United States dollar, in the other through an implied tariff rate that the protectionist legislation proposes, payable to the United States Treasury. As stated above, protection for a specific industry can be analyzed independently of the exchange rate regime. In particular, from the producer's point of view, protectionism is the more feared of the possible American policy responses in that it would represent an abdication of the role the United States has played as protagonist for free trade.

In contrast, from the portfolio holder's point of view the concern is that the United States will behave irresponsibly in its role as "world central bank" by bringing about a rapid inflation. Protectionist legislation tends to maintain the value of the United States dollar in terms of foreign currency, so that its purchasing power is stabilized for foreign holders. If, instead, an expansionary monetary policy is undertaken, with its consequent inflationary effects, then the real value of these dollar holdings will be eroded. The enormous size of American capital account surpluses in recent years indicates that dollar holdings outside the country are by no means negligible. Indeed, the United States recently became a net debtor economy, which is a highly unusual situation for the richest country in the world. As the interest burden of government debt mounts, the United States will be tempted to use inflation to reduce its burden. So far the Federal Reserve appears to have resisted this temptation, but the outlook for the future is far from clear.[20]

To summarize, United States policy initiatives have had a major impact on other countries, and the impact has been positive for them. But in the United States it has created a situation of domestic incoherence with the administration, the Federal Reserve, and Congress battling in different directions. The resolution of such chaos often involves policies that place burdens on foreign countries. In the present case the resolution of this problem will likely involve either inflation or protectionism. It is the possibility of the enactment of these policies and the abdication by the United States of its responsibility to the international economy which causes foreign countries to be uncomfortable with the current American gamble.

7. Conclusions

During the last four decades the United States has moved slowly but unmistakably towards being an open economy. In this transition period Canadian economists made enormous contributions in providing policy advice on matters of international finance. These contributions were based on the Mundell-Fleming model which emphasized the role of the exchange rate in a world of close economic integration.

Recent United States financial policy is based on a very loose fiscal stance, which favours defence and high technology service sectors at the expense of traditional sectors. Consistent with the conclusions of this model, the exchange rate forced on the American economy a more rapid and more painful adjustment than would have occurred under fixed exchange rates. While there are benefits in the present situation for Canada, the imbalances in the United States are widely cited as justification for action directed toward the foreign sector. Such policies as have been proposed would undermine either the international monetary system or international trading arrangements.

Notes

1. Harry Johnson has described the dilemmas that faced Canada in the 1950s in *The Canadian Quandary* (Toronto: McClelland & Stewart, 1977). In many dimensions this discussion could be repeated for the United States in the 1970s and 1980s.

2. The freedom of capital movements between the United States and Canada is detailed in Paul Wonnacott's *The Canadian Dollar* (Toronto: University of Toronto Press, 1960). In contrast, Europe during much of this time had extensive capital controls.

3. Flexible exchange rate episodes in the nineteenth century coincided with major wars: the Napoleonic War, the American Civil War. In the twentieth century, many currencies floated during the world wars, before the return to gold in the 1920s, and during the Great Depression. In all these cases, the important influence upon the expected value of the exchange rate was the value at which convertibility would ultimately be restored.

4. The Salter-Swann model (named after W.E. Salter and T.W. Swann for their writing in the late 1950s) pointed out the usefulness of the distinction between traded and non-traded goods. The Scandinavian model introduced markets for factors of production (labour and capital), putting an emphasis on possible productivity growth rate differences between these sectors. The Dutch disease model calls attention to the fact that in an open economy a boom in one (natural resource) sector can cause a depression in another (manufacturing sector). Other countries which have faced such mineral booms are: Canada, 1971–73; Australia, 1973–76; the United Kingdom and Norway, 1976–82.

5. Harry Johnson during most of this period was professor of economics at the University of Chicago and was the originator of the monetary approach to the balance of payments. McKinnon is professor of economics at Stanford University and is an important contributor to the literature on money and economic development. Mundell is widely known for his theoretical work. On policy issues he developed the notion of growth and the balance of payments that postponed the devaluation of the United States dollar relative to gold until 1971. He is widely cited as the guru behind supply-side economics, and he has contributed to the current tax simplification plan in the United States. Chipman is professor of economics at the University of Minnesota. Penner has held a number of positions in policy-making bodies. He is currently head of the

Congressional Budget Office. Viner wrote his Ph.D. thesis on the Canadian balance of payments and held professorships at Chicago and Princeton.

6. One of the most important contributions by these authors, especially by McKinnon and Mundell, is the concept of an "optimal currency area." See, in particular, Robert Mundell, "A Theory of Optimal Currency Areas," *American Economic Review*, 51 (1961), pp. 657-664. The conclusion of the article is that from the point of economic efficiency alone the North American continent should have "east dollars" and "west dollars" rather than the "north dollars" (Canada) and "south dollars" (U.S.) that we now have. Jane Jacobs has recently introduced this idea into the urban economics literature. See her *Cities and the Wealth of Nations: Principles of Economic Life* (New York: Random House, 1984).

7. This observation is central to the absorption approach to the current account. For a discussion of this approach and the consequences of payments imbalances, see Harry Johnson, "Towards a General Theory of the Balance of Payments," in H.G. Johnson, *International Trade and Economic Growth* (Cambridge: Harvard University Press, 1961), pp. 153-168.

8. There are a number of reasons why this statement needs to be qualified. Economic growth may permit a country to have a current account deficit indefinitely. Exchange rate changes may cause revaluation effects. Accounting problems arise in trying to distinguish between payments for servicing a debt and repayment of the principal.

9. For a comprehensive discussion of the development of open economy macroeconomic models, see R.I. McKinnon, "The Exchange Rate and Macroeconomic Policy: Changing Postwar Perceptions," *Journal of Economic Literature*, 19: pp. 531-557, 1981, or P.B. Kenen, "Macroeconomic Theory and Policy: How the Closed Economy was Opened," in R.W. Jones and P.B. Kenen eds., *Handbook of International Economics*, Vol. II, (Amsterdam: North-Holland, 1984-1985), pp. 625-677.

10. This discussion follows the analysis by Robert Mundell, *International Economics* (New York: Macmillan, 1968), Ch. 17 and 18. For a review similar to what is undertaken here, see Douglas Purvis, "Public Sector Deficits, International Capital Movements, and the Domestic Economy: The Medium-term is the Message," The 1985 Harold Innis Memorial Lecture, in *The Canadian Journal of Economics* XVIII, No. 4, Nov., 1985. p. 11.

11. This conclusion can be made rigorous by a comparison of the equilibrium generated under fixed exchange rates with that under flexible exchange rates. A useful model for this purpose is Russell Boyer, "Financial Policies in the Open Economy," *Economica*, 45 (Feb. 1977), pp. 39-58.

12. Accusations that this has always been the intention of the Reagan administration (with the Laffer curve merely providing a smoke screen) have resurfaced with the failure of budget negotiations in the United States Congress during the summer of 1985.

13. Robert Barro, "Are Government Bonds Net Wealth?" *Journal of Political Economy*, 82 (Nov./Dec. 1974), pp. 1095-1118, provides an analysis of the circumstances under which the size of the government deficit is irrelevant. The similar effects of tax levies and deficit financing is called Ricardian Equivalence.

14. For a thoughtful review of the issues raised by monetary policy since 1979 see Bennett McCallum, "Monetarist Rules in the Light of Recent Experience," *American Economic Review*, Papers and Proceedings, (May 1984), pp. 388-391.

15. Two qualifications should be made to this statement. The importance of the United States dollar in financing world trade has been increasing. See Stanley Black, "International Money and International Monetary Arrangements," in R.W. Jones and P.B. Kenen eds., *Handbook of International Economics*, Vol. II, (Amsterdam: North-Holland, 1984-1985), pp. 1153-1193. This suggests, on the basis of the "safe-haven" argument put forward by administration spokesmen, that demand has risen at a more rapid rate than domestic considerations alone portray.

The second qualification concerns the attitudes shown by the Federal Reserve System. Most economists acknowledge that current perceptions of the rate of growth of the money supply in the future have an important role to play in the economy. In this dimension Paul Volcker, Head of the Board of Governors of the Federal Reserve System, has kept money fairly tight since his attitude and actions seem to suggest that he will not allow serious inflation to occur in the future.

16. This conclusion is derived in Russell Boyer, *op. cit.*

17. We should bear in mind that these industries would have expanded even more had there not been restrictions on them in the form of Voluntary Export Restraints.

18. The useful distinction between expenditure-reducing policies and expenditure-switching policies was made by Harry Johnson, *op. cit.*

19. The main effect of comprehensive protectionist legislation under floating exchange rates is to strengthen the currency on the foreign exchange market. An important determinant of the current value of the exchange rate is policies that are likely to be enacted in the future. This suggests that part of the reason that the dollar is so strong is the anticipation of this legislation. Rather than "countering" the dollar overvaluation, such legislation would "justify" the dollar's current value. Furthermore, were it not anticipated, such legislation would not be necessary.

20. This point has been emphasized recently by David Laidler, "International Monetary Institutions and Deficits," in James M. Buchanan and Charles K. Rowley, eds., *Toward a Political Economy of Budget Deficits* (Oxford: Basil Blackwell, 1986).

Canada–United States Relations and the Global Trading System

John Whalley

This chapter will deal with Canada–United States trade issues within the context of the global economy and the pressures on the global trading system, as we move from the negotiations in the Tokyo Round on into what may or may not be a future round of negotiations under the General Agreement on Tariffs and Trade (GATT). Our emerging and changing relationship with the United States on trade matters will be considered in this context, and we will touch on some of the multilateral dimensions of our bilateral trade relationship with the United States.

This is very much an economist's view of the issues. We all know, and are all acutely aware, that there are many other dimensions to our trading relationship with the Americans. Questions about sovereignty, for instance, are central to any policy decisions which may be made in these areas. Although we will not dwell on them, it does not mean that they are not important; indeed, they are vitally important to the policy debate on trade issues. Also, the discussion will be restricted to trade questions covering tariffs, non-tariff barriers and the like. This essay will not discuss international financial issues even though, when one looks at the current situation, the pressures that high interest rates in the United States create for protectionist policies there are clearly substantial. Environmental problems are also of crucial importance; indeed, some would argue that acid rain is one of the central issues underlying the Canada–United States relationship.

The central theme of this essay is that in looking at all Canada–United States trade issues, one cannot ignore the wider global trading system. If one goes back over the Canadian debates on trade issues to 1867 or 1879 and the National Policy, to 1911 and the reciprocity debates, and to more recent discussions, the wider dimension of global trading arrangements and their influence on the Canada–United States relationship has never been absent. In our present environment, there are also global issues which affect the way in which Canadians have to deal with the Americans in our bilateral trade relationship.

Perhaps most important is the way wider global arrangements affect our strategy towards negotiating better access, and improvements in security of access to American markets. Many people in Canada involved in policy debates often regard trade policy as discrete. The choices are sometimes posed in terms of the question: "Should Canada have bilateral free trade or not?" In fact things are much more complex. Canada already has a distinct bilateral trade relationship with the Americans quite separate from our multilateral obligations. This has been emerging since 1935, when Canada first entered into bilateral arrangements with the United States, and subsequently through a series of further bilateral negotiations such as the Auto Pact of 1965. In 1984, Canada signed a special safeguards notification agreement with the Americans, a form of early warning system on safeguard measures. Since 1947 and the signing of the GATT, Canadians have tended to focus much more heavily on multilateral rather than bilateral negotiations. Advocates of free trade with the Americans are, in fact (and sometimes unknowingly), suggesting only a change in emphasis.[1] No one seems to be suggesting we abandon our multilateral obligations. There is, therefore, already a bilateral focus to our trade policies; the issue is what the balance should be between bilateralism and multilateralism in our trade strategy, not whether there should be any bilateral component.

In looking at Canada–United States trade relations and the way they interact with the global trading system, Canadians should not think in simple terms of an exclusive bilateral or multilateral focus in our policies. Not only are these not mutually exclusive, they currently coexist. The issues are: what is the appropriate balance between the two; and are they complementary or competitive?

One can, for instance, argue that an increased bilateral focus in our trade policies could accelerate multilateral trade negotiations under the GATT. Some argue that this is what happened in the early 1960s with the formation of the European Economic Community (EEC) and the Dillon GATT Round which followed. There are others, however, who argue that we currently face a fragmenting global environment, and increased bilateralism by us will accelerate this process. The global trading system, as it has emerged since 1947 through the multilateralism under the GATT, is showing evidence of fragmentation into regional trade arrangements, through trade measures which are being used outside of the GATT agreements, such as the growing use of non-tariff measures. One can therefore argue that if there is an increased bilateral focus in our trade policies towards the Americans, it could lead to a further fragmentation in the global trading system, which itself is so central to smaller countries like Canada.

Such matters are not simple; they are complex and involve difficult strategic issues. Also related is the fact that there are developments underway in the global trading system which Canadians have not really experienced in the past. They further affect the trade relationship with the United States. The most direct and obvious are the pressures from the world beyond, as they make an impact on the United States while secondary effects rebound onto Canada. The most important of such changes are taking place in the developing world and especially in the newly industrialized countries, which are growing rapidly and penetrating the American markets. As this happens, industries are slow to adjust and adapt to this new competition, so the political pressures for protection grow. Since we depend heavily on access to markets in the United States, protectionist barriers against developing countries also affect Canada.

Within the last two years, for example, there have been pressures in the United States for safeguard measures in steel. The United States has already moved in this area since the election of 1984, as witnessed by quotas on steel pipes which are causing major problems with the Europeans. Another case is copper. At one point in 1984 it looked as if the United States was going to impose quotas on copper for similar domestic reasons, although in the end this did not happen.

In approaching our trade relations with the United States, we have to be aware that activities by other countries are triggering trade policy actions in the United States that are causing problems for Canada. But this is not the only trade problem Canadians have in dealing with the United States. The origins of many other trade measures are much more contained within the Canada–United States relationship, such as the imposition of counter-vailing duties by the United States on products which they view us as subsidizing. Pressures on the Canadian softwood lumber industry continue to mount. But these aspects of the Canada–United States relationship illustrate the linkages to the wider global environment.

In the next ten to twenty years, the major trading developments will very clearly be in the third world. The latter itself is a heterogeneous group of countries. There are countries which have very poor growth performance, particularly in Africa. Latin America in the last few years has experienced negative growth in a number of countries that were growing rapidly in the 1970s before the debt crisis hit. In contrast, growth in the Asia-Pacific region is rapid.

Trade policies towards the developing world are going to be the key issue again facing the global economy during the next generation. This situation creates a special problem for Canada and also poses problems for our trade relations with the United States. Unlike the Americans or the Europeans, Canada has only a small share of total trade with the developing countries. The Europeans have a much larger fraction of their trade with the developing world—around 35 to 40 per cent. The reason for this is clear. Our major exports are raw materials and agricultural products. The developing countries tend to be our competitors in the export markets upon which we rely. There are pressures for changes in trade policy towards the developing world, motivated by genuine and appropriate concerns of compassion for these countries. But, as Canadians, we have to be aware that positive selectivity in trade policies in their favour (giving them preferential access to certain markets, and in particular to the American market) is going to complicate our relations with all our trading partners and especially with the United States. Therefore, what we are looking at is a complex set of developments. The global trading system is central to our trade relations with the Americans; we ignore it at our peril.

If one looks at the global economy as a single system, it can be divided up into a number of different regions. First, there is the division between the developed and the less developed countries. In the developed world the large blocs are the European Economic Community, the United States, and Japan, which between them account for a large portion of world income and trade. Among the smaller countries, Canada is one of the more important. We rank seventh in terms of size among members of the Organization for Economic Co-operation and Development (OECD). Canada is not a small country in its absolute size, but it is relatively small compared to the larger units.

The less developed countries can be classified on a geographical basis. Countries of the Asia-Pacific region are growing rapidly, and are introducing cheaper products into our markets. Latin American countries, which had experienced strong growth through the 1960s and 1970s, are now encountering massive debt problems. There have been large reductions in their import volumes in the last several years. India, China, Pakistan, and Bangladesh are the large population countries where there are significant degrees of poverty. Of course, China is emerging very rapidly now; it may have something like 4 per cent real growth per capita in 1984. Sub-Saharan Africa is the worst region in terms of performance, and in terms of trade volumes it is very small.

In looking at trade shares for larger countries, this trade tends to be relatively less important than for the small countries. For the United States, Japan, and the EEC (taken as a single unit), only a little over 10 per cent of Gross National Product is actually traded. Trade issues tend to be relatively less important for these countries than for Canada. Canada trades over 30 per cent of its GNP thus making trade issues correspondingly more important.

Moreover, these trade shares are changing over time. Over a period of about twenty years the fraction of GNP traded in the United States has doubled. Growth of world trade has been larger than growth rates of GNP in all these regions. Over very long periods of time, world trade is growing at about 4 per cent in real terms, whereas world growth may be averaging about 1.5 to 2 per cent per year.

Looking specifically at Canada and the United States, few are aware of how the Canadian share of trade with the Americans has been changing. Everybody states that about 75 per cent of Canadian exports enter the United States market. That is true, but at the end of World War II Canada was a large net importer from the United States. In fact only about 30 per cent of Canadian exports were to the American market after the war. This began growing in the 1960s. The Auto Pact, negotiated in 1965, produced a significant change in our trade share with the United States. It really propelled Canada to the point where we stand today. About 25 per cent of total trade with the United States is in automobiles and parts. This, therefore, emphasizes an important feature of the relationship, the importance of de facto bilateral arrangements that we have negotiated with the Americans. One can indeed argue that the Auto Pact is the biggest change in trade policies in the postwar period and thus is a major feature in bilateral trade policies.

Conversely, the United States share of trade with Canada has been falling. In the 1950s the export share with Canada was in the region of 30 per cent. Since then the total trade share and GNP have both grown, and in turn the United States has been penetrating other export markets. Now less than 20 per cent of United States exports come into Canada, which is not as important a market for the Americans as it was fifteen or twenty years ago. It is still significant, but the fraction of American exports that come into Canada is currently of the same order of magnitude as the fraction of United States exports going to the developing countries. This must be made clear in dealing with the Americans on trade issues. The United States is fundamentally important to Canada, and Canada is significant to the Americans, but it is not as crucial a market as in the past.

Beyond this picture of trade shares, and reflecting on some of the trade policies that operate in various countries, one sees again the linkages between Canada–United States trade issues and the global environment by presenting a schematic view of the world. Among the developed countries tariffs are now relatively low. They have been reduced through the various agreements that we have negotiated under the GATT since 1947. All tariffs on manufactures by the end of the implementation of the Tokyo Round in 1987 may average around 4 to 5 per cent. Other trade issues, such as non-tariff barriers (NTBs), have become more important as tariffs have been reduced. Some people even believe that NTBs have grown in significance because countries have participated in the tariff-cutting negotiating rounds under the GATT.[2] They have reduced their tariffs and hoped that other countries would in fact take the process seriously, but have offset the effects of tariff reduction with their own non-tariff barriers. It is contentious whether that has actually happened, since there are a number of problems in the measurement of these effects.

There is a long list of non-tariff barriers, beginning with quotas, many of which apply to textiles and clothing, and some of which apply to steel. There are Voluntary Export Restraints (VERs) and Orderly Marketing Agreements (OMAs). Many of these involve the Japanese and the Americans, but now the Europeans are increasing their activities in this area. Procurement practices concern the ways in which governments restrict their purchases of products to domestic suppliers. An attempt to deal with this problem in the Tokyo Round only addressed part of the problem. There are also various kinds of administrative measures and standards, and all manner of devices that are very subtle. For example, several years ago the French decided that all video cassette recorders coming into the country had to clear customs in Poitiers. Since there were only two customs officials there at the time, the product took a long time to reach the consumer. This kind of trade measure is effective, if one wants to achieve trade restrictions.

Among the developing countries, however, the situation on trade measures is very different. They typically have high tariffs which are a heritage of their import substitution policies. Many of them were adopted in the 1930s and 1940s and then maintained in the postcolonial period. They continued because of the reactions of these countries to the balance of payment crises they faced in the 1950s. There are also quantitative restrictions, quotas, and licencing arrangements that, in many countries, are so penal that they are impossible as export markets for the consumer goods of other countries. Trade restrictions also apply to many capital goods. In addition, some countries have rigid foreign exchange rationing procedures. On balance, these are very heavily regulated markets that exporters from developed countries find very hard to penetrate.

Global Institutions and the Trading System

A further feature of the global trading system is the institutions that manage and regulate trade. Four are worth brief mention: the GATT is probably the most important and is the framework through which Canadians have negotiated on trade issues in the postwar period; the United Nations Conference on Trade and Development (UNCTAD) is an organization oriented towards the developing countries; the International Monetary Fund (IMF) was originally organized to maintain the fixed exchange rate system; and finally, the World Bank is the main facilitator of project-specific financial assistance to the developing world.[3]

In terms of trade issues with the Americans the GATT is most important. Some of the issues with the GATT illustrate its impact on current Canada–United States questions. The GATT is a set of trade agreements between contracting parties. There were twenty-three signatories to the first agreement in 1947, which was viewed as only an initial one. The GATT was simply meant to record the outcome of the first tariff-cutting conference, until there was agreement on a wider set of arrangements. Since this subsequent set of arrangements never materialized, the GATT has become Canada's main trade vehicle. There are now eighty-nine signatories and thirty more countries which, de facto, are members.

The best way to understand the GATT is through the articles which control and restrain various trade measures. It was an outgrowth of the bilateral agreements which the United States entered into in the 1930s, based on President Franklin Roosevelt's "good neighbour" policy. The intent was to reduce trade barriers, which were regarded as one of the reasons for the onset of the Great Depression, an economic depression many blamed on the passage of the Smoot-Hawley Tariff of 1930 by the United States Congress. The GATT has changed a great deal since it was originally formed. It has evolved into a series of negotiating principles and rules of operation that create the constraints on our current global trading system.

There are two basic principles underlying the GATT that must be kept in mind. First, all trade should take place on the basis of non-discrimination. This is a central GATT tenet, which leads to the so-called most-favoured-nation principle. This means that trade measures used by one country should not discriminate among other countries. Canada should not use trade measures which permit imports from the Americans, but not a comparable amount from the Europeans. Any geographically discriminatory trade measures are against the spirit of the GATT, so there is a conflict between a bilateral focus in our trade policies and the GATT.

The second basic principle is national treatment. Whenever goods cross a national border and have cleared whatever tariff walls are in the way, they should receive the same treatment as all other products. There should not be discriminatory trade measures and regulations beyond the tariff and other measures which apply at the border. Trade restriction should be in the form of visible tariff barriers which can potentially be negotiated away.

The GATT as it stands in principle and the GATT as it has evolved in practice are very different. The discriminatory trade arrangements that have evolved since 1947 are accommodated within the GATT. It accepted the formation of the EEC and recently accepted the bilateral trade arrangement between Australia and New Zealand.[4] National treatment has been modified in its application because of the growth of all kinds of measures which are used outside the GATT system. Nonetheless, there has been an ongoing process of trade liberalization within the GATT, the net effect of which has been to produce a series of negotiations on the topic. The two most important of the seven negotiating rounds within this framework since 1947 have been the Kennedy and Tokyo Rounds—one in the 1960s and the other in the 1970s.

Many issues currently facing the GATT rebound on Canada and the United States and the way in which our mutual trade relations are likely to evolve. The first is the inability of the GATT to limit significantly the use of non-tariff barriers. Some people involved with the GATT view it in a very pessimistic light at the present time. In particular, the inability to deal with the issue of quotas and the growth of safeguard measures is in contradiction to the original spirit of the agreement. The need to control safeguard measures is very closely related to wider questions of non-tariff barriers. Generally speaking, countries facing large amounts of import competition have been unwilling to accept the adjustments which import competition implies. They have adopted various temporary measures designed to ease the transitional problems created by import penetration, but, in many cases, these temporary measures have become permanent.

The classic case of this process is the treatment of textiles. In 1961 the developed and the developing countries negotiated a short term agreement on cotton textiles. It was meant to be in effect for six months but is still with us today and has grown substantially in scope from its original design. Many argue that the measures which the Americans have just introduced on steel are evidence that we are moving towards the same kind of managed trade arrangement for steel as we have had in textiles since 1961. In turn, the arrangements with steel between the Americans and the Europeans have a very long history, going back even to the 1930s.

There is also a need to integrate the developing countries more fully into the GATT framework. The trade negotiations which have taken place in the GATT have largely excluded them for some very complex reasons. Generally speaking, considerable support exists in the developed world for bringing the developing countries more fully into the global trading system, but there is also a lot of scepticism. Many of the developing countries view the GATT as a rich countries' club that simply produces trade liberalization for those products which are of importance to developed countries.[5] Again, Canada–United States relations become directly involved in these issues.

Finally, there is the issue of certain countries using trade measures in a selective manner. One of the major disputes in the negotiations during the Tokyo Round involved the desire of the Europeans to apply safeguard measures selectively. The issue prevented a safeguards code being concluded during those negotiations, and it is still a central problem .

These issues facing the GATT will likely be converted into concerns that a future round of trade negotiations under the GATT will have to confront. Again, many are central to Canada–United States questions. Whether or not a future round will actually take place is uncertain at the present time. Some commentators suggest a set of pre-round negotiations, which could get under way around 1987 and last about three years, leading to an actual round of negotiations starting in 1990, which may last another ten years.

What are some of the issues which might arise in such a round? A major concern is agriculture. It has been largely excluded from most previous trade negotiations in the GATT and has not been attacked in any central way. Agricultural trade is one of the most distorted areas of world trade, primarily because of the domestic policies used by many countries to regulate agriculture and to intervene in that sector. The Common Agricultural Policy in the EEC is something which the Americans feel strongly about, as indeed do the Canadians. There is likely to be a determined attempt by the Americans to put this item on the agenda, which, in turn, may well be strongly resisted by the Europeans. Canada has a community of interest on this issue with the Americans.

Another prospective issue is trade in services. Trade liberalization thus far under the GATT has focused on trade in commodities; yet there is a wide array of service trade issues involving investment, banking, insurance, financial questions, transborder data flows, transborder communication issues, and other matters. The Americans in particular feel strongly that these issues should be on the agenda for a future round of trade negotiations. The position of Canada is somewhat complex. In fact, it is not clear what an appropriate Canadian response is to these questions, given that Canada tends to be a net importer of services.

A third issue is safeguards. The need for a stronger safeguard code is felt particularly by countries like Canada. The use of safeguard measures in United States markets is currently affecting Canada directly. We pushed strongly for a new safeguard code in the negotiations during the Tokyo Round and were unsuccessful. Many feel that this will be a central issue during the next round.

There are also trade-related investment issues. How should investment flows across national borders be handled? Canada has recently been the subject of an American reference to a GATT panel on the issue of how various features of the Foreign Investment Review Agency (FIRA) apply to domestic content provisions. This resulted in Canada making a change in its FIRA regulations by replacing it with Investment Canada, but the Americans would like a wider set of codes to be negotiated on trade-related investment issues.[6]

However, in addition to the GATT, there is another trading system which, for want of a better term, I will call the non-GATT system. The non-GATT system is growing very substantially in size. Perhaps as much as 50 per cent of world trade now takes place outside of GATT rules, or indeed in open defiance of GATT rules. This is difficult to measure but economists agree that it is very large.

There is a series of trade measures not covered by the GATT involving quantitative restrictions, Voluntary Export Restraints, Orderly Marketing Agreements, and all the state trading practices, which involve many developing countries and the centrally planned countries, and, indeed, some of the state trading agencies in the developed world. In addition, a whole series of regional arrangements is contrary to the spirit of the GATT, although technically compatible with it. They include the EEC, developed in the 1960s; EFTA, the European Free Trade Association, a response of the other European countries to the evolution of the EEC; CARICO, a small common market amongst Caribbean countries; LAFTA, the Latin America Free Trade Association; ASEAN, the Association of South East Asian Nations; and the Australia–New Zealand free trade arrangement. The 1984 trade bill in the United States authorized a free trade arrangement between the United States and Israel, which may be relatively unimportant in quantitative terms, but is further evidence of the growth of these regional arrangements. The agreement was concluded in February, 1985. The Caribbean Basin Initiative is another of the regionally discriminatory trade arrangements.

Canada is unique among large developed countries in either not being part of one of these regional arrangements, or in turn not having access to a large domestic market of one hundred million or more. The Japanese have such a market; the Europeans are already involved in these regional arrangements; the United States, of course, has a large domestic market. This growth of regional arrangements, most of which have been made compatible with GATT in one way or another, is another feature of the way the current global trading system has evolved.

Bilateral Canada–United States Arrangements

The Canadian bilateral arrangements with the Americans are a further part of the trading environment and complement the multilateral system under the GATT. In many ways, the fundamental change in Canadian trade policies occurred in the 1930s, which is often not recognized. In 1935, Canada concluded a bilateral trade agreement with the Americans on tariff reductions. This really marked the major change in trade policies relative to 1879 and the National Policy, which had been the source of Canadian protectionism developed around the turn of the century.

Since 1935, in addition to the multilateral obligations that Canada has entered into under the GATT, the country has increasingly moved towards bilateral accommodations and arrangements of various types. These do not cover all the products that Canada trades with the Americans, but they are significant. In addition to the original bilateral agreements on tariff reductions, the Defence Production Sharing Arrangement (1959) covers contracting agreements on defence products. Although originally initiated in wartime by the Hyde Park Agreement of 1941, it is nonetheless still significant today. The Auto Pact is one of the most important trade agreements because it covers so much of our trade. As evidence of this continuing trend, there is also the Safeguards Notification Agreement concluded in 1984. Although relatively small, it provides for notification to the other country in the event of planned introduction of safeguard measures, and it is further evidence of a bilateral relationship being worked out in addition to multilateral obligations.

Implications for the Canada–United States Relationship

All this, then, is a picture of the way the global trading system is evolving. It is necessary to place this in the context of Canada–United States relations, drawing out what all this implies, and then look at a few of the options that Canada will probably have to confront in the years ahead.

The first point, which I have already stressed, is that Canadians have had a mixed relationship with the Americans in terms of bilateralism and multilateralism since 1935. The issues Canada now faces include: how do we manage our relationship; how do we decide on the balance of the appropriate types of relationships we have with the United States; and how do we conduct these relationships in light of the changes which are both taking place now and will take place in the future of the global trading system?

Secondly, we have the paradox of size and the way that considerations of size are manifest in the global trading system. The whole global trading system as it has unfolded in the GATT is one of paradox. It is a strange arrangement in the sense that the smaller countries tend to gain most through the trade liberalization that occurs under it. As tariffs have been lowered as a result of these trade negotiations, the smaller countries have benefited most by increased access to the larger markets, such as the United States and the EEC. Multilateral trade negotiations have been very beneficial to Canada.

On the other hand, the large countries determine and largely drive this whole arrangement. They initiate the negotiating rounds and their votes count in determining what actually happens in the negotiations. What are the implications for Canada of the fact that the main beneficiaries are not the countries which initiate things? In dealing with the United States, it is clear that its foreign policy interests and trade policies are inseparable. The drive towards the GATT in 1947 was a continuation of bilateral attempts undertaken in the 1930s and was part of the American attempt to rebuild the non-communist world at that time and to move forward in a more cooperative series of arrangements with the allies in trade and other matters. From the American point of view, this process has always been part of the GATT. Thus, to a large country, trade policy becomes more and more involved with foreign policy. The smaller a country is, the more the economic dimensions of foreign policy come to dominate.

So too in Canada's relations with the Americans, it must be clear that from an American point of view their interests may well be far more dominated by foreign policy concerns than more narrow economic concerns. From a Canadian point of view, we should recognize that our economic interests are central in dealing with these trade issues.

The third point is that Canada should recognize that any future round of trade negotiations under the GATT may well be as much concerned with repairing and re-invigorating the current trading system as moving forward towards new trade liberalizing measures. There is now a degree of disrespect for the multilateral framework of the GATT. The growth of trade measures outside of the GATT framework means that this lack of respect is undermining the multilateralism that has dominated the postwar world. Again, Canada has to make judgments as to how to proceed in our arrangements with the Americans, as we move through this set of negotiations ourselves. How far do we move on the bilateral and multilateral fronts?

Finally, and perhaps most importantly, it is clear that there has been a distinct change in the attitude towards trade policy among practitioners of United States trade policy. The protectionist attitude of politicians is less important than that of officials in the executive branch of government. There is no doubt that the people who actually conduct trade policy on a day-to-day basis, have become convinced of the need for a new United States assertiveness in trade policy matters. This, in turn, is part of a wider set of changes taking place in the United States, leading generally towards a more assertive foreign trade policy. It is very clear that the focus is no longer on "good neighbours" but on "levelling the playing field" for fair trade. This occurs by the use of aggressive reciprocity and by the use of trade measures to force access in foreign markets. There is discussion only with like-minded powers. Again, this trend runs counter to the strong American commitment to global institutions and multilateralism, which grew out of the 1940s.

This situation leaves Canadians with room both for opportunities and anxieties. Canada can gain advantages if it wishes to deal with the Americans on a more flexible basis. On the other hand, one can point to an erosion of multilateralism in the global trading system and in turn more widely in the whole geo-political system, and the threats that might possibly imply for smaller countries such as Canada. But the facts of the situation are fairly clear; change is taking place.

The global trading system and the way the global trading system fits alongside our bilateral relationship is central to the issues on which Canadians must deal with Americans. Whether Canada likes it or not, this linkage is inescapable, and it will help us and our neighbours to the south to recognize this fact.

Notes

1. See, Duncan M. McMonagle, "Provinces Ask Quick Start to Trade Talks," and Orland French "Trade Winds Confusing," *The Globe and Mail*, 23 August 1985.
2. See, Colleen Hamilton and John Whalley, "Non-Tariff Barriers and Canadian Trade Policy: Summary of the Proceedings of a Research Symposium," Vol. 10: Canada and the Multinational Trading System, *Report, Royal Commission on the Economic Union and Development Prospects for Canada* (Ottawa: Minister of Supply and Services Canada, 1985).
3. The original rationale of the IMF has largely disappeared with the end of the Bretton Woods Agreement (1944) in 1971. Its role and concern is now much more focused toward the developing world.
4. The *Australian–New Zealand Closer Economic Relations Trade Agreement* was concluded on 28 March 1983.
5. The GATT opened preliminary negotiations on 30 September 1985, in Geneva. There was a controversial American initiative on the table aimed at freeing world trade in services, which most third world nations opposed. The United States has demanded the inclusion of trade in such things as banking, insurance, and telecommunications services which account for 60 per cent of United States employment.
6. Investment Canada came into existence on 30 June 1985, under the authority of the Investment Canada Act. Already, it has been criticized by American officials. See J. Levington "Washington Fuming over Ottawa Plan for the Bank Business," *The Globe and Mail*, 30 September 1985.

CHAPTER 6

Bilateral Free Trade with the United States

Bruce W. Wilkinson

1. Introduction

If we look at the United States economy from a Canadian perspective with regard to trade issues, we have to address the issue of bilateral free trade between Canada and the United States, what the American response might be to any initiatives Canada puts forth, and what the implications of this response might be for Canada.

In this essay, we will examine the supposition that if Canada approaches the Americans to negotiate a bilateral free trade agreement, it definitely risks losing much of its political sovereignty and could end up being politically absorbed into the United States.[1] Whether this outcome occurs depends not just on internal Canadian policies and desires but also, and more importantly, on the motives and aspirations of the United States, now and in the future, and the steps that nation may wish to take to fulfill its aspirations. We will examine a number of issues that are worth consideration by Canada with respect to any bilateral free trade agreement with the United States. In so doing, we will compare what seems to be a common and overly optimistic perception by Canadian economists as to what Canada might be able to achieve in negotiations, with what is a more realistic expectation of the outcome of the process—that bilateral free trade is only a reasonable way to proceed, if we are not too concerned about possible, eventual political union with the United States. If that is a major concern to Canadians, then we might be well advised to be patient and work through the General Agreement on Tariffs and Trade (GATT) for another multilateral round of negotiations.

2. A Brief Review of the Risks of Bilateral Free Trade

First, United States ownership and control of Canadian industry is likely to increase in the short run as a consequence of a bilateral free trade agreement.

In the long run, even though capital/output ratios may be decreased in manufacturing and aggregate savings may be increased so that more minority interests may be purchased in foreign-controlled companies, the foreign control of these companies is unlikely to be decreased from what it was in the short run. Thus, the concentration of much of the decision-making regarding research and development, production, and world marketing will be in non-Canadian hands.

Secondly, Canadians may develop an inflated view of what Canada can hope to gain from bilateral free trade as a result of relying solely upon estimates of gains by models which do *not* take into account the realities of what the American bargaining expectations and styles are likely to be. This may make Canadians disillusioned and more willing to consider closer political ties with the United States. We shall look at this subject much more closely below.

Thirdly, in contrast to the view that Canada will be stronger and more independent economically and therefore politically, the likelihood is that, as we extend our manufacturing runs of standardized, often mass-produced products and rely even more on United States markets, we will be more vulnerable to any American moves to abrogate the bilateral free trade agreement. Our product lines would tend to be more like those the newly industrialized countries are producing, and we would not have the marketing channels readily available in other lands to shift easily from reliance upon the Americans. We could not withhold our resource exports from the United States either because, with many of our manufactured exports in jeopardy, we would be heavily dependent upon continuing export revenues from resources.

Fourthly, in contrast to those who have stated that free trade types of arrangements have *never* led to political absorption or affiliation, the fact is that it has happened *at least twice*. One of these occasions occurred in 1871 when the Zollverein, which was formed in 1834, became under strong Prussian leadership, the Germany that we knew earlier in this century. With regard to negotiations among the individual states one historian put it this way: "On all important matters the Prussian point of view prevailed."[2] This came about because of the economic dominance of Prussia within the customs union.[3]

The second occasion, much closer to home, was the transformation of Hawaii from an independent nation to a possession of the United States in 1898 and finally into the fiftieth state in 1959. Hawaiian interests wanted tariff-free access to the United States for their sugar. Negotiations for a reciprocity agreement were pursued in the 1850s, but the United States Senate failed to ratify the agreement reached. With the serious depression in 1866/67, Hawaii once again sought reciprocity. The Hawaiian authorities recognized that once they had achieved it, should the United States subsequently desire to abrogate the treaty, there would be much economic pressure on them to seek annexation to the United States so that they could have permanent free access for their products to that nation. As for the

United States, one historian wrote, "both those who favoured and those who opposed the treaty had the same ultimate objective in mind—annexation of the archipelago; they differed only in the method that they thought would best achieve it."[4] In any event, a reciprocity treaty was finally signed with Hawaii in 1875.

Hawaiian sugar exports in particular expanded greatly over the ensuing two decades. The merchandise trade balance alone involved a modest export surplus for Hawaii. But if one were to add in all service payments for freight, shipping, banking, insurance, and dividends, the United States had the export surplus. Nevertheless, many in the United States argued that it was losing from the agreement and that there should be some compensation or the agreement should be terminated.[5] The arguments went back and forth, but after William McKinley became President in 1896, a joint resolution was passed by the Senate and the House of Representatives and signed by the president to annex Hawaii without so much as a plebiscite in Hawaii. Reciprocity did lead to annexation. Other lands were also annexed by the United States over the ensuing several months: Guam, the Philippines, Puerto Rico, and Wake Island.

3. The Current Situation

In this historical context, consider the Canadian situation vis-à-vis the United States. In terms of commodities, mostly raw materials and their products, the reciprocity agreement that Hawaii signed with the United States in 1875 was not unlike the Elgin-March 1854 reciprocity agreement between Canada and the United States. Also in the 1860s, one of the motives of the expansionist members in the United States for abrogating the Canada–United States treaty was the hope "that the resulting dislocation of Canadian commerce might quicken natural impulses for voluntary annexation."[6] However, Canadian exports to the United States at that time amounted to only about 40 per cent of total exports, much less than the 76 per cent today, or the even higher percentage that would result if a bilateral free trade agreement were signed with the United States. Our vulnerability to abrogation was much less then than it would be now. Just as one of the main motives for Hawaii to seek reciprocity with the Americans in the last century was economic depression, so it is in Canada today. With unemployment persisting at about 10 per cent, some see bilateral free trade as a means of eradicating much of Canada's unemployment.

From a perspective of what the United States response might be, let us turn to some specific issues that must be dealt with in negotiating a bilateral free trade agreement.

(a) Buy Domestic Policies

Consider first the matter of buy domestic policies. There seems to be a belief in Canada that it is simply a matter of the two countries bilaterally agreeing to give each other's companies freedom to bid on government purchases with no margin of preference to domestic suppliers. Of course this view recognizes that in both countries it would be necessary to include all three levels of governments. In Canada, for example, it would require the agreement of the provinces and municipalities. When this particular reality is brought home to some of the provincial governments, there may be less enthusiasm for bilateral free trade than there is at the moment. Achieving such an agreement, therefore, may not be easy.

More important in my judgment, however, is the fact that the United States is unlikely to see bilateral removal of buy domestic rules as an equal trade-off. If, for example, in the United States this implies access to bidding on $20 billion of government purchases whereas in Canada the corresponding figure is $1 billion, the United States will, in all probability, want some compensation elsewhere in the agreement. The costs, then, of eliminating buy domestic policies vis-à-vis one another could be very expensive for Canada, economically, and in the long run, perhaps politically.

In contrast, if Canada were patient enough to wait for a new round of GATT talks to begin, then, when the United States permits access to $20 billion of government purchases, Canada would not have to provide *all* the compensation for this privilege. The United States would be compensated because the other industrial nations in the GATT would also be granting access to their government purchases. Canada, in exchange for surrendering its own buy domestic policies, would obtain access to many nations. The gains could be considerable, without the risks and costs associated with a purely bilateral free trade agreement. We will return to this argument later in the essay.

There may be some who would argue that in a bilateral free trade agreement American demands on Canada regarding buy domestic policies would not be as great as I suggest, but the evidence suggests otherwise. Recently, the senior assistant to the United States Special Trade Representative was quoted as stating that the United States would consider Canadian proposals for bilateral free trade "as long as they are commercially balanced," which implies that they should be of like advantage to each nation.[7] That this is the prevailing United States view becomes even clearer as we consider some of the other areas requiring negotiation.

(b) Service Trade

One of these matters relates to the flow of services, including information and communications. The most contentious issue with regard to information and services generally is the 1975 Canadian Bill C-58, which removed the right of Canadian firms to deduct, as an expense for income tax purposes, expenditures for advertising on United States media such as border television stations. As John Meisel has pointed out, advertising expenditures in 1975 on United States stations were reduced by only about $15 million.[8] A more recent estimate for 1982 suggests the total was about $30 million. But considered from any perspective, the sum involved is minuscule compared to the overall trade flows between our two countries. Yet American threats of retaliation have involved penalizing Canada in amounts up to forty times the value of the advertising lost, such as eliminating tax deductions for United States firms buying Canada's videotext technology, Telidon.

One would have thought that the retaliatory provision in section 232 of the United States Trade and Tariff Act of 1984, which denies the right to deduct for income tax purposes any expenditures on advertising in foreign media by United States firms when such advertising is directed at United States viewers or listeners, would have settled the matter. This amendment was specifically directed at Canada, since it applies only to countries which do the same to the United States. Yet just recently, a representative of the American border broadcasters has been talking to United States government officials about possible additional measures of retaliation against Canada, which might include tighter restraints against Canadians owning property, newspapers, other media, or other investments in United States firms.[9] This type of American response, if enacted, would go much beyond "commercially balanced" types of arrangements into swift congressional retaliation (or executive action) against those who do not see things the American way. Thus, as I will enlarge upon below, Canada probably needs the type of protection that the GATT can offer.

Consider some other United States positions on trade in services. The 1984 Trade and Tariff Act (section 305) makes it very clear that the United States views *any* restrictions on service trade as un-American, including the transfer of information in or out of another country, or the use of data processing facilities within or outside a country, as well as any restrictions on United States firms being established or operating in foreign markets. It follows that any acts taken by Canada with regard to controlling information or data flows, which may be deemed necessary to preserve Canadian cultural autonomy or political sovereignty, would thus violate United States law and could be the cause of retaliation. This section of the Trade and Tariff Act could also be interpreted to mean that the United States would expect Canada to relax any and all laws regarding restrictions on foreign ownership of the news media.

(c) Industrial Development Policies

Under bilateral free trade Canada is also likely to find its policies on regional development grants or the encouragement of particular industries subject to United States consent. The American bilateral free trade agreement with Israel clearly must be used as an indicator of what the American position would be in relation to Canada. To illustrate: a provision of much greater importance to Israel than to the United States is the fact that unilateral help to infant industries will be permitted only to 1990.[10] Thereafter, any such actions by Israel will have to receive the agreement or endorsement of the United States. In other words, under bilateral free trade, we would have to expect that domestic proposals by the Canadian Department of Regional and Industrial Expansion would eventually come to be routed through the United States government.

Section 305 of the 1984 Trade and Tariff Act also makes it clear that the United States wants to remove all policies by Canada or other foreign countries which discourage American investment, or encourage the development of domestic high technology industries, and/or discourage in any way the purchase of American high technology products in favour of domestic ones. In contrast, many American states, as well as the federal government, have laws restricting foreign ownership and control. This section emphasizes the importance of allowing the market to operate and fits with the often-voiced American view of wanting to "play on a level field."

However, what Americans seem to forget, as do many Canadians glibly endorsing bilateral free trade, is the problem that even if the field is level, it does not have eleven approximately evenly-matched players on each end. Rather, one end has about 240 million people and many of the largest and most powerful corporations in the world; on the other end of the field are 25 million people and a large number of corporations which are still small and/or inefficient. It is not an evenly-matched game. No wonder the United States sometimes feels the playing field is upward sloping.

"Letting the market work" may often mean letting United States interests prevail. This attitude is certainly reflected in section 304 of the 1984 Act which amends the Trade Act of 1974. It instructs the president to take action to protect United States interests not only when another nation is violating some trade agreement but also whenever a foreign country does anything that, in the eyes of the United States, "is unjustifiable, unreasonable, or discriminatory and burdens or restricts United States commerce." For an action to be labelled "unreasonable" it need not violate United States international legal rights but must merely be deemed by the United States government to be "unfair and inequitable." That is, the United States decides what is unfair and inequitable. Also, the president is enabled to retaliate on a country-specific basis if desired, and retaliation need not be limited to the industry or goods involved but can be against any other sector or set of commodities the president chooses.

(d) Natural Resource Policies

It is well known that the U.S. House of Representatives overwhelmingly supported a natural resource provision for inclusion in the 1984 Trade Act. This would have allowed the United States to impose countervailing duties on any product which had used natural resource inputs priced lower than the price these resources had when sold by that country to the United States. Apparently, it was primarily agricultural interests, which feared foreign retaliation and increases in the prices of fertilizer to United States farmers, that were able to have this provision removed. Nevertheless, its advocates indicated that they would try again to reintroduce a similar legislative provision.[11]

With this attitude in the House of Representatives and with some support in the Senate, the obvious question arises, "What chance is there for the ratification of any bilateral free trade treaty with Canada if it does *not* include restrictions on the pricing of Canadian natural resource inputs into products going to the United States?" If such a clause was included in the treaty, it could adversely affect the chances of the Alberta petrochemical industry being able to export to the United States. Former Premier Peter Lougheed's support for bilateral free trade might not be as great then as it is currently. It could also adversely affect Quebec exports of products requiring substantial amounts of cheap hydro-electricity.

Notice the type of assumption implied by the American position on resource inputs: a nation would not be permitted to exercise fully its *comparative* advantage in natural resources. It could be deemed unfair or unreasonable or discriminatory to do so. One can visualize all sorts of difficulties here. Suppose a corporation owns both the abundant, cheap raw material and a plant processing this raw material. If the company wished to export some of the raw material and also use some of it internally for processing, it would be restricted in its internal pricing policies to charging itself the same price it charged the Americans or else face countervailing duties or other United States government retaliation. How far is the already long arm of the United States going to stretch?

One can better understand the basic United States position regarding these resource pricing matters by looking at four commodities—natural gas, lumber, steel, and copper. It was only a year or two ago that the United States was complaining that exports of Canadian *natural gas* were priced too high. It was prepared to take retaliatory action. Canada subsequently allowed the export price to be reduced, and gas exports increased. But it was not long before there were complaints from some quarters that Canadian prices were too low and that there should be some restrictions on them.[12]

As for *lumber*, Canadian firms are not subsidized. They are not charging American buyers more than domestic ones. They are simply charging rock-bottom prices in order to survive in a tough domestic and international market. In other words, they are operating in the market and letting the market work. But there is now heavy American pressure, particularly from congressmen in the north-western states, as well as from the chairman of the House of Representatives trade subcommittee, Sam Gibbons (D.–Fla.), to limit the Canadian share of the United States market to a certain percentage based on historical averages.[13] In other words, in spite of the usual United States endorsement of "letting the market work," when the impersonal market works against the United States, pressures arise repeatedly from vested interests to restrict market forces. Can Canada reasonably expect that this would be any different under bilateral free trade?

The same type of problem arises with respect to *steel*. The 1984 Trade Act (section 803) indicates that the foreign share of steel in the United States should not exceed 20.2 per cent. Canadian steel is not subsidized. It is an efficient industry. Yet, because of the recent Trade Act, it faces potential American constraints.

Finally, let us consider *copper*. The 1984 Act (section 247) authorized the president to negotiate production restraints on copper with other producing countries so as to help raise the world copper prices, keep remaining United States copper producers in operation, and thus "achieve a secure domestic supply of copper." Notice how "security of supply" enters the picture here, as well as something approaching an international copper cartel.

4. The Future

In pulling these various observations together, what can we conclude? First, there will be no "free lunch" for Canada in any bilateral free trade agreement. We need to be cautious, as former United States Trade Representative William Brock so kindly warned us.[14] For every gain Canada receives, the Americans are going to expect something in return. Also, Canada should not expect to be able to retain safeguard provisions preventing complete destruction of a Canadian industry without the Americans wanting the same. One wonders, therefore, how or why Canada should expect to have a 5 per cent gain in employment in the short run as some analysts have predicted.[15] Therefore, Canada should not allow itself to be stampeded into negotiating a bilateral free trade arrangement by statements that "the window into the United States is only a small one, and it is closing soon."[16]

Nor should we be panicked by statements uttered by some highly placed Canadians that non-tariff measures (NTMs) such as quotas or voluntary restraint measures have been rising so rapidly as to offset the gains that have occurred via the Tokyo Round tariff reductions.[17] The facts do not support this. The rise in the real volume of world trade by 9 per cent in 1984 is one such fact. The work by Morici and Megna on the United States shows that tariffs are being lowered in the United States as a consequence of the Tokyo Round. At the same time their estimates also suggest that by 1985 the tariff equivalent of NTMs will be less than in 1976. This is as we should expect, because a number of agreements were negotiated that relate to the reduction in or control of NTMs. The Customs Valuation Agreement established a standardized system for the valuation of commodities for customs purposes and required the discontinuance of artificial valuation practices such as the American Selling Price, Wine Gallon Assessment, and Final List methods. The Procurement Code, although it still excludes some commodities important to Canada such as telecommunications, surface transportation, and heavy electrical generation and transmission equipment, nevertheless does reduce the effects of United States federal buy domestic measures by about two-thirds.[18] Product Standards were also brought under the GATT by the Agreement on Technical Barriers. The GATT system for refereeing disagreements was made more explicit and enhanced for operational purposes during the Tokyo Round as well. The acceptance by the United States of the need to show injury when instituting countervailing duties was also a step forward, as was the United States agreement not to attach new buy domestic clauses to federal assistance to state and municipal governments for purchasing civil aircraft and components. These types of measures have all shown progress in reducing NTMs and complement the various articles in the GATT that restrict or limit NTMs.

A good argument can thus be made that GATT still plays a vital role in limiting the rise of new trade restrictions. The developed nations, including the United States, are all very much aware of the international chaos that would result within and among developed and developing countries if they start to ignore the GATT in a wholesale fashion.

Although the Bonn Summit of 1985 did not produce an agreement for a new GATT round to start at a specific date in 1986, as many had hoped it would, it is not valid to suggest that the GATT is going to collapse and that Canada had better "leap fast through a small window" into supposedly outstretched American arms. In spite of the much-publicized international hindrances to trade, it is still true that trade is freer today than probably at any time since early in this century, if not before. The decline in transportation costs over this period also means that natural barriers to trade are far less today as well.

The GATT system also provides a means of neutralizing discrepancies in power between individual parties to a dispute, such as the discrepancies discussed here between Canada and the United States. This is evident in the adjudication of dispute mechanism which was clarified and strengthened in the Tokyo Round. There are five possible phases, if a bilateral dispute is not settled in one of the earlier stages:

1. deliberation between the two parties
2. review by the GATT Council
3. review of the issue by an appointed working party or panel
4. examination and weighing of the panel report by the GATT Council
5. discriminatory retaliation against the defendant as approved by the Council.

During the Tokyo Round, Canada and the United States agreed that if one member wished to go to a panel, the other would support this desire. The total weight of the GATT is behind the panel system.

Thus, as long as Canada remains fully in the GATT there are important restraints on American use of NTMs against Canada. Also, in most instances, other nations will be involved as well in any new measures the United States may adopt. This will strengthen Canada's position. If Canada limits itself to bilateral free trade with the United States, the real discrepancy in power will be evident. It is naive, for the type of reasons indicated earlier, to think that any bilateral free trade agreement will result in both Canada and the United States being willing to give one another a "blanket exemption" to all NTMs, including countervail, possible quantitative restrictions, safeguard provisions, and the like. American hands would not be tied as much as they are now under the GATT.

Canada could easily end up surrendering control over resource pricing, guaranteeing access to a variety of Canadian resources on American terms, losing control of information and communication services, and/or a host of other things in return for increased access of Canadian manufacturing to the American market. More generally, contrary to the popular view that because there is a highly protectionist mood in Congress, Canada should try to negotiate bilateral free trade, one could just as easily, if not more easily, argue that now is just the time for Canada not to be negotiating a bilateral free trade arrangement with the United States. The costs are likely to be too great. Greater dependence upon the United States and political vulnerability could be the result.

We therefore might do better by exercising more patience and working through the GATT system. Included in this could be a greater willingness on Canada's part to invoke our full GATT rights when we are an injured party, as we failed to do when the United States imposed restrictions on uranium imports and the EEC gave fish tariff preferences to Norway, adversely affecting the Canadian fish market in the EEC. We might also find that with the increased use of computerized control in production, manufacturing may increasingly become less dependent upon long production runs in order to be competitive.

Only if there is no particular concern about preserving what is left of our culture and political independence would there be nothing wrong with negotiating for bilateral free trade immediately. It may be the easiest route to follow in the short run, even though it may be costly in the long run. That has often been the Canadian way of doing things.

Notes

1. Bruce W. Wilkinson, "Canada–US Free Trade and Canadian Economic, Cultural and Political Sovereignty." A paper prepared for the conference: Canadian Trade at a Crossroads: Options for New International Agreements, 16-17 April 1985, Ontario Economic Council.

2. W.O. Henderson, *The Zollverein* (Cambridge: The Cambridge University Press, 1939) p. 315.

3. The only difference between a customs union and a free trade area is that in a customs union, over time, the countries develop a common external tariff. In a free trade area this does not necessarily occur completely, although it will on a range of products.

4. Merze Tate, *Hawaii: Reciprocity or Annexation* (East Lansing: Michigan State University Press, 1968) p. 76.

5. See *Ibid.*

6. *Ibid.*, p. 49.

7. "U.S. Willing to Trade Ideas," *The Globe and Mail*, 6 May 1985, p. 3.

8. John Meisel, "Escaping Extinction: Cultural Defence of an Undefended Border," in this volume.

9. "Canada Urged to Change TV Ways," *The Globe and Mail*, 6 May 1985.

10. This agreement was concluded in February, 1985, after about two years of negotiation. This limitation on support for infant industries is an example of the United States imposing its will on Israeli legislative processes so as to preclude Israeli government subsidies leading to possible new competition to American industry.

11. *Cargill Bulletin*, November, 1984, pp. 1 and 12.

12. This position is reflected in the May, 1985, U.S. Federal Energy Regulatory Commission proposal that cheap Canadian gas be merged with higher priced American gas. "Old," cheap

U.S. gas would be handled separately. The effect would be to stimulate consumption of less expensive U.S. gas at the expense of Canadian supplies. See "U.S. Gas Proposals worry NEB, Industry," *The Globe and Mail*, 16 July 1985.

13. "Canadian Lumber Facing U.S. Seige," *The Globe and Mail*, 13 June 1985. Note also that the bill which Gibbons is sponsoring would define any stumpage fees charged lumber harvesters by governments that were below those charged in the United States, as subsidies subject to countervail by the United States.

14. "U.S. Says Trade Pact to Set Good Example," *The Globe and Mail*, 13 March 1985.

15. Professor Richard Harris made this prediction at the Ontario Economic Council Conference, "Canadian Trade at a Crossroads: Options for New International Agreements," 16-17 April 1985.

16. A statement to this effect was made by a member of the United States State Department at the conference mentioned in n. 15.

17. For example see, "Notes for a Speech by The Honourable James Kelleher," Minister for International Trade, to the World Trade Centre, Montreal, 1 April 1985, p. 1; and "Notes for an Address by The Honourable James Kelleher," Minister for International Trade, to the World Trade Conference, Chicago, 18 April 1985, p. 4.

18. As this sentence suggests, the Procurement Code provides for reductions in discrimination against imports by government purchasers.

A Business Perspective on the Canada–United States Relationship

Harold E. Wyatt

The relationship that we in Canada enjoy with the United States is far too precious to be left to chance. Perhaps a person from the business sector can ask the questions that no one else is asking. Let us start with some of the major irritants that exist between our two countries and propose some of the solutions we must reach for co-operatively.

It is no secret that relationships between Canada and the United States have "blown hot and cold." We have had good times and bad. When things have been favourable to Canada, the United States has complained, and of course the reverse is also true. It depends whose ox is being gored. For a number of years the classic example was the Canada/United States Auto Pact. Yet the beneficiary of this arrangement was often decided by the size of car in vogue at that moment, which in turn has been decided since the early 1970s on the whims of the Organization of Petroleum Exporting Countries.

In Canada we need to take a longer-term view in a dispassionate manner. We need objective input into our assessments of American policy and American politicians. We need more people asking questions, and we need many more providing answers. And we, as business people, need the research data that can come from long-term studies of international business cycles and fluctuating political relationships. Such research data are among the services made available by the Center of Canadian Studies at Johns Hopkins University in Baltimore. There is a need for a similar research centre in Canada now and in the foreseeable future. But to allow such a relationship to hinge on the vagaries of shifting political views, changing trade climates, or on poor information, misinformation, or no information, could quickly undermine this special relationship. Both nations would lose if we allowed more divisive postures to develop and become entrenched.

These thoughts are based on experience in business, and on interaction with representatives of business in the United States, through the Committee on Canada–United States Relations of the Chamber of Commerce, the board of the American Management Association, and the boards of Canadian subsidiaries of United States companies.

This article may provide some answers on our transborder relationships, but it should also raise some questions. After a relationship that has lasted more than two centuries, both countries should be taking a hard look, not only at what we do well together, but also at the irritants and the source of these irritants.

Someone once described our relationship this way: "When the United States sneezes, Canada catches a cold." While there is an element of truth to that statement, perhaps we can think of our relationship in more picturesque and pragmatic terms. Although the United States is ten times the size of Canada in most things except land mass, in terms of influence our relationship is more like an association between an elephant and a flea. If one can picture the North American continent as a giant waterbed, when the elephant rolls over, the flea has a rather difficult time reorienting. And as one can imagine, the ripple effect from even the slightest change in position is going to be more significant and threatening to the flea than it ever would be to the elephant. In fact, many of the stability-threatening ripples rolling into Canada in the past have not been considered particularly significant by the Americans, simply because of the pachyderm standards of their country. This difference in *scale* is one of the reasons why we still have our disagreements. It is hard for us to achieve prominence or equality when we are forever in their shadow. Some people call it being overlooked or ignored. Others, more kindly, call it benign neglect.

It has been said the United States does not consider Canada an equal partner. There is no doubt that we are unequal partners. But the fact that we *are* partners, whether by choice or chance, is of positive consequence for us. We must work at this partnership. As an exporting nation which depends on sales outside the country for survival, we are sitting on the doorstep of the richest consumer society the world has ever known. They speak one of Canada's official languages and they even look, and in many ways act like us. The monetary system is similar in denomination—if not in value. We watch the same kind of violence on television, eat the same kind of polyunsaturated, sugar-free, vitamin-added food, and shop at the same kind of chain stores for the same type of merchandise. So our similarities should be a starting point for discussion, right? Wrong!

The starting point for any research or any discussion about our transborder relationship must start with the premise that *we are not the same.* While we share many things in common, including much of our European ancestry, it is important for the United States to know that Canadians are most concerned about maintaining a separate identity. We want to be known as Canadians and not North Americans. Perhaps this is part of the problem, because we have not really defined what a Canadian is to ourselves, let alone others. And yet we become upset if people refer to us as Americans. It is an easy mistake to make if one does not happen to be from Canada or the United States.

Initially the best place to start differentiating between Canada and the United States is to look at some of the things we have in common, the ties that bind. We share a common heritage, the same continent, and the same basic language. We share, very unequally, in defence. We also share a border that is 5 500 miles on one side, and 8 891 kilometres on the other (known as the longest undefended border in the world). We also share trade to the extent of $120 billion. And in 1985, with trade growing at the rate of 30 per cent on both sides, this total jumped well above that level. From Canada's point of view almost 80 per cent of our total trade is with the United States. Roughly one-third to one-half of the goods consumed in Canada originate there. The United States exports more goods to Canada than it does to Japan, or about one-fifth its total exports. In fact, the United States does more trade with Ontario than it does with Japan! At the other end of the country, the United States does more trade with British Columbia than it does with China. Perhaps I can add perspective this way: American trade with Canada is twice as large as its trade with Japan, three times as large as its trade with Mexico, and almost as large as its trade with all ten countries of the European Economic Community combined. In practice, United States/Canada trade is the largest bilateral economic relationship in the world. We are each other's best customer, and each other's prime investor.

What we need to work at is being each other's best friend. The United States now has about $50 billion of direct investment in Canada, around 20 per cent of all American foreign investment, and Canada has $15 billion in the United States, representing 50 per cent of Canadian foreign investment. While these enormous numbers should provide an underlying foundation for building better relations, this has not always been the case. The fact that Canadians work so hard to emphasize their differences creates tensions. We can become sensitive to minor issues that can quickly be blown out of proportion. We do not always temper our emotion with reality. Sometimes we lose sight of the fact that one in every five dollars earned in Canada comes from trade with the United States. We also forget that in our manufacturing sector one job in every three depends on that trade. This means that while we want to be independent, outspoken, and admired, we dearly want to remain on the waterbed.

The opposite end of that equation for many Canadians suggests that without a strong voice, without that separate identity, we can be taken for granted and lumped together as North Americans. The operative word here is *compromise*. Compromise can lead to *balance*. We have to arrange and distinguish between our wants and needs. We have to separate what we want from what we need! Maybe the appropriate time has arrived, and the next few years will prove interesting. We have witnessed the passing of one era with the resignation of Prime Minister Trudeau, and the beginning of a new one with the election in 1984 of the Progressive Conservatives led by Brian Mulroney. They hold a massive parliamentary majority.[1] President Reagan will be in the White House until 1989. All of this means that we are in a period of reassessment and reflection. The new shape of the relationship has not yet been established, and there could not be a better time to decide an appropriate course for the future.

From the perspective of the business community, relations between our two countries over the last two decades have been a veritable roller-coaster ride. Volatile relations, whatever else they might achieve, are just plain bad business. They breed a climate of uncertainty and mistrust which frightens off investors and turns clients away. As Canadians, we may have a variety of national policies we want to pursue. This is our prerogative. But despite the worthiness of those policies, the balance, distinguishing between wants and needs, means that we must be mindful that our existence is interwoven into the fabric of the American economy. Everything we do which affects that economic relationship will inevitably have an impact on our ability to produce wealth and on the quality of our lives. We must recognize that our needs, our "must haves" are a priority for the Canadian future.

It still amazes me how little Canadians are aware of the importance of the United States to our prosperity. It is equally amazing how much less aware Americans are of the role Canada plays in their economy, which means we should seize every opportunity we can to remind them of it. Canadians cannot afford to take the special relationship for granted as we grope towards a national identity and try to exercise Canadian sovereignty. It is equally obvious that we cannot conduct our life only by what we think the Americans may want us to do. The voyage of the *Polar Sea* through the Northwest Passage perhaps highlights the Canadian dilemma on the Arctic shores.[2]

But every policy has its costs, and we should at all times be aware of the cost and be clear about whether we are willing to make such policy payments. The one thing we cannot do is to embark on a policy one day and then retreat the next, because we cannot afford to be unpredictable. We have done so at times with tax concessions, with the Foreign Investment Review Agency (FIRA), and with the National Energy Program.[3] Not only is this bad politics, but it demoralizes the whole country, and creates the kind of instability which poisons friendships. It also creates a lingering climate of uncertainty which eventually exacerbates our economic problems. Fortunately the present government has sought to allay American misgivings by announcing that Canada is once again "open for business," although we have yet to see what this means in practice in the areas of investment and ownership.

Over the last two decades the biggest sin of Canadians has been indecision. We have not been able to make up our minds about our relationship with the United States. Canadians are constantly equivocating and engaging in self-analysis:

- Are the Americans friends to be trusted, or competitors to be feared?
- Have Canadians matured enough as a nation to feel confident in our identity or are we still insecure and afraid of assimilation?
- Are Canadians just as productive, aggressive, and enterprising as the Americans, so that we can meet them face-to-face?

• Are Canadians so small, frail, and dependent that we can only survive by shutting ourselves off from the United States?

And perhaps the ultimate question–is there, or should there be, a special relationship between Canada and the United States, or should the two countries treat each other exactly as they would any other country?

Despite uncertainty at any given moment, Canadians have behaved as if there were clear answers, deciding on policies and pursuing them regardless of the consequences, only to appear bewildered when the cost became too steep, or we came upon an unpredicted set of responses. At the end of a decade of FIRA and five years of the National Energy Program, we are no closer, today, to answering the basic questions about our national existence. But we have experienced the cost to our economy, and to each of us individually, in terms of our standard of living. Such nationalistic policies do not justify the long-term costs.

There were also errors made on the American side. One need not search far to find examples of unilateral American policies, suddenly adopted, which only augmented Canada's feeling of insecurity. For example, in August 1971, President Nixon suddenly announced that the United States was going off the gold standard, and temporary surcharges of 10 per cent would be imposed on all goods coming into the United States. In fact the United States may have had good economic reasons for doing this, but, given our large exports to the United States, the shock of this unanticipated announcement on Canada was profound.

At about the same time, the United States introduced its DISC program, the Domestic International Sales Corporation. This system of tax deferrals gave American companies operating in Canada considerable advantages over their Canadian competitors. Despite our protests, and those of just about every other trading partner of the United States, the DISC program continued. It was only after a decade, and after a GATT tribunal found that it contravened the provisions of the General Agreement on Tariffs and Trade, that the DISC program was discontinued. It was a major irritant to many of America's trading partners, but for Canada, with so many United States companies operating within its economy, it was a major attack on the ability of Canadian companies to compete.

There are many other American irritants which encourage a more strident tone to our Canadian nationalism. One need only mention acid rain and its threat to personal health and to our natural resources. It is a problem which Canada cannot overcome by itself, and yet the United States seems unwilling to address the problem with the same seriousness and urgency that we feel it deserves.

Perhaps more technical, but certainly no less galling, has been the extraterritorial application of United States law. The problem has been compounded by the attempts of the United States to enforce American policy through the subsidiaries of American companies operating abroad. From the establishment of the coordinating commission on exports to the Soviet Bloc—at the height of the Cold War—Canadians have argued about the kinds of goods which should, or should not, be exported to the communist world. A recent example was the dispute over sanctions against the Soviet natural gas pipeline. In that case, foreign firms were denied access to data bases stored in the United States, and companies contracting for deliveries from American firms found those contracts abrogated. We have also argued about the kinds of goods which we feel can be exported to non-communist countries. An earlier example occurred when Canadians were prevented from selling Canadian-built trucks to Arab countries at a time when Canada had no problems dealing with the Arabs. Because Canadian companies are so closely tied to American ones, and because so many enterprises operating in Canada are subsidiaries of American parents, this kind of policy is especially unsettling for Canadians.

More recently we have seen the case where the Bank of Nova Scotia, which has branches in both Florida and the Cayman Islands, was a captive of American law. A Florida court, investigating charges against persons suspected of drug smuggling, ordered the Florida branch of the Bank of Nova Scotia to produce records from its branch in the Cayman Islands. Since the law of the Cayman Islands is very strict on bank secrecy, the Bank of Nova Scotia was placed in an impossible position—either break Cayman Islands law, or disobey the subpoena of the Florida court. In the end, the bank was given permission by the Cayman Islands government to produce the records in Florida, but this was not until the bank had been fined $1.8 million. Was this fair? Was it reasonable? Would it have been tolerated by the United States, if the situation was reversed? Few Canadians wish to aid and abet criminal activity, but neither do they wish to relinquish their sovereignty to the jurisdiction of American courts. But, as might be expected, in his own territory the elephant does pretty well what he pleases.

I have spent some time on the irritants, because it is important to realize that not every problem in the Canadian-American relationship originates in Canada. When it comes from ill-considered actions in the United States or knee-jerk reactions, it only reinforces the Canadian sense of insecurity, and we respond by adopting policies that may not be in our own best interests.

We saw this happen throughout the 1970s, and it took a major effort to restore a modicum of stability. In 1984, the United States was urged to impose countervailing duties on steel imports from Canada. Canada was not dumping steel and was not the cause—or even part—of the problem. The discussions became inflammatory until it was pointed out that imposition of duties would affect companies like Stelco. What was so special about Stelco? It exported to a United States plant the only available steel wire which could be used in the manufacture of tires. If the supply of steel wire was halted, many of the jobs in the tire plant would be lost. It was also pointed out by lobbyists for the steel industry that the coal used in the Canadian furnaces came from the United States. Any added duties on Canadian steel could affect a considerable number of mining jobs in a depressed sector of the American economy. Once this scenario was outlined the rhetoric became less heated.

Another example is the softwood lumber industry in Canada, which for years has exported to the American market. When sales in the United States declined drastically, lumber people from the north-western states quickly looked for a way to stanch the flow of red ink by lobbying for action against Canadian imports. They claim that the stumpage fees provide an unfair advantage. If they are successful, the result will be higher costs with subsequent fewer starts in housing and commercial construction in the United States. This would be followed by a corresponding decline in employment opportunities there, and a parallel decline in employment in the Canadian lumber industry. But, rather than outline each example in detail, let us quickly run through the list of problems Canadians have faced over the years.

Protectionism

Canadians, amongst others, have perceived the United States to be moving in a distinctly protectionist direction, with numerous petitions to the Department of Industry, Trade and Commerce for relief against imports, and to Congress for a variety of protectionist measures. Among the particularly difficult issues are non-tariff barriers, which are hard to identify, let alone turn back. These include tax measures, credit subsidies, direct subsidies, health and safety legislation, procurement practices, "buy domestic" legislation, and local content rules.

One disturbing recent trend has been the tendency of the United States Congress, reacting to special interests, to link non-related issues. For example, in retaliation for Canadian tax measures relating to transborder advertising, designed to keep Canadian advertisers using Canadian stations, Senator Patrick Moynihan has threatened legislation which would affect Canada's Telidon operations in the United States, a matter worth about forty times as much in trade to Canada.[4] When the ripples grow forty-fold, the surface of the waterbed starts to resemble a storm in the North Atlantic.

While the United States views these actions as protection, Canadians see them as domination. Understandably we feel resentful that we have to protect our heritage and history. It is sad, but true, that Canadian children know more about Wyatt Earp than they ever will about Jerry Potts. Yet both were cowboys, both were pioneers in the West. "Wild Bill" Hickok is a household name in Canada because of films, radio, and television. Colonel MacLeod is the name of a school in Calgary, and the name of a major thoroughfare. The doughty colonel restored peace and brought order to western Canada with his troop of North West Mounted Police one hundred years ago. One became a legend, the other became almost invisible. Along the same lines, most Canadian youths have heard the story of the Alamo, time and again. But ask American children, or even Canadian children for that matter, where Duck Lake is, or Batoche, and they look at you quizzically. Yet Louis Riel is a Canadian folk hero. His uprising at Batoche was a major event in Canadian history but, sadly, very few know the story even in Canada. And until recently, most Canadian people could name more United States presidents than they could Canadian prime ministers, and not just because we had Pierre Trudeau and Mackenzie King for so long. This occurs because of the dominance of the American communications media—radio, television, newspapers, magazines and books. It is simply crowding out Canadian content.

Extraterritoriality

I gave examples of extraterritoriality earlier. The United States still reserves the right to act unilaterally to prevent subsidiaries in foreign countries from exporting to the Soviet Bloc and to parts of the Arab world as well. Indeed, the United States uses those subsidiaries to force other countries to follow American foreign policy. This costs Canadian jobs and causes trade deficits and a weakened Canadian dollar. The United States also reserves the right to subpoena documents from foreign countries through American courts, as if those courts had jurisdiction over foreign governments.

Taxation

Several of the states in the United States use the unitary method of taxation, by which a tax bill in an American state is assessed not on the basis of a company's operations in that state, but on its global operations, deeming the in-state operations to be only a percentage. This can be applied regardless of whether the company makes any profit in that state or not. This amounts to taxation without representation.

Canadian Cultural Policy

Along with the border broadcasting issue, regulations of the Canadian Radio-Television and Telecommunications Commission, and postal rates for foreign magazines, there are numerous issues which the Canadian government has decreed to be domestic cultural policy. These were designed to protect broadcasters and publishers in this country from their huge southern competitors. As a result *Time* magazine and *Reader's Digest* no longer have Canadian editions although the former is contemplating another attempt. The Americans have viewed these actions as economic protectionism. Needless to say, nearly all Canadians viewed the United States reaction with alarm, because of the threat of retaliation.

Investment Policy

People such as former United States Ambassador to Canada, Paul Robinson, voiced bitter opposition to FIRA. Now the title has been changed, along with its mandate, to Investment Canada. Its new mandate is to encourage greater foreign investment. But who were the major beneficiaries when Petro-Canada paid $343 million to take over the shares of Atlantic Richfield, or $1.5 billion to buy out Pacific Petroleum, 46 per cent owned by Phillips Petroleum? American shareholders were the clear beneficiaries. To be fair, Petro-Canada spread our wealth around the world. It paid $1.4 billion to the 51 per cent shareholders of Petro Fina in Belgium and $577 million for the refining and marketing arm of British Petroleum. Its last acquisition, worth some $886 million, was the purchase of Gulf's downstream operations from Canada's Olympia and York who had purchased all of Gulf Canada's assets from Chevron of California.

While we are often on the receiving end when people start pointing fingers, we should remember that the United States has very serious barriers to foreign investment, such as the Securities and Exchange Commission, and stringent anti-trust laws. In fact some states, such as Oklahoma, do not allow any foreigners to own land at all. This has created misery for Canadian developers. What has been overlooked in the verbal battles is that the Canadian economy has the highest degree of foreign ownership of any OECD country, and that changed only slightly because of FIRA. Compounding that, we find that foreign subsidiaries in Canada tend to import more and export less, and yet our survival hinges on exports.

Acid Rain

This issue will continue to be a problem as long as the United States is content only to study it and not to act. Our health and theirs, and the resources of both countries, are at stake. It is up to us to lobby our case until the Americans recognize that it is in their own national interest to take this problem seriously. The prime minister has appointed former Ontario premier, Bill Davis, as an "acid rain envoy" to the United States, his counterpart being Drew Lewis, former Secretary of Transportation. Davis is on record as wanting to tackle the problems immediately, without waiting, as the Reagan administration prefers, for more research data.

Energy Issues

A decade ago, when the oil crisis was at its peak, each country became very protective over its energy resources. It now turns out that Canada has more energy than we thought, and a good argument could be made to coordinate energy exploitation so we could be receiving more of the economic benefits. Canada is moving towards considerable deregulation of oil and gas prices, and we may want to consider a free market in energy for North America.

Free Trade

This is probably the most controversial issue of all. It is probable that some kind of trade liberalization is coming. The question is how this will be achieved. The United States wants to liberalize trade bilaterally as an example to other countries to roll back international protectionism. This may be Canada's strong card, since the United States has to demonstrate to others that the agreement has worked to Canada's advantage. The trade liberalization currently being discussed covers two areas: sectoral, which has many difficulties; and free trade with opt-out, which has almost as many. The Mulroney government has made this a priority, which is good. There is one danger, however. The United States has, by various American accounts, been falling behind in terms of world competitiveness. It will not help Canadians to become competitive in a market which is itself non-competitive, since we will still have to face the Japanese, the Koreans, the Taiwanese, and the people from Hong Kong and Singapore.

Transborder Data Flows

This issue holds special significance for Canada, because the regulations in Canada are considerably different from those in the United States. Canadian regulations restrict many aspects of data flow in ways that do not occur down south. In the United States, it is possible to procure various types of data easily, mixing all kinds of retail and commercial components together. In the process, large companies have developed that are like department stores of data. Canadian companies, which are more restricted, would find it difficult to compete and would lose business to the United States. The more Canadian information that is transmitted there, the more it is pro-cessed, and then sold back to us in forms like mailing lists. It is not the free flow of data itself that is objectionable, but the one-way flow of data, or a one-way flow of jobs or money. Indeed, so important are the issues of transborder data flows, and world trade in other services, that the United States has made access to foreign markets a prerequisite for entering into the next round of GATT negotiations scheduled for 1986/87.

Another similar example is that telephone calls from point-to-point in Canada are often routed through the United States, because it is cheaper. We are back to the question of scale and deregulation in such matters. It is not so much an issue of data flow as it is an issue of service. We must ask: who will supply the equipment? Who will run the systems? Who will control the systems? Who will gain from the systems? These are the signif-icant questions for Canada, because our hope for the future is to be able to adapt technology. We cannot do that if we do not have access to hardware and software.

Conclusions

It is obvious in today's highly competitive international environment that we can no longer afford to waste our time and resources on petty disputes. This does not mean selling out to the United States, but managing our friendship better. There are a few basic things we can do that would go a long way towards improving the climate between the two countries. In the first place, we need a significant change of attitude on the American side. Americans must realize once and for all that Canada is not just a paler version of their country. At every opportunity we must let Americans know in a friendly but firm way that this country really is different. It is different in history, culture, and geography. And although we share a basic language, we are different in total language, since too many times we forget that one-third of Canada's population speaks French as their mother tongue, and Spanish is quickly becoming a second language in the United States, despite attempts to make English the official language.

The second item is a change of attitude on the Canadian side. We need to have more faith in ourselves as a nation. We need more confidence in our culture and identity, and to be more certain about how we want to work with our southern neighbour. I do not want to speak about patriotism, because that is something which cannot be bought or sold and it certainly cannot be legislated. We all have to decide how we feel about the country in which we live and how much we are prepared to sacrifice for it. Canada needs more patriotism and pride.

We need to concentrate on organizing our economic life better so that we can compete with anyone in the world. If we can do that, then perhaps the flea will gain respect, if not stature, and we can meet the United States with more confidence and on more equal terms. In Canada, we need to think more about developing world-class companies, big enough to compete effectively, and substantial enough to fund the complex kind of research and development which is needed in today's world. We need better economic coordination. That means more consultation and improved consultation between business, government, and labour. We need to work out appropriate strategic goals for ourselves and to waste less time arguing. This does not call for love or respect but enlightened self-interest. We also have to realize that we cannot be out of step with the rest of the world when it comes to salaries and wages.

At present, both we and the United States are paying salaries to our labour forces ranging anywhere from four to ten times as much as some of our Asian competitors. We cannot maintain this discrepancy. Even more ominous for Canada is the difference in salary scales between Canada and the United States for basically the same kinds of work. If we want to be independent, yet remain interdependent, we must examine all aspects of Canadian business, labour, and management. We must seek ways that will allow us to offer quality products and services at a competitive price. To do this, we need to involve every single Canadian in making Canada competitive and successful again. We have to demonstrate to people that they do have a stake and a share in the success of this country and that the quality of their lives depends on the quality of their efforts.

There are thus two major changes needed to improve Canadian-American relations: a change in the attitude of Americans to Canada; and a change in the attitude of Canadians towards themselves. But there are also a number of practical things we can do to foster a better climate of cooperation and consultation. Perhaps the most important is to anticipate problems long before they become serious barriers to consultation. This is where university research centres can play a valuable role. We need people who have the time and the objectivity to look at the broader picture. We need people who can analyze, assess, and advise. We need people who can project, prognosticate and predict. In other words we need people who can look at the previous dilemmas, help us design solutions, and tell us the best method to achieve our goals. Thorough research and quiet diplomacy allow both sides to consult well in advance of any conflict and, if necessary, they allow us to do it in an effective way. We may need less inflammatory public rhetoric and more of the hard diplomatic donkey work which goes on behind the scenes. Although few seem to appreciate such work, it is how most difficult problems are actually solved.

Furthermore, because of the complexity of the relationship between Canada and the United States, we can assume that there will always be something to discuss, and that there will inevitably be differences of opinion. We are going to have to learn how to lobby in Washington. If we cannot influence the House of Representatives and the Senate, then irrational and costly legislation could be passed, such as we have seen recently dealing with softwood lumber, surface transportation, fisheries, the Garrison Dam, copper imports, American- or state-buying preference, trucking deregulation, and many other matters. So let us prepare ourselves for continuous negotiation and the exertion of new and imaginative efforts at all levels of the American policy process. Let us broaden the range of institutions which carry on these negotiations by creating bodies such as the International Joint Commission.

The Department of External Affairs and the prime minister have the ultimate and final authority in dealing with any foreign power. However, there are other channels of communication that can play an effective part. One of these is the Committee on Canada–United States Relations of the Canadian and United States Chambers of Commerce. In that committee, business people and economists from either side of the border have the opportunity to sit down with each other, twice a year, to exchange views, make suggestions, and then take their thoughts back to their respective governments. This is non-governmental diplomacy. It never makes the headlines of a newspaper, but it has worked well for over half a century, and the two governments seem to appreciate the added perspective which it gives them as they talk to each other. Let us have many of these points at which Canadians and Americans can talk to one another. And, if we are going to argue, let us argue for regulations that will ensure that as North Americans we become best friends—as well as best customers. Let both countries develop a promising future, working alongside each other, not looking over or around barriers at each other. We are only "two feet" from success, but we have got to get up and use them. I think that Canadian research on the United States can help Canada and the United States to "use them" to the better advantage of our two nations.

Notes

1. The distribution of seats in the House of Commons in 1980 was: Liberals, 147; Progressive Conservatives, 103; New Democrats, 32. After the 1984 election where 50 per cent of the population voted for the Progressive Conservative party, it was: Progressive Conservatives, 211, Liberals, 40, New Democrats, 30, Independent, 1. Especially surprising was the support accorded Mr. Mulroney in the province of Quebec where Progressive Conservative seats went from 1 to 58, while Liberal support fell from 74 to 17 seats.
2. The issue revolved around the fact that the U.S. government did not request permission from the Canadian government for the voyage because it considers the Northwest Passage

international waters. Canada unilaterally granted permission and was allowed three observers on board. Canada considers the waters to be territorial and thus the voyage could be viewed as a threat to Canadian sovereignty. See Franklyn Griffiths, "Time to Ante Up in the Arctic Game," *The Globe and Mail*, 22 August 1985.

3. The Foreign Investment Review Agency was established in 1973 to act as a gatekeeper to foreign investment in Canada. It was a major irritant to Americans. On 30 June 1985 it was replaced by Investment Canada. The Progressive Conservative Industry Minister, Sinclair Stevens, stated that the Investment Canada Act " . . . reflects Canadians new spirit of enterprise" which would promote Canada as a safe and profitable place to invest.

The National Energy Program was announced in October, 1980, by the Liberal Minister of Finance, Allen MacEachen. It was an attempt to Canadianize oil and gas resources which were then 77.7 per cent controlled by foreigners with 72 per cent ownership. Prime Minister Mulroney's government has been dismantling this program. Canadian ownership is about 48 per cent since Olympia and York and then Petro-Canada purchased Gulf Canada in mid–1985, from Chevron of California.

4. The law (Bill C-58) made advertisements on United States border television a non-tax-deductible corporate expense for Canadian advertisers. Under the Trade Act, section 301, Reagan recommended mirror legislation to Congress. See S. Clarkson, *Canada and the Reagan Challenge* rev. ed., (Toronto: James Lorimer and Company, 1985) pp. 120-124, 140-141.

PART III

American Society and Culture

Because the overriding theme of this section is potentially all-encompassing, it should come as no surprise that the authors included here deal with a diversity of topics. Nor should it come as a surprise that Canadians, often sensitive to the overwhelming cultural influence of the United States, should reflect upon the repercussions this has in their daily lives. The Americanization of a society presumes the absorption of cultural values often foreign to the host country. Yet there is hardly a society in the world that has not been touched by the consumer goods and the media services provided by the United States. The messages beamed across the world draw us into the American Dream. If this may be called cultural imperialism, it is a form of influence usually gained not through force but most often through persuasion. Canadians are not alone in their wariness of, nor their determination to embrace, the values of American democracy and the benefits of the market-place economy.

Chapter 8 effectively serves as an introduction to this section, because Denis Smith forthrightly declares that the "political separation of the two countries will be maintained." Given this however, he is concerned about the relative lack of Canadian scholarship related to the United States. He queries why we have produced so few commentators on the American way of life. "Are we inside or outside observers of the United States?" he asks. Even so, there is "the potential richness of Canadian study of the United States, if we encourage it from our various regional points of view." Smith discusses three reasons why he feels Canadians are reluctant to engage in such an endeavour, but concludes that "we have a unique perspective and we should exploit it."

In Chapter 9, Stuart Smith, professing a "modest attitude toward nationalism," contends that "the differences between our societies are very small and subtle." Paying particular attention to the role of technology, he begins by discussing two risks (or threats) to the continued independence of Canada: the integration of our economies; and the desire for a standard of living equivalent to that of the Americans. Canada risks political union precisely because it is a resource based economy. One solution which avoids such a possibility is the recognition of the importance of the newest high-technology industries. To move along with the United States, which Smith believes is reasserting its leadership in the high-technology enterprise, requires governmental support in Canada if it hopes to remain internationally competitive as a trading nation. In the end he demands that government make some tough choices. Does the government continue to support mainly resource industries, or does it recognize the problems and attempt to create a new future? "What is needed is a diversification strategy emphasizing advanced technology." This is Smith's seemingly simple answer, but one which clearly needs the force of a political agenda from federal and provincial governments.

Peter Buitenhuis, in Chapter 10, addresses the question of Canadian studies of the United States from the point of view of a literary scholar. "The most compelling reasons for the lack of growth ... are Canadian nationalism and the pervasive sense that we are so close." Having asserted that "a recurrent fantasy of Canadians, especially some of our writers, is to erect an enormous wall along the United States–Canadian border," Buitenhuis skilfully makes a study of the "literary relationships between English Canada and the United States" from "loyalist times to the present." Emphasis is placed "on the tortured decade of the 1960s." But his main contention, as reflected in the title of his essay, is the fact that Canadians writing about the United States, "are entering not so much another country, but their own minds"—namely the funhouse. "Canadian writers have been *better* off when they have entered that funhouse and, after having been lost, found themselves." We are given a formal invitation to "listen to the best contemporary American writers with the same intensity as we now, as scholars and students, listen to the classic American writers for what they can tell us about what is really going on in that country's psyche."

As an interesting contrast, or perhaps an example of the "wall" which surrounds Canada, John Meisel gives us, in Chapter 11, an overview born of experience of the problems associated with living across an "undefended border." His concern is with the cultural integrity of Canada, especially as it is manifested in the communications networks which help tie the country together. In placing less emphasis on economic issues, he concedes to taking a "sectoral approach." He argues that because of the dominance of the American media, "our cultural development may be stunted .... There is ... a well grounded fear that ... our perceptions, values, ideas, and priorities will become so dominated by those of our neighbours that the distinctiveness of Canada will . . . vanish." He links this cultural dilemma to the field of communications and the dependency of Canadians on chauvinistic American culture, especially with regard to television. Meisel then shows us the domestic, transnational, and international implications of such dependency, within the context of Canada's broadcast policy as defined by the regulatory agency, the Canadian Radio-Television and Telecommunications Commission (CRTC). The historical and analytical discussion arising out of the preceding issues gives us a fascinating insight as to how it is possible for Canadians to "escape from extinction."

Moving to Chapter 12 we are forced to come face to face with the view of William Johnson, which contradicts the theses of such authors as Meisel and Wyatt more than any other piece in this book. Johnson asserts that "Canada, in reality, in substance, does not exist. What exists, in reality, is Canadians. 'Canada' is a legal fiction." He thus takes strong issue with Wyatt who claims that Canadians and Americans are not the same, and with Meisel who contends that there is a Canadian culture which is distinctive enough to warrant preservation. To Johnson, "Canadian culture is real and strong, but it exists only marginally by its distinctiveness." And to explode the notion that Canadians are different culturally because of the presence of a large French minority Johnson (who has had considerable working experience in Quebec) states that "some 99 per cent of Québécois culture is shared; it is not unique." He throws a challenge to cultural nationalists. "The burden of proof must lie on those who would promote exclusiveness, barriers, tariffs, immobilities, and rigidities" between the United States and Canada. John Meisel's "rejoinder" which follows as Chapter 13 takes issue with Johnson's views.

tario into New England and the Midwest. Some Edmontonians took escapist weekends in Great Falls, Montana. The forty-ninth parallel hardly existed in our imaginations and, after 1941, it seemed to disappear altogether when the B-17s and Tomahawk fighters arrived in Edmonton—and then thousands of U.S. troops for the duration of the war. For a teenager all that seemed entirely natural and unproblematic. Toronto and Ottawa were distant and alien, just as Washington and New York were for our Montana neighbours. That degree of intermixing of the two societies, both of them new and resource-based societies in the West, has had a profound and continuing influence on political and social assumptions in the prairies; and those assumptions, in turn, have complicated the political life of Canada, as it has become more nationally self-conscious and mature in the last three decades.

These personal reflections lead to an initial conclusion about Canadian perspectives on the United States: while the American presence has been near to us all, there are obviously important regional distinctions among our perspectives on the United States, the result of contrasting regional experiences of the American nation. The view from the Maritimes, Quebec, and Ontario is as idiosyncratic as the view from Alberta, and each area can offer its own distinct insights. What that suggests to me is the potential richness of *Canadian* study of the United States, if we encourage it from our various regional points of view. The more common choice of Canadian regional scholars until now has been to examine Canadian subjects with American regional influences in mind, rather than American subjects from a Canadian regional perspective. It may be true that the historical influences have mostly flowed one way with, for example, the arrival of the Loyalists in Upper Canada and the Maritimes, or the spillover of the progressive movement in the west, but the application of our Canadian perspectives to American subjects, where we have had similar experiences of settlement and industrial and resource development, should certainly offer fresh illumination on many subjects of American enquiry. Some possibilities come immediately to mind. Where are the studies by Quebec scholars of the French-speaking minorities of New England, or on a larger scale, of American policies of cultural assimilation in general? Where are the studies by Canadian authors of American regional politics? On the national level, where are the Canadian contributions to American constitutional studies, or foreign policy studies, or to scholarship on American transportation and resource development? There are some striking exceptions to this Canadian scholarly neglect of big American subjects, in the writings of the economists Jacob Viner and John Kenneth Galbraith, for example; or in Ted Chamberlin's book on native policy in the United States and Canada, *The Harrowing of Eden*;[2] or in Thomas Berger's current commission of enquiry into the Alaskan native land settlement.[3] And there are, of course, the three great Canadian originals with their startling insights into imperial America: Harold Innis, Marshall McLuhan, and George Grant (only one of whom has reached the American audience). But those exceptions are certainly unusual.

There is surely something very curious about the fact that this most dynamic society has drawn observers in their hordes from across the globe to dissect it, but has not attracted the same interest from the closest neighbours. Canada has not had an Alexis de Tocqueville, a James Bryce, a Denis Brogan, or a Marcus Cunliffe; an Alistair Cooke, or Alastair Buchan, or Henry Brandon, or Henry Fairlie, or Louis Heren. Scarcely any of our scholars or journalists have attempted to see the United States as a whole and to deal with the central issues of its history and culture. (There was one journalistic exception in Max Freedman, but he wrote for the *Manchester Guardian* rather than for Canadian enlightenment.) We may say simply that we have been too busy in the young life of Canadian scholarship and journalism to turn to many subjects beyond the life of our own national community, but the explanation of our neglect goes deeper than that.

The failure to analyze the United States can be partially explained on the grounds that, until recently, Canada lacked the educational and cultural apparatus to prepare individuals of talent to undertake such enquiries at home, let alone to do so abroad. Our institutions of higher learning and our educated population have just been too sparse to produce such riches. If that is the chief explanation of the failure, we should soon have evidence that it has been overcome, since we now possess the developed apparatus of higher education to produce some Bryces, Brogans, and Brandons (although we still lack the intensive publishing industries, both scholarly and popular, that complement the universities in Britain and Western Europe). Perhaps it is now only a matter of waiting, complacently and confidently, for our inspired studies of the United States to appear.

But this is unlikely. Scholarly interest and fashion do not develop autonomously from the broader movements of popular interest in the community in which the scholarship is produced, and that may be one key to the reluctance of Canadian academics and journalists to plunge seriously into writing about major American subjects. There are at least three distinct aspects to this Canadian reluctance. Two of them arise from a kind of McLuhanite immersion in American society which makes that society largely invisible to us. We are so close to it, we are so fully a part of it, that we cannot see it whole as independent observers. We cannot leave the fishbowl to look in, as Europeans can, from the perspective of a few thousand kilometres.

But Americans somehow manage to gain a critical perspective on themselves, just as we do increasingly on ourselves. So why do Canadians find it so difficult to achieve that perspective in relation to the United States? A further reason for the lapse may be that we have not found it necessary. Americans reflect on their own society as part of an internal debate that leads to action; Europeans have reflected on the United States for generations, because it was a new giant on the horizon that had turned away from the Old World and threatened its power and self-confidence. While, as Canadians, we feel that we are inside the American nation and can hear the national debate going on around us, we know, too, both that our contributions will not make much difference if we do make them, and that Americans can be counted on to make their own pungent and telling comments from all angles on their own national issues. We are so close that we can take a free ride. Other foreign observers, standing at a greater distance or writing for audiences at a greater distance, cannot take for granted that the domestic American conversation will be heard abroad, so they have to reconstruct and analyze it, just for the sake of elementary understanding.

The third reason for our collective reluctance to enter the great debate about American issues is more tentative—though perhaps more crucial. This is the matter of cultural confidence and its relationship to power. The prominent place occupied by British and European commentators in the debate on America derives not simply from the highly developed state of their journalism, scholarship, and publishing, but from the original position of these countries as leading societies in relation to America. They had already established their political and cultural positions in the world when the United States was a mere upstart, and although their empires have faded, their cultural pretensions, their assumed superiority, their established cultural competence, have not. They go on observing and commenting because they have always assumed, in relation to the United States, that they have a right and a responsibility to do so.

We, on the other hand, come from a more modest background. In relation to the United States we are the upstarts. We existed originally on the imperial fringe, not at the centre, and both empires have departed. (Donald Creighton would say that they abandoned us;[4] Hugh MacLennan has told us that we are the descendants of defeated nations and continue to act that way.)[5] We have been left alone to our own devices in the American shadow, without much experience and without much power. While we may privately have comforted ourselves on the superiority of our manners and our ordered constitution (in contrast to the American condition of constant risk and near-anarchy), we have never assumed our role as legitimate commentators on the American scene, as the Europeans did from the beginning.

By an act of will, by belief in our own competence, and by the application of sufficient resources to the cause, we may at last be overcoming this absence of inherited cultural confidence in relation to the United States. That would be an admirable change if we can bring it about. The change will not be entirely a matter of will, and it can only go so far: Canada is not a great power, is unlikely to be one, and its literary and scholarly self-confidence are not going to be buoyed up by the presence in the background of the Royal Navy or the National Aeronautics and Space Administration (although a powerful Arctic icebreaker would help). But we can do enough things well to give us the assurance that others might benefit by our observations. The study of the United States is one of the most fascinating and important subjects, in all its aspects, that academics and journalists must undertake in the modern world. It is high time that Canadians plunged fully into it. As Canadians we are, and will remain, both inside and outside the United States. We have a unique perspective and we should exploit it.

Notes

1. "Namerica, Namerica," *The Economist*, 6 April 1985.

2. Ted Chamberlin, *The Harrowing of Eden* (New York: Seabury Press, 1975).

3. Thomas R. Berger, *Village Journey: The Report of the Alaska Native Review Commission* (New York: Hill and Wang, 1985).

4. See Donald Creighton, *The Passionate Observer: Selected Writings* (Toronto: McClelland & Stewart, 1980).

5. Hugh MacLennan, "Scotland's Fate, Canada's Lesson," *Maclean's*, October, 1973, pp. 27-29 and 94-98.

The American Challenge and Canadian Interests

Stuart L. Smith

Nationalism is not the highest of human achievements nor is it a virtue. It may well be that the only good thing to be said for Canadian nationalism is that it is not American nationalism. In other words, the most attractive feature of Canadian nationalism is its modesty; its weakness is the best thing about it. Unfortunately, this modest attitude toward nationalism, while it is the main component that makes it worth preserving, is probably the one component that makes it very hard to keep. That is the paradox of Canada.

Yet modern changes in the world economic structure, particularly the role of technology, have led to a situation where the continued existence of Canada beyond a couple of generations is open to serious question. Most Canadians want to be Canadians, and Americans seem happy to let us be so. I do not know any Americans who would want to absorb Canada; the question is whether we will, at some point, insist that they take us. The differences between our societies are very small and subtle. Still, most of us would like to retain a separate identity on this part of North America. We want friendly, family-style relations with the United States; we feel great affection and admiration for our American friends and relatives. We have managed to be close but separate; we are similar but still somewhat distinctive.

It is somewhat of an achievement for us. We are an under-populated nation living next to a very great country, the greatest economic and military power in world history. It is partly because Americans have been so understanding and partly because Canadians have been so resolute, that Canadians have succeeded in creating a separate nation. But let us recognize that we have always paid an economic price for this nation; it has never made economic sense. It would always have made more sense financially to trade north and south and to integrate our economies, ultimately becoming one country. Under such circumstances even fewer people would be trying to make a living in the colder half of the continent.

The Canadian economy has been less productive than that of the Americans, yet our standard of living has only been slightly lower than that of

128

the United States. If the price of independence could be afforded, it could be afforded for one reason only: Canada is a rich storehouse of natural resources. That is the only reason Canadians can afford the luxury of independent nationhood in the northern half of North America. That is the raison d'être of this country, and Canadians have to face the fact. I include in the term "natural resources" the Canadian ingenuity in finding and exploiting those resources and even "creating" new ones (as in agriculture).[1] We collect rents on these resources that have been sufficient to keep our living standards close to the level of the United States. But what happens if the resource rents are no longer sufficient to mask our inefficiency or uncompetitiveness in other fields? In such a circumstance, there are two risks to our continued independence.

The first risk, and there are signs of this already, is a chain of events by which Canadians would try to compensate for the lack of a globally competitive industrial structure by linking their economy even more closely to the very successful economy south of the border. Gradually, Canadians would relinquish control over monetary policy, trade policy and eventually, I suspect, fiscal policies. Soon it would dawn on Canadians that going to the polls to elect a government in Ottawa would be rather a waste of time. We would then insist on an arrangement whereby Canadians had political representation in the United States. Whatever Canadian symbols would remain, in time Canada would become integrated politically.

The second risk would stem from not maintaining a living standard comparable to the American one. This would lead to the loss of our innovative and well-educated people. It would produce a brain drain in the country as the best people left. Eventually, the Canadian government would face pressure from within for access to the ordinary jobs and the other benefits in the stronger economy. Those who come from Newfoundland will understand how that feels. Newfoundlanders wanted access to Canadian jobs and to Canadian benefits. In fact, they gained access, but what happened? Those who stayed in Newfoundland benefited to some extent; thousands who left Newfoundland and moved to Cambridge, Ontario, for instance, benefited even more, getting jobs at good salaries which they were not able to match in Newfoundland. I suspect therefore that if we fall too far behind, Canada will move toward political union. Canadians pay a price for independence but, with the present economic pattern, that price can only be paid so long as we receive the economic rents from our resources and so long as our standard of living does not fall too far behind that of the United States.

If natural resources were to become insufficient to compensate for relative weakness in our more advanced industries, then Canadians would face a challenge. Canada would either have to improve its capacity to compete in modern industry and world markets or it would eventually join the United States.

What is the outlook for resources? Technology and other factors have changed the world's economic situation so that Canadians can no longer depend on natural resources to carry them the way they did in the past. New technology has meant that one can receive more function out of less raw material. First, there is down-sizing, conservation and efficiency. Second, new technology is substituting for traditional resources. We now have advanced industrial materials replacing the usual materials that Canadians produce: fibre optics, composites, and plastics are replacing copper, wood, and metal. Third, there is severe competition from other countries in the world where other resource deposits exist. Some of these are Third World countries that desperately need foreign currency and therefore produce at very low prices. Canada can compete with difficulty but, even then, there is a downward pressure on prices. And finally, there are some supply problems looming in the future. I refer to difficulty in managing our fisheries, soil erosion in agriculture, acid rain affecting the lakes and trees, and poor forest management. All in all, I do not think Canada can live as well in the future as we have in the past, if we rely as much on our natural resources.

The major trend in the world economy is the emergence of the newly industrializing countries (NIC's), breaking what used to be referred to as "the Atlantic monopoly." Technology can now move to lower wage areas, partly because the technology is simpler, but mainly because these low wage areas have the education and management ability to operate the technology very effectively. There is still a discrepancy between the high levels of education and the low level of wages. There is a lag period until the wages catch up, during which time they are powerful competitors indeed, particularly where standardized products are being produced. Even when those wages do catch up, there will be other countries following along the same route. So, Canadians have to recognize that such competition will be around for some while.

The high wage countries will therefore lose the production of standardized products; they will have to compete by offering products and services that are research- and knowledge-dependent. Not all the high wage countries are going to succeed in doing this. Not all will crawl through what I call the "knowledge-intensive escape hatch." If we look at Canada and the United States in this regard, we have good news and bad news in Canada. The good news is that we do not have to shift completely into the new "high value-added" industries as quickly as some other countries. Canadians still have ample resources which will certainly sustain us a while longer. The bad news is that the resource sector is in relative decline. In a sense, that is even worse news because, if it disappeared overnight, we would know that something drastic had happened, and the government could act to change the economy. Instead, because the process is gradual, people still think that they can just drive the old horse a little harder, and it will eventually do what it did in the past. They do not realize that there is a fundamental change occurring in the world economy.

The other bad news revolves around the fact that, as a resource dependent economy, we have developed habits which are exactly the wrong ones for entering the new, higher-technology industries. Canadians have learned to fight over the division of the economic rents rather than to work together to create new opportunities. We have the habit of being neither research-intensive nor export-oriented. Canadians have too many foreign-owned branch plants that have no mandate to export and that rarely develop or design new higher-technology goods. Nor do we know how to finance them. We are used to financing real estate and mines, i.e., tangible assets, but the idea of intellectual property is new. Canadian universities are not used to working with our industries the way universities do in the United States.

The United States has surged ahead in the new economy. It has taken the challenge from Japan and has regarded this almost as another "Sputnik." Thousands of new companies are moving into new, higher-technology in-dustries. It is my view that the United States is moving ahead so quickly that it is leaving all the rest of the advanced world far behind. People try to explain why the United States can have a huge government deficit, a huge trade deficit, and high real interest rates and still have enormously high investment and a booming economy, along with a very high dollar. A fore-caster who said five years ago that we would see very high interest rates and yet have booming equity investments would have been given very little credence. A forecast that predicted the biggest government deficit in history and the biggest trade deficit in history, and a currency which was zooming upwards, would have been highly questionable. Yet, all of this is happening.

What is the explanation for this reverse of accepted patterns that even a lay person can recognize? It seems that the world has decided that the United States is going to win the high-technology race. Japan was the early leader and is now stalled, Europe is falling behind, the United States is winning and Canada, of course, is watching. The United States seems to be making the transition successfully. The huge trade deficit in the United States is all in traditional industries. Americans seem to be letting those traditional industries sink or swim against foreign competition, while they run a high government deficit to maintain employment. Much American and foreign investment is going into new technology. Americans have an innovative, entrepreneurial society; they are flexible, aggressive and have new ideas; they give young people their head. They will probably succeed. The inter-national investment community senses this and is betting accordingly.

We can now see why we should be concerned about Canada's national survival. It is probable that Canada will be uncompetitive in the traditional industries and will be faced with having to leapfrog over the relatively weak secondary manufacturing sector into highly advanced industries. This is very difficult to do. Normally, if one enters into the high value-added in-dustry, it is medium value-added industry that takes a little jump upwards. It is not low value-added that jumps to high technology. But in our medium sector, Canada is usually foreign-owned, branch-plant, not oriented toward the export market and not very research-intensive. Canadian trade figures indicate that the higher the technology, the higher the deficit. In Canada, we have to make a fundamental change, and the economy is not geared to do that.

Market forces, left to themselves, will not bring about this needed change in Canada's economy. Those with money to invest in new high-technology ventures will rarely do so in Canada. It is easier to invest in companies that are already a few steps up the ladder, and they can be found in the United States by the hundreds. It is very difficult to start from a standing position as new Canadian companies usually must do. Our venture capital companies know this. For example, in the big venture capital fund that was set up by Inco and some investment companies, 70 to 80 per cent of the money is going to the United States.[2] That is natural, since the action is there.

Market forces will not permit us to attract much of that investment in Canada. By looking at the Toronto Stock Exchange one can see where Canadian money is invested, and it is not generally in higher technology. Like it or not, Canadians are going to have to use government, just as we have always had to do in this country, as a counterbalance to the weight of market forces favouring the United States. But, the political trend of both major parties, the demand from business (largely continental in orientation), the theories of most economists (who believe in free markets), the demand from the United States government—all are against the use of government. Yet, even in the United States, the effect of defence spending is enormous. Even one-twentieth of that amount of government stimulus would make a significant difference for high-technology companies. All the trends are against using government. They point towards leaving change to the market. Governments do not want to make choices. Nevertheless, choices are being made. We are investing in double-tracking the railways in Canada to the west coast, but we are double-tracking not to move microchips but to move resource products! It is a choice; the choice to support the resource sector. But when one tries to get a choice to use investments from the government for the high technology sector, one is told, "We do not make choices." The result is foreseeable.

What is needed is a diversification strategy emphasizing advanced technology. A second possible strategy is to muddle through and trust to luck. We may, in fact, be lucky. Resources might become valuable again. This has happened in Canada before. Conventional wars and the rebuilding of Europe created resource booms. Maybe water will be a valuable commodity. Perhaps the greenhouse effect will warm up Canada and bring the United States population here!

The third alternative, and the one we seem headed for if we do not make some changes, is to join the United States. This could be accomplished either by the complete integration of our economies, followed by political integration, or by falling so far behind their advancing economy that we really have no choice but to demand free movement of people across the border to compete for the jobs that are there. It is not inconceivable that some politician twenty-five years from now, will say, in effect, "You've got our goods, you've got our money, we demand you take our people." And when the United States finally agrees, that person will be acclaimed. That is what may happen. Nobody will be opposed to it. Maybe that is not so terrible. Borders change with history and, if we lose our national identity, it is not a tragedy—but it is certainly a loss.

However, if Canadians truly understood the road we are on, perhaps they would be willing to adopt policies which would change that direction. They might be willing to adopt certain industrial policies that had as their purpose the building up of new industries in Canada to help us compete in the new global economy. But as long as they do not know what is happening, they will be like a frog that you put in a very hot bath. If you raise the temperature very slowly, one degree at a time, you can eventually boil the frog to death. If you raise it ten or fifteen degrees at once, it gets the idea and jumps out of the water! It might just be that if Canadians understood the choices, we might find the political will to adopt some policies so that we can continue to be the best of friends with the United States but not necessarily part of it.

Notes

1. Two great success stories of Canadian agricultural science in the areas of grain are Marquis, a wheat strain developed from 1903 to 1908 and distributed widely by 1911; and Canola, a seed and oil meal developed from the rape plant in the 1960s. It has become a major crop on the prairies since the mid–1970s.

2. Comments by President of SB Capital Corporation, Ottawa, November, 1984.

CHAPTER 10

Canada's America, or Lost in the Funhouse

Peter Buitenhuis

Two of the most compelling reasons for the lack of growth in Canadian studies of the United States are Canadian nationalism and the pervasive sense that we are so close to the United States that we have no perspective on that country. From where we sit, studying the United States is rather like looking through our next door neighbour's window with an astral telescope: we have an especially good view of his warts, but it is hard to see his whole face. Perhaps that is why we have not produced commentators of the stature of Alexis de Tocqueville or Alistair Cooke. Marshall McLuhan has often been cited as an exception to this rule, but he is more the genius-critic of modern technology, which, although it may be the dominant American mode, is not generically, nor by any means exclusively, an American phenomenon.

Yet everyone agrees that there is a real need for informed comment about the United States from Canada. As the American author Sylvia Wright said at a Harvard seminar in 1977:

> I have come to feel that one thing we desperately need today is a much more distinguished—a higher quality of—anti-Americanism, expressed with more elegance, developed with more logic, and elaborated with more humor. It is time, I think, for Americans to be rigorous about the sort of anti-Americanism they will accept. Canadians in the main have not been good enough at this.[1]

We can only bow our heads in assent at this just rebuke.

A recurrent fantasy of Canadians, especially of some of our writers, is to erect an enormous wall along the United States–Canadian border, as the Chinese did 500 years ago against the northern barbarians. Ironically, it was an American, the commentator Richard H. Rovere, who most compellingly evoked this fantasy in an article he wrote for *Maclean's* in 1960: "What would happen in Canada if full sovereignty were invoked and the southern border were sealed tight against American mass culture—if the airwaves were jammed, if all our comic books were embargoed, if only the purest and most uplifting of American cultural commodities were allowed entry? Native industries would take over, obviously. Cut off from American junk, Canada would have to produce her own."[2] We know, of course, that if this were to happen Canadian junk would be no better than American junk; the chances are it would be a lot worse. But, the arguments run, it would at least be our own junk. Canadian writers have sometimes wished that even the most uplifting of American cultural commodities could be embargoed. In a whimsical poem, F.R. Scott satirizes this desire. It is titled "The Call of the Wild."[3]

> *Make me over, Mother Nature,*
> *Take the knowledge from my eyes,*
> *Put me back among the pine trees*
> *Where the simple are the wise.*
>
> *Clear away all evil influence*
> *That can hurt me from the States*
> *Keep me pure among the beaver*
> *With un-Freudian loves and hates,*
>
> *Where my Conrads are not Aiken*
> *Where John Bishop's Peales don't sound,*
> *Where the Ransoms are not Crowing*
> *And the Ezras do not Pound.*

The wall is the recurrent fantasy of Canadian nationalists, whether they be economic nationalists who want to erect tariff walls or controls against capital influx, media nationalists who want continually to raise Canadian content in broadcast policy, or literary nationalists who want to declare a moratorium against the importation of American writers and their works. Of course, fantasy crumbles when faced with the realities of modern economics, broadcasting, and literature.

What I want to do in this essay is study some of the realities of literary relationships between English Canada and the United States (highly selectively) from the beginnings in Loyalist times to the present, placing most of my emphasis on the tortured decade of the 1960s. Fortunately for my purpose, a Canadian academic, James Doyle, has already surveyed the scene from the other side of the border in *North of America: Images of Canada in the Literature of the United States, 1775–1900*. Doyle points out that Canada has usually figured in American literature as a "vague, peripheral, and ambiguous concept."[4] When not simply seeking to annex Canada, nineteenth century American writers, according to Doyle, tried to ignore a country which is "a reminder of alternatives, some of which seem wrong, but many of which too often present disturbing possibilities of United States error and failure." In the twentieth century, on the other hand, Doyle adds,

American writers' "interest is frequently directed towards denying the distinctions between the two countries."[5]

It seems that the reverse of all this is true about Canadian images of the United States. The influence of the United States has always been inescapable. The historian J.M.S. Careless ended an article by writing that he was tempted to conclude "that there could not be a Canada without the United States . . . ," and added, piquantly, "and may not be a Canada with one."[6] As Margaret Atwood discerningly noted in the "Afterword" to her *Journals of Susanna Moodie*, "If the national mental illness of the United States is megalomania, that of Canada is paranoid schizophrenia."[7] In the earlier days of Canada, the schizophrenia was fairly simple to define. Over against the absorptive and domineering power of the new United States, the Canadian could put the power and the glory of Great Britain. Libertarian republicanism and egalitarian democracy could be countered by monarchy and parliamentary institutions: the Crown could stand up against the Eagle. In literary terms, Shakespeare could be placed against Emerson, Wordsworth against Whitman. In Charles Mair's anachronistic verse drama, *Tecumseh* (1886),[8] General Brock tells his young republican friend, Lefroy, in Shakespearian blank verse:

> *The kingly function is the soul of state,*
> *The crown the emblem of authority,*
> *And loyalty the symbol of all faith.*
> *Omitting these, man's government decays—*
> *His family falls into revolt and ruin.*

The low buffoons in the play, appropriately enough, are "Yankee ruffians."

After the war of 1812, Britain's influence on the colony steadily diminished while that of the United States grew correspondingly. What was a collection of small and separated enclaves to do in the face of this growing power, in the absence of other alternatives? The paranoid reaction of Canadian writers then, and even some time after Confederation, was either to deny the existence of the United States or to acknowledge its power and deny its relevance. Moreover, I have discovered in my readings of Canadian writings about the United States that, in true paranoid style, their authors are entering not so much another country but their own minds, which is why I have subtitled this essay "Lost in the Funhouse." This is the title of a short piece by the American writer John Barth. The protagonist of the story, a young boy, wanders in the wilderness of distorting mirrors in the funhouse and wonders at "the endless replication of his image," adding that "the necessity of an observer makes perfect observation impossible." At last he thinks he sees his way out by following his older brother and his girl friend, whom he covets: "Then he set his mouth and followed after, as he supposed, took a wrong turn, strayed into the pass *wherein he lingers yet*."[9]

This has often been the paranoiac fear of Canadian writers when confronted by the United States and by the work of its writers. My central contention is that, on the whole, Canadian writers have been *better* off when they have entered that funhouse and, after having been lost, found themselves. They have been *worse* off when they have denied the presence of the funhouse altogether.

As we know, there is generally some basis for a mental illness. A paranoid usually has some real enemies and a megalomaniac often has some real power. The most notorious of the American literary megalomaniacs, Walt Whitman, the singer of "these States," effortlessly absorbed Kanada, which for some unknown metamorphic reason he always spelled with a "K", into the United States. In the poem "On Journeys Through the States,"[10] we find the lines:

> We dwell awhile in every city and town,
> We pass through Kanada, the North-east, the vast valley of the
>   Mississippi, and the Southern States,
> We confer on equal terms with each of the States . . .

In "By Blue Ontario's Shore,"[11] Walt goes even further than this to incorporate not only Canada's lands, but also Canada's poets, into his vision of America:

> Bards with songs as from burning coals or the lightning's fork'd stripes!
> Ample Ohio's, Kanada's bards—bards of California! inland
>   bards—bards of the war!
> You by my charm I invoke.

We might be tempted to remark in response to this, something like Hotspur's response to Glendower, "Aye, but will they come when you invoke them?" There is no denying that Walt is Manifest Destiny with a vengeance. This sort of thing has no doubt repelled many Canadian writers in the past. Contemporary Canadian reviewers did not take kindly to his work; they referred to his "sins of grossness and coarseness of style"[12] and to his "rampant bestiality . . . so far from poetry that it is not even verse."[13] Yet it seems to me that Whitman was from the beginning potentially the most liberating and the most relevant writer for Canadian poets, not only for his democratic vision, but also for his catholicity, his generosity of spirit, and his open but rhythmical forms.

Whitman has by no means been the only one to appropriate Canada's bards. In his travel book, *A Trip Around Lake Huron*, the Canadian poet David McFadden noticed a roadside park near Cheboygan, Michigan, dedicated "in honour of the great American poet, Bliss Carman (1861–1929)."[14] Any of us here can cite instances of such casual megalomania, literary and otherwise. My favourite is the habit of American scholars and editors when sending me manuscripts to assess; they include postage prepaid—in U.S. stamps. Even a scrupulous scholar like Warwick Wadlington in his 1975 study, *The Confidence Game in American Literature*, discusses Sam Slick without mentioning the fact that his creator was a Nova Scotian.[15] Is it any wonder then that we suffer from paranoid schizophrenia?

One of the most effective counters to such misappropriation is satire. It is surely one of the wonders of Canadian literature that the inventor of the best-known literary Yankee should be born in 1796 in Windsor, Nova Scotia, of true-blue Loyalist stock. Thomas Chandler Haliburton went into the funhouse with his eyes open for, as Constance Rourke has shown in her seminal book, *American Humor*, Sam Slick had his origins in stage Yankees going back to Royall Tyler's play *The Contrast* (1787).[16] Sam's direct ancestor was Major Jack Downey, the creation of Seba Smith of the state of Maine. Downey's salty and funny observations, couched in the form of monologues, first appeared in the local newspaper and were widely copied. Sam Slick also first appeared in the newspaper, but in Haliburton's hands the monologue became a dialogue, since his purpose was more complex than that of Smith. True to the paranoia, he was interested not so much in the Yankees as in the Bluenoses; his primary purpose was to satirize his fellow Nova Scotians out of their idleness and complacency.

One of the earliest pieces, "The American Eagle," contains a wonderfully boastful encomium by Sam of both the flag and the power of America. This is countered by his interlocutor, the English squire, in a finely sarcastic comment based on the absurdity of the emblem on the naval buttons of the United States: an eagle carrying an anchor in its claws. But Sam has the last word:

> If that Eagle is represented as trying what *he cant do*, its an honorable ambition arter all, but these blue noses wont try what *they can do . . . An owl should be their emblem* and the motto "*he sleeps all the days of his life*"—the whole country is like this night, beautiful to look at, but silent as the grave, still as death, asleep, becalmed . . . .[17]

The squire does not reply to this sally because Haliburton has achieved his main purpose of lampooning his fellow Bluenoses. But he had at the same time penned a perfect picture of the megalomania, the aggressiveness, the complacency, and the unthinking patriotism that makes of the United States such a strong, but at the same time, such a dangerous ally.

What might have remained a purely parochial piece of writing, wherein Haliburton would have lingered yet, became universal because of the character of Sam Slick. The necessity of an observer, to use Barth's words, made perfect observation impossible, but ended in a character who transcended the columns of a newspaper, travelled through the states and to the Court of St. James in England, ending up in a series of bound books.

Haliburton created the character of the sharp-dealing, fast-talking Yankee pedlar for all the world, and went beyond that to represent another American strain, the frontier boaster and tale-spinner. Sam claims:

> It isn't every day that you see a genuine Yankee Doodle, I calculate! Oh no. Now look at me. I'm cast iron all over, and pieced with rock . . . I'm half fire, half love, and a little touch of thunder bolt! . . . I am Sam

Slick the Yankee pedlar—I can ride on a flash of lightning and catch
a thunderbolt in my fist ... .[18]

Sam Slick passes by osmosis into the humour of Artemus Ward, Bret Harte,
and Mark Twain, not to mention Herman Melville of *The Confidence Man*—
a testament to the true reciprocity of literary relations, which know no
borders.

This Haliburton, who created the character of the egalitarian Yankee and
his dialect so authentically, was a profound conservative who ended his
legal career as a judge on the Supreme Court of Nova Scotia, and his political
career in the British House of Commons. He was a member of that elite
who later moved the Maritimes into Confederation. As everyone knows,
Confederation was the consequence of more paranoia—the belief that the
United States, having successfully concluded the Civil War, would move to
consolidate its empire by annexing Canada. It needed only a few feeble
Fenian raids to goad the colonies into action. The road led from the legislative buildings in Prince Edward Island to Quebec, to Kingston, and finally
to Ottawa. John A. Macdonald and his Conservatives built the railway to
the west coast, again to conserve the country from American expansion in
the West.

The so-called Confederation poets, Lampman, Carman, and Roberts, were
as conservative as the politicians. They looked backwards, to the English
romantics, Wordsworth, Shelley, and Keats, and to their British contem-
poraries, Tennyson and Browning, for their sources and inspiration when
they came to interpret the Canadian landscape and character. Even their
titles give their sources away: Roberts's "Ode to Drowsihood" and "The
Solitary Woodsman" are as Keatsian and Wordsworthian as one would expect.[19] Lampman's titles are not as tell-tale, but if you listen to his rhythms
and diction, the origins are clear enough. Shelley's "Ode to the West Wind"
blows through Lampman's "Storm:"[20]

> *So day and night, O Wind, with hiss and moan you fleet*
> *Where once long gone on many a green-leafed day*
> *Your gentler brethren wandered with light feet*
> *And sang, with voices soft and sweet as they ...*

Occasionally Lampman breaks through this soft romantic haze to visions
more terrible and appropriate to Canadian reality, as in "The City of the
End of Things," which has echoes of Edgar Allan Poe.[21]

Even Bliss Carman, who used to be called the Canadian Whitman, is more
like Yeats of the Celtic twilight. In "A Vagabond Song,"[22] you hear the voice
of "The Lake Isle of Innisfree:"

> *There is something in October sets the gypsy blood astir.*
> *We must rise and follow her,*
> *When from every hill of flame*
> *She calls and calls each vagabond by name.*

Every writer must start somewhere, choose, or be chosen by, an influence. With judgment and luck he makes the choice appropriate to his time and place and his own voice. After that there should take place that painful period which Harold Bloom calls "the anxiety of influence," in which he both fights against and assimilates that influence.[23]

The Confederation poets did not have the judgment or luck to choose the right influences, nor did they transcend those they did choose. The English romantics had little to say to the northern environment, the vast spaces, the immigrants flooding into the cities and to the west. The Confederation poets would surely have been better off with Walt Whitman. Let us take a moment to record that his work was available and being promoted by a man from a most conservative profession in the most conservative of cities, Dr. R.M. Bucke of London, Ontario. Bucke first heard of Whitman's work in 1867 and wrote to a friend in 1869: "Have you seen that here is the modern poet? Especially the American poet, the only one so far, the founder of American literature as Goethe was of German literature . . . .that here in fact is a mastermind in literature . . . ."[24] It seems that few Canadians listened to this most persistent and dedicated advocate of Whitman's work.

Turning to the twentieth century and to the most characteristically Canadian novelists of the 1940s and 1950s, Hugh MacLennan and Morley Callaghan, we find again that these writers did not have the judgment or luck to choose the right sources of influence. Callaghan in particular had his chances. He went to the Pierian spring of the whole modern movement— Paris in the late 1920s, where the Ezras were Pounding, and James Joyce was rejoicing. There also were Gertrude Stein, Ford Madox Ford, Ernest Hemingway, and F. Scott Fitzgerald. But Callaghan did not drink deep of the spring; in fact he barely tasted it. He writes in his memoir, *That Summer in Paris*, "The plain truth was, as I saw it, Gertrude Stein had nothing whatever to say."[25] Callaghan claims to have admired Joyce greatly, and yet this is what he writes about him: "Joyce in exile had gone deeply, too deeply, into himself. But what if he had stayed in Dublin?"[26] During that summer in Paris, Callaghan was quite close to Hemingway and Fitzgerald, yet he seems to have learned little from them, except a certain economy with words. Speaking of his wife, Loretto, Callaghan writes: "And she asked if Scott and Ernest too were in flight, and I said, yes, they were. Ernest would never again write about his own country, and Scott, as long as possible, would go on drinking and rushing to the Riviera."[27] With these surly words, Callaghan writes off the whole, later, fine achievement of these two writers. Psychologically, Morley Callaghan stayed in Toronto, did not broaden his talent, and fatefully limited his achievement.

Similarly, Hugh MacLennan had his chances to listen to the modern masters, particularly Henry James, Joyce, and Hemingway, but chose instead John Galsworthy, Thomas Hardy, and Arnold Bennett. He worked with narrative techniques more appropriate to nineteenth century realities than twentieth century uncertainties. In the few essays about literature that MacLennan has published, he reveals far more about his own limitations than he does about the qualities of his subjects. For example, he criticizes the style of Henry James as being "quite out of tune with the frantic rhythms of our time."[28] Of Hemingway, he writes, "As a prose writer he is superb; as a novelist he must be regarded as little better than second-rate."[29] He goes on to claim that most of the great novelists were indifferent to style, and in so doing unconsciously reveals that he was never interested in developing the techniques which could have enabled him to explore the depths of his own materials.

In his own novel explicitly about, and partly set in, the United States, *The Precipice*, MacLennan had a potentially rich subject: the exploration not of two solitudes but two puritanisms, and their effects on the psyches of the two nations. After promising so much, the novel delivers relatively little, as the author goes inward to his own preoccupations rather than outward into the minds of his characters. The point of view is diffuse and the novel tends to degenerate into a series of lectures on "the unwillingness to be content" that drives Americans. "First the Lord had hounded them," MacLennan editorializes, "and when the Lord grew remote, they had hounded themselves."[30]

Henry James, Ezra Pound, Gertrude Stein, and T.S. Eliot had done much to bring about the modernist movement by 1920, but it was not until after World War II that the full effect of these American writers was felt by Canadian poets and novelists. A.J.M. Smith, F.R. Scott, Louis Dudek, and Sheila Watson, among others, translated modernist techniques into Canadian content. The effect of the modernist movement was strong throughout the 1960s, a period of immense turbulence and change everywhere, overshadowed increasingly by the cloud of the war in Vietnam.

The war became one of the strongest forces in promoting Canadian nationalism, which has traditionally been a form of anti-Americanism. At the height of the controversy over Vietnam, Mel Hurtig asked Al Purdy to put together an anthology of Canadian reactions to the United States. It was published in 1968 under the title *The New Romans: Candid Opinions of the U.S.* Here are fifty pieces by the best known Canadian writers, academics, and commentators, ranging from George Grant on the right to Barry Lord on the left.

The New Romans is a fascinating and instructive anthology, which has the distinction of containing some of the worst verse ever published in Canada. It reveals that paranoia, guilt, and rage were strong elements in the national psyche at the time, and that, even more than usual, authors, in writing about the United States, were writing about themselves. Opinion was extreme. On the one hand there is Raymond Souster's long "Death Chant for Mr. Johnson's America."[31] The first eight lines will be sufficient indication of the rest:

> America
> you seem to be dying
> America
> moving across the forty-ninth parallel each day a stronger

> *more death-laden stench; wafting inshore from off the Great*
> *Lakes the same unmistakable stink, so unlike the*
> *usual putrefaction of these waters*
> *America*

On the other hand, right next to Souster's effort is this one by Irving Layton: "Hymn to the Republic."[32] Again a mercifully brief extract:

> *They say you have too many hydrogen bombs*
> *I do not think so: you do not have enough.*
>
> *They say you are too rich and too powerful.*
> *I do not think so: you are not rich and powerful enough.*

It goes on in this way for some time and at length concludes:

> *I'm sorry for you, America*
> *You deserve grander neighbours*
> *than assholes covered with ten-gallon hats!*
> *Shine on, glorious republic, shine forever.*

Although this is a parody of Walt Whitman, I do not think that it is meant to be a parody of Whitman's rhetoric, but simply an imitation of it. Layton turns both barrels of that rhetoric on his fellow Canadians for their parochial and mealy-mouthed criticism of their great neighbour.

Among the posturing and rhetoric of *The New Romans*, there are some excellent insights about America and its influence. In a brief essay George Grant conveys the essence of his two critiques of the liberal ideology, *Lament for a Nation* and *Technology and Empire*.[33] For him the Vietnam War was a natural outgrowth of a society whose moral roots led to the exaltation of affluent technology. Grant's philosophy has been one of the main springs of Canadian nationalist writings and provides a genuine link to the loyalist strain from which grew Haliburton's satire. Like him, he comes out of a conservative and religious tradition with its roots in Anglican royalism—the tradition to which T.S. Eliot attached himself after moving to England. It is a melancholy fact that this tradition has not strongly manifested itself in modern Canadian literary expression. One major exception to this is Scott Symons, whose limited-edition book *Civic Square* is a powerful, if inchoate, attack on what he thinks to be the whole sell-out by Canadian liberals to American interests.[34]

The fact is that the liberal tradition, even when it has been masked by political conservatism, has triumphed in Canada as well as in the United States. This is why many of the paranoiac utterances of *The New Romans* are also agonized ones, for the schizophrenia of that condition has no other self with which to identify. The liberal historian William Kilbourn admits that his complex emotions about the United States stem from what he calls sibling jealousy. He looks on the United States, not Great Britain, as his place of origin, for his ancestors lived there for many generations. In other words, in Kilbourn's mind, the Loyalist tradition has died out, and much of his identity is tied up with America. So that country has become, for him, Canada's cultural asylum, just as Canada has been political asylum for dodgers of the American way of life, from the Loyalists through the fugitive slaves, to draft evaders from the Vietnam War.

After enumerating his American cultural heroes, from Thomas Jefferson to Franklin D. Roosevelt, from Nathaniel Hawthorne to Bob Dylan, Kilbourn concludes: "America gives the Canadian writer a usable major past to nourish both his craft and his way of seeing things.... As for speech, Huckleberry Finn invented the American dialect for Canadians as well as for his countrymen."[35] Kilbourn speaks for a generation of Canadians who grew up knowing the American classic writers, and finding in them better guides to their ideas and conduct than the British writers they studied in the schools and universities.

One of the most effective of all the pieces in *The New Romans* is a poem by George Jonas. Unlike most of the other contributors to this book, Jonas is not "hung up" on the neuroses of the Canadian psyche with respect to the United States. He escaped from Hungary during the Soviet invasion of 1956, so knows about imperialistic aggression at first hand. His poem is called "American Girl: A Canadian View."[36]

> *It is reassuring*
> *To spend part of a night*
> *With an American girl.*
>
> *Chances are she will not resemble*
> *The leaders of her nation*
> *In speech, figure or stance:*
>
> *If she has imperialistic designs*
> *She may draw you without a struggle*
> *Into her sphere of influence.*
>
> *Then you'll find her battledress*
> *Fit for her private battles,*
> *See not her battleships but hear her battlecries,*
> *And melt (perhaps with a wistful smile)*
> *Before the native napalm of her eyes.*
>
> *But she'll seem to be prepared*
> *To give as well as to accept*
> *Some foreign aid*

And by midnight or so
While the fires of her manifest destiny smoulder
You'll be all ready to slip across
The world's longest undefended border.

Here the political rhetoric is skilfully subverted into sexual politics. The issues, under Jonas' cool and detached gaze, assume a different perspective when an international transaction is transformed into a personal one.

Jonas has seized on a paradox that lies at the heart of the Canadian-American relationship—that the personal encounter can be so warm and friendly, while the national one can appear to be so hostile and threatening. The nationalist cry is to build up those walls; the individual response is to tear them down.

Lionel Kearns put the paradox well in his poem "International Incident:"[37]

I was drinking the American's beer
and talking loud and saying things
that seemed unpleasantly true
I was drinking the American's beer
and shouting we should legislate against
foreign take-overs and US control
of colleges, media, land, us
I was drinking the American's beer
and telling him it was all his fault
yes I was drinking the American's beer
and reminding him that it sure takes guts
to be so hostile to your host, but he
thought I was talking about my hostility.

Kearns has entered the funhouse and encountered not the American but himself, but he has at least had the grace and irony to admit it.

The issue of the funhouse of American literature and its effects on Canadian literature is at the heart of the case study with which I want to conclude. In 1963 the Vancouver Poetry Conference took place. It was largely organized by Warren Tallman, an American professor of English at the University of British Columbia. Among the visitors were Charles Olson, Robert Duncan, Allen Ginsberg, Robert Creeley, and Denise Levertov, American poets all owing a great deal to the Pound-Eliot tradition, and some of whom were identified with the Black Mountain school. This Poetry Conference was only a large event in a series of visits by American poets dating back to 1961 when Duncan gave three lectures in Vancouver. Out of Tallman's devotion to this new poetry and these visits came the magazine, *Tish*, founded by Tallman's students, Frank Davey, George Bowering, Fred Wah, Gladys Hindmarch and others.

The emergence of this group of poets is interesting for many reasons, not the least of which is the attack made on it by the Canadian nationalist, Robin Mathews, and his student Keith Richardson, who in 1976 published *Poetry and the Colonized Mind: Tish*. In his preface to the book, Mathews claimed that the *Tish* movement was one more lost round in the battle for a Canadian poetic. An earlier round was lost, he claimed, when in Montreal in the 1930s and 1940s John Sutherland and Raymond Souster advocated following American models.

Richardson makes a sustained attack on the *Tish* movement as a sell-out to American ideas and cultural nationalism. He points out that one of the chief influences on the group, Charles Olson, did not believe in national boundaries. Another luminary, Robin Blaser, a San Francisco poet who later became a member of the English Department at Simon Fraser, wrote in his journal, *The Pacific Nation*, "authors who count take responsibility for a map which is addressed to travellers of the earth, the world, and the spirit."

Robin Mathews asserted that "major work needs to be done to examine the reasons why Canadian poets forsook Canadian tradition, denigrated Canadian achievement—achievement of high level—and sought to supplant the Canadian with the U.S. tradition."[38]

This is to beg the question with a vengeance. What is the Canadian tradition? The Confederation poets could hardly be of much help to poets coming of age in the 1960s. If we look at later periods, such as 1930–1960, we can hardly find a Canadian tradition but only poets or groups of poets who draw eclectically from many sources, European and American. The appeal of Olson, Duncan, Creeley and others to the Vancouver poets lay in their freshness and spontaneity. The Americans had learned from Pound and Eliot, but they had rejected the formalism, the elitism, even the authoritarianism of their predecessors. Moreover, these poets were highly critical of many aspects of American life and ideology, a fact that Mathews and Richardson quite fail to mention. According to Warren Tallman, these poets were leading "poetry out of an age of perception into a new age of proprioception."[39]

What is proprioception? It is the attempt to see the surrounding world from within the objective self, or "sensibility within the organism." Ezra Pound locates himself in history and appropriates it for his own purpose. More relevantly for the Vancouver poets, Olson located himself in Gloucester, Massachusetts, and worked from within its local history, its speech, its legends and gossip, its seacoast, and its streets to create the Gloucester of the *Maximus* poems. Like Whitman, Olson broke away from traditional poetic form and bodied his poetry in the syntax and idioms of speech. The voice of the poet becomes all-important: the voice of the poet speaking directly to the reader. The poet also sometimes manipulates the texture of the poem, using the form to express the immediacy of the experience and at the same time point up the inevitable artificiality of form. In other words, proprioception is moving beyond the formalism of modernism to what has come to be loosely called post-modernism, which capitalizes on the fact that, in Barth's words, "the necessity for an observer makes perfect observation impossible." If one reads aloud from the *Maximus* poems, one can hear what kind of command of idiom and texture Olson has.[40]

MAXIMUS, TO GLOUCESTER, LETTER 19 (A PASTORAL LETTER

relating

to the care of souls,

it says)

      He had smiled at us,

      each time we were in town, inquired

      how the baby was, had two cents

      for the weather, wore

      (besides his automobile)

      good clothes.

                    And a pink face.

      It was yesterday

      it all came out. The gambit

      (as he crossed the street,

      after us): "I don't believe

      I know your name." Given.

      How do you do,

      how do you do. And then:

      "Pardon me, but

      what church

      do you belong to,

      may I ask?"

And the whole street, the town, the cities, the nation

blinked, in the afternoon sun, as the gun

was held at them. And I wavered

in the thought.

      I sd, you may, sir.

      He sd, what, sir.

      I sd, none,

      sir.

And the light was back.

For I am no merchant.

Nor so young I need to take a stance

to a loaded

smile.

I have known the face
of God.
And turned away,
turned,
as He did,
his backside.
2. *And now it is noon*
of a cloudy sunday.
And a bird sings
loudly

And my daughter, naked
on the porch, sings
as best she can, and loudly,
back
   She wears her own face
   as we do not,
   until we cease to wear
   the clouds
   of all confusion,
   of all confusers
   who wear the false face
   He never wore, Whose
   is terrible. Is
   perfection

This American movement is antagonistic to what it calls humanism—the kind of subjectivism that is identified with specific political programs or concerns. Following this line, the Vancouver poets have often quarrelled with Irving Layton and other easterners who insist on political engagement. We have seen such humanism already in the poems for and against the United States by Layton and Souster already quoted. Such poetry moves too easily into posturing, rhetoric, and preaching. Humanism has tempted even such a fine poet as Dennis Lee, as in this excerpt from Section 5 of *Civil Elegies*: [41]

In a bad time, people, from an outpost of empire I write
bewildered, though on about living. It is to set down a nation's
failure of nerve; I mean complicity, which is signified by the
gaseous stain above us. For a man who
fries the skin of kids with burning jelly is a
criminal . . . .

And the consenting citizens of a minor and docile colony
are cogs in a useful tool . . .

Bowering, Davey, Kearns, Daphne Marlatt, and other young poets on the west coast all got into the American proprioception funhouse, went weaving through the distorting mirrors, and learned many things about poetry in the process, particularly about the long poem. The long poem as written by this group is not like the narrative poem by E.J. Pratt, which was in turn derived from Browning and Hardy; it is disjunctive, often fragmentary, mirroring in its structure more the movement of mind than the progress of story. The important point, however, is that the Vancouver poets did not linger in that funhouse, but found instead a better image of themselves, and better techniques of representing their own place and time. So we have Marlatt's *Steveston*, a vivid reflection of the small fishing town south of Vancouver, and George Bowering's *Kerrisdale Elegies*, published in 1984.

In the *Elegies*, Bowering has rid himself of many of the idiosyncracies of style and attitude that tended to clutter some of his earlier work. The title ironically echoes Dennis Lee's, but more seriously refers to Rainer Maria Rilke's *Duino Elegies*, which supply models for the meditative, sombre, and yet often quite lyrical styles of Bowering's poem. Significantly, too, the epigraph for *Kerrisdale Elegies* is a poem by Emily Dickinson. Some of that New England poet's concision and verbal dexterity also find their way into Bowering's *Elegies*.

Kerrisdale is the pleasant residential middle-class area of Vancouver in which Bowering lives. On the surface it is a bourgeois, rather boring neighbourhood, "where mothers in velvet jogging suits push prams," but inside is the shadow of its past, as well as Bowering's own past, his personal and family history, his loves, and his fear of death. External and internal reality move in and out in a complex pattern of image and meditation which make brief quotation difficult. However, here is a passage from *Elegy Seven*:[42]

No more love poems for you,
                    dear old voice,
you've outgrown them here on this street of leaves.
I know,
        I know, you can still do it,
                    turn words
as those swallows turn quick in the air they know.
But each of them falls and is eaten
                    and you
are only consumed.
Remember that big house at 38th and Larch?
Look now:
        a translucent spectre rises there,
                    comfortable

as the notion of home still building in your brain.

So all your neighbours have built this city block,
ethereal as their own passing conversations.
                                                    They
would put leaves on their naked pear trees.
They build a stadium of the heart downtown,
and will never find their way to the game.

Thomas Chandler Haliburton and George Bowering are only two of many I could have mentioned, including Leonard Cohen, Robert Kroetsch, and Michael Ondaatje, who have plunged into the American funhouse and found their ways out to write more discerningly not only about the United States, but also about their own land. They have come to terms, to a greater or lesser degree, with the paranoiac schizophrenia that is the inheritance of Canadians, and learned to cope with detachment and irony, or satire and burlesque, with our megalomaniac neighbour to the south.

There is another justification for our writers, as for everybody else, to read American writers. This was articulated by David McFadden in the book referred to earlier, *A Trip Around Lake Huron*. Musing on the role that the American poets William Carlos Williams, Olson, and Duncan have played in Canadian poetry, McFadden asserts that it is important for the poets of the weaker countries to listen to those of the stronger ones, for in their work lies the key to survival. The seers, he goes on, are often rejected by that which tends to suppress weakness in a strong country: "That weakness must be seized and understood," McFadden concludes. "Only in that way will we become strong."[43]

I believe that McFadden was using the wrong word when he talked about weakness. What he meant surely was sensitivity, awareness, the apprehensions of psychic terrors and destructive impulses, which great writers like Poe and Melville, Stephen and Hart Crane, Henry James, and Dickinson reveal. Those apprehensions are often met by neglect and rejection by the public at the time. McFadden is saying, quite rightly, that we must listen to the best contemporary American writers with the same intensity as we now, as scholars and students, listen to the classic American writers for what they can tell us about what is really going on in that country's psyche. For they are, as Ezra Pound put it so succinctly, "the antennae of the race."[44]

Notes

I would like to acknowledge, with thanks, the advice of my colleagues in the English Department at Simon Fraser University: George Bowering, Sandra Djwa, Lionel Kearns, Bruce Nesbitt, and David Stouck. This is not to say that they all agree with the views expressed in this essay.
1. Elliot J. Feldman and Neil Nevitte, eds., *The Future of North America: Canada, the United States, and Quebec Nationalism*, (Cambridge, Mass.: Harvard Studies in International Affairs, 1979), No. 42, p. 59.

2. *Maclean's* magazine, 5 November 1960, p. 36.

3. *The Collected Poems of F.R. Scott* (Toronto: McClelland & Stewart, 1981), p. 255. Reprinted by permission of McClelland and Stewart Ltd., the Canadian publishers.

4. James Doyle, *North of America: Images of Canada in the Literature of the United States, 1775–1900* (Toronto: ECW Press, 1983), p. 1.

5. *Ibid*, p. 146.

6. Al Purdy, ed., *The New Romans: Candid Canadian Opinions of the U.S.*, (Edmonton: M.G. Hurtig Ltd., 1968), p. 134.

7. *The Journals of Susanna Moodie: Poems by Margaret Atwood* (Toronto: Oxford University Press, 1970), p. 62.

8. Quoted by Norman Shrive in his *Charles Mair, Literary Nationalist* (Toronto: University of Toronto Press, 1965), p. 182.

9. John Barth, *Lost in the Funhouse: Fiction for Print, Tape, Live Voice* (New York: Doubleday, 1973), p. 10.

10. Walt Whitman in Sculley Bradley and Harold W. Blodgett, eds., *Leaves of Grass: Authoritative Texts, Prefaces, Whitman on His Art, Criticism*, (New York: W.W. Norton, 1973), p. 10.

11. *Ibid.*, p. 355.

12. K.S. MacLean, "Walt Whitman and His Poems," *Rose-Belford's Canadian Monthly and National Review*, V (July, 1880), p. 34.

13. Anonymous review of H.B. Forman, *Our Living Poets, an Essay in Criticism*, in *Canadian Monthly and National Review*, I (March, 1872), p. 279.

14. David McFadden, *A Trip Around Lake Huron* (Toronto: Coach House Press, 1980), p. 57.

15. Warwick Wadlington, *The Confidence Game in American Literature* (Princeton: Princeton University Press, 1975), p. 11.

16. Constance Rourke, *American Humor: A Study in the National Character* (New York: Doubleday, 1953), pp. 24-32.

17. Thomas Chandler Haliburton, *Recollections of Nova Scotia: The Clockmaker, or the sayings and doings of Samuel Slick, of Slickville* (First Series, No. 1-21), ed. with an introduction and notes by Bruce Nesbitt (Ottawa: Tecumseh Press, 1984), pp. 62-63.

18. Quoted by Constance Rourke in *American Humor*, p. 66.

19. Carl F. Klinck and Reginald E. Watters, eds., *The Canadian Anthology* (Toronto: Gage, 1974), pp. 100 and 106.

20. *Ibid.*, p. 125.

21. *Ibid.*, p. 131.

22. *Ibid.*, p. 114.

23. Harold Bloom, *The Anxiety of Influence* (New York: Oxford University Press, 1973), pp. 1-16.

24. R.M. Bucke, *Medical Mystic: Letters of Dr. R.M. Bucke to Walt Whitman and his Friends*, selected and ed. by Artem Lozynsky, with a foreword by Gay Wilson Allen (Detroit: Wayne State University Press, 1977), p. 25.

25. Morley Callaghan, *That Summer in Paris: Memoirs of Tangled Friendships with Hemingway, Fitzgerald, and Some Others* (New York: Coward-McCann, 1963), p. 184.

26. *Ibid.*, p. 230.

27. *Ibid.*, p. 229.

28. Hugh MacLennan, "Homage to Hemingway," in *Thirty and Three*, ed. Dorothy Duncan (Toronto: Macmillan, 1954), p. 95.

29. *Ibid.*, 85-86.

30. Hugh MacLennan, *The Precipice* (Toronto: Collins, 1948), p. 278.

31. *The New Romans*, p. 65.

32. *Ibid.*, pp. 62-64. Reprinted by permission of Irving Layton.

33. *Ibid.*, pp. 39-41.

34. Scott Symons, *Civic Square* (Toronto: McClelland & Stewart, n.d.), limited facsimile edition.

35. *The New Romans*, p. 56.

36. *Ibid.*, p. 53. Reprinted with permission of George Jonas from *The Happy Hungry Man* (Toronto: House of Anansi Press, 1970).

37. Lionel Kearns, *Practicing Up to be Human* (Toronto: Coach House Press, 1978). Reprinted by permission of the author.

38. Keith Richardson, *Poetry and the Colonised Mind*, with a preface by Robin Mathews (Ottawa: Mosaic Press, 1976), pp. 68 and 69.

39. Warren Tallman, "Wonder Merchants: Modernist poetry in Vancouver during the 1960s," *Boundary 2*, Vol. III, No. 1 (Fall, 1974) p. 39.

40. Charles Olson, *The Maximus Poems* (New York: Jargon/Corinth Books, 1960), pp. 87-88. Reprinted by permission of the University of California Press.

41. Dennis Lee, from "Elegy #5," *Civil Elegies and Other Poems* (Toronto: House of Anansi Press, 1972), p. 47.

42. George Bowering, *Kerrisdale Elegies* (Toronto: Coach House Press, 1984), pp. 33, 93 and 99. Reprinted with permission of the author.

43. *A Trip Around Lake Huron*, p. 68.

44. Ezra Pound, *Literary Essays* (London: Faber and Faber, 1954), p. 297.

Escaping Extinction: Cultural Defence of an Undefended Border

John Meisel

Much has been written, and even more said, about what constitutes the Canadian character, what identifies the quintessential Canadian. A definitive answer continues to elude us, but two features clearly emerge as dominant elements in the make-up of both French- and English-speaking members of our family: we are constantly brooding over who we are, what gives us our Canadian character, and what makes us different from other nationals. Most other nationals never think about such things, or take the answers for granted. Secondly, we share a keen awareness of, interest in, and concern with all things American, that is, with the United States of America. Popular culture, sports, politics, even tourist attractions south of the border are part of the mental map of most Canadians and are frequently as important to us, if not more so, than corresponding indigenous realities. Inside every Canadian, whether she or he knows it or not, there is, in fact, an American. The magnitude and effect of this American presence in us all varies considerably from person to person, but it is ubiquitous and inescapable.

The economic dependence of Canada on the United States only exacerbates this state of affairs. Economic issues usually arouse the greatest interest and controversy; they are viewed from a variety of perspectives, depending on current problems and fashions. Right now, everyone is "atwitter" about sectoral free trade, and it is an awesome matter, to be sure. But other aspects of our uneasily shared and separated lives are equally important. We shall deal with one of these and shall take a leaf out of the economists' book by also adopting a sectoral approach. The sector explored in this essay is our culture and our cultural relations, particularly one manifestation of them.

You may think that the wording of the title—"Escaping Extinction"—is a trifle hysterical and that to link Canadians, even if only potentially, to the dinosaur, the passenger pigeon, or the dodo ignores the fact that there is a dance or two left in us yet. But it was chosen after reflection which was certainly measured and (as my grey locks and furrowed brow indicate) also mature. The greatest threat to Canada lies in the possibility (some might even say probability) that, as the result of the strong presence of American influences, our cultural development may be stunted. United States styles, ideas, and products are never far away. There is, alas, a well-grounded fear that as a consequence, our perceptions, values, ideas, and priorities will become so dominated by those of our neighbours that the distinctiveness of Canada will, to all intents and purposes, vanish. The danger is greater with respect to anglophones than francophones, but even the latter have cause for alarm.

Canada's cultural vulnerability vis-à-vis the United States is manifest everywhere. Book publishing, the periodical press, film production and distribution, comic books, the record industry, theatre, dance, popular and so-called classical music—all have been dominated by foreign influences in Canada. The indigenous product has had an exceedingly hard time getting started and surviving. This was so, in English Canada at least, largely because of the absence of a suitable native infrastructure and of an indigenous tradition, and because of the easy accessibility of, first, British cultural goods, and later, United States counterparts. The facts are only too well known, even if the solutions do not always leap readily to mind.

No form of cultural activity so clearly displays Canada's cultural dilemmas, and their implications for Canadian-American relations, as the field of communications. This critical and ever more important area is immensely complex. It encompasses such diverse aspects as transborder data flows, the transnational character of satellite footprints, the allocation of scarce slots for communications birds in the geostationary orbit, and the implications of one country's being dependent on another with respect to computer hardware and software. More important still, it embraces the field of broadcasting, the focus of our concerns in this essay.

All of broadcasting, but television in particular, has the most far-reaching effect on the minds of individuals and therefore on the nature of human society. Television is by far the most popular of all the media, engaging, on the average, the attention of Canadians for more than three hours a day. Children spend more time before the little screen than in the presence of teachers. Dominant perceptions of ourselves, of others, of this country and its neighbours, of desirable life-styles, of national and world affairs, of different ethnic, religious, and social groups, of the diverse regions at home and abroad—perceptions of all these things are profoundly influenced by the programming available and watched on television. No wonder then that this medium is a uniquely powerful force in the socialization of individuals and in the formation of collective attitudes, values, and aspirations.

And television is, as we all know, predominantly, even overwhelmingly American. This fact is of absolutely central significance in the state and development not only of Canada's culture but also of the country's perception of, and relations with, the United States. It is, therefore, imperative that we understand fully why we are so dependent on our neighbour and what we can do to ensure that the electronic media serve the best individual and collective interests of Canadians.

There are at least six major factors explaining why Canada is so vulnerable to the television world of the United States. First, the physical proximity of so many Canadians to the United States border places a vast majority of the population within the reception area of American signals with the aid of only a cheap rooftop antenna. New technologies, particularly cable, and, more recently, satellites, have placed almost the whole of the country within reach of American programming. Secondly, 80 per cent of Canadians speak English and therefore have no problem in savouring the goodies produced south of the border.

Thirdly, the American entertainment industry is the most vital and vivacious in the world. Growing largely out of the enormously successful and widely applauded American film industry, television programs and stars have found easy acceptance everywhere. American television has from the beginning, and until the advent of the Public Broadcasting System (PBS) in the late 1960s, been conceived as a commercial medium whose major role is to deliver audiences to advertisers. The content has therefore been designed, and with consummate skill, to appeal to the largest possible audiences. While this may leave something to be desired aesthetically, or in terms of the educational potential of the medium, it has unquestionably produced immensely popular shows. The format and type of drama originated by the American entertainment industry have in the most recent era created a new universal art form which is claiming something close to a worldwide audience. Successful genres of drama as typified by "Dallas," for example, have not only led to imitations domestically and massive sales in scores of countries, but are actually being copied in communities that in no way resemble the United States. America, having given us the western, has now presented the world with a vastly popular new theatrical form claiming widespread acceptance.

The fourth cause of Canada's vulnerability to United States television is probably the most telling. It concerns the economics of television programming and particularly of drama production. It costs about $1 million to produce a one-hour show like "Dallas." American networks can afford this expense, because it can be amortized in their vast and rich domestic market. Having paid for themselves at home, these programs can then be offered to foreign (including Canadian) purchasers for from 3 to 6 per cent of their cost.[1] Although the money spent on a program certainly does not guarantee its quality, it is impossible to present, consistently, shows comparable to the best American dramas without spending very large sums on them. But the size of the Canadian market does not permit the same investment in indigenous productions as is possible in the United States. Even the CBC can only afford to offer its English viewers less than two hours of original Canadian drama a week. The rest of the time the insatiable hunger for entertainment of our audiences can only be met from foreign sources or old stock.

As for the private broadcasters, their involvement in the production of Canadian drama is insignificant. One reason is obvious: they can acquire the rights to wildly popular American shows for very much less than the cost of comparable Canadian ones. It therefore makes very little *economic* sense for commercial broadcasters to try to program Canadian dramas. The importance of this matter cannot be exaggerated. Fifty per cent of Canadian viewing hours are devoted to drama, but only 4 per cent of the available shows in this category are Canadian. Films, soap operas, situation comedies, and television plays are at least as important in influencing perceptions and values as public affairs, and yet the menu offered our viewers in this most popular type of programming is almost totally foreign, in part because of the facts just described.

Historical antecedents are also responsible for the strong presence in Canadian homes of American programs. They are the fifth factor we need to note. Television made its way south of the forty-ninth parallel in the 1940s: "The year 1948 is commonly accepted as the turning point when TV emerged as a mass medium and the United States networks changed their emphasis from radio to television."[2] Canada only authorized the new medium in 1952, after the release of the Report of the Massey Commission.[3] In the first instance, only the CBC and its affiliates provided service, but in the early 1960s CTV was licensed and provided an alternative source of programs in many parts of the country. Television broadcasting was, of course, regulated in hopes that the broadcasting system would, in the words of the 1958 Broadcasting Act, be "basically Canadian in content and character."

Viewers who bought sets before the inauguration of the CBC's service were able to watch United States shows, and this, in a sense, established expectations and patterns which could not be ignored later. Both the CBC and the private broadcasters realized that they would only win and hold viewers, so many of whom could receive signals from south of the border, if they themselves offered many of the most popular American programs; the appetite for these, therefore, became deeply ingrained. Free marketers argue that in commercial broadcasting it is the viewers' tastes which determine programming. In fact, of course, the reverse normally occurs. The shows available shape tastes, and in our case it was essentially American television fare which formed the preferences of Canadian audiences.

This brings me to the sixth factor accounting for our vulnerability to American cultural influences. It would be foolish to ascribe the popularity of entertainment provided by CBS, NBC, ABC or PBS to its being crammed down reluctant Canadian throats. On the contrary, a great many Canadians have an avid thirst for most things American and feel perfectly at home surrounded by them. This applies not only to anglophones but also to francophones, as their mass annual exodus to Florida, among other things, shows. The fact that these sentiments are induced in part by the hype emanating from Hollywood and the United States entertainment industry makes the Canadian empathy no less genuinely felt.

Although we have inadequate evidence to permit firm assertions, it looks as if the affinity for our neighbour's culture is not shared equally among all groups of Canadians. A mass/élite dichotomy is evident, with the better educated, higher-income groups being more sensitive to Canadian-American cultural differences and more interested in indigenous cultural products. One consequence of this phenomenon is that the more low-brow an American cultural activity, the wider its appeal in Canada. Similarly, it is largely Canadians with middle- and upper-class backgrounds and with middle- and highbrow tastes who are concerned with the health and viability of Canadian culture. A nationalist foreign cultural policy is therefore more likely to appeal to a minority of the population.

Canadians not only like American programs, they also believe that they are entitled to have full access to them. They may not share their southern neighbours' conviction that they have an inalienable right to carry a gun, but they make up for it by insisting that they must not be deprived of all the gun-play being shown on American television. This strongly held view compelled the Canadian Radio-Television and Telecommunications Commission (CRTC) to allow Canadian cable systems to carry the programs of American stations, and it has weakened the government's will to block the widespread pirating of American shows carried on satellites. Not only individuals and companies but also municipalities, sometimes supported by Members of Parliament and provincial governments, have resorted to the unauthorized reception of United States signals, many of which, as I just noted, are meant to be available only to bona fide subscribers. There is, in short, an enormous interest in United States programming which reflects the liking of countless Canadians for the United States and the responsiveness among them to the diverse facets of American life.

The result of being so exposed to other people's electronic offerings is that it is extremely difficult for our own programs to be made and to be aired. Many of our most gifted writers, performers, and technicians are consequently forced to find work abroad, where they come to reflect the realities and perspectives of another country. Under these circumstances it becomes extremely difficult for very large numbers of Canadians to know the highly textured and varied character of their own land and to allow their imaginations to roam at home rather than abroad. This makes it hard not only to recognize one's own national interest but also to pursue it. American popular culture, and particularly television, is thus an immense Trojan horse enabling foreign concerns and priorities to infiltrate our very minds and beings.

Lest that martial metaphor of the Trojan horse give rise to a misunderstanding, I hasten to add that the nationalist, pro-Canadian stance espoused here in no way reflects an anti-American sentiment. Although the overall quality of American television may not fully satisfy, many of its programs are good. In any event, Canadians should not be deprived of the opportunity of watching whatever they please from abroad so long as a reasonable chance is provided for their own shows to be available. This, in a nutshell, is the problem: given the potent forces favouring the foreign product and the latter's plentiful supply, what can be done to create conditions in which Canadians can make genuine choices between foreign and domestic offerings? When only 4 per cent of drama available is Canadian, such a choice simply does not exist.

Canada has laboured hard and long in an effort to find a solution to the dilemma. No less than six Royal Commissions and special committees of inquiry, as well as seemingly endless parliamentary probings, have struggled with the problem, and we are still without a sure-fire remedy.[4]

The issue has both domestic and international dimensions. Students of international affairs now draw important distinctions between the field of *international* relations, which focuses on the interaction between states speaking through their governments, and *transnational* relations, which deal with all manner of individual, corporate, and other contacts across boundaries. Our broadcasting conundrum has both transnational and international aspects, as well as purely domestic elements. To examine it is, in fact, a nearly perfect means of exploring the perspectives the two countries adopt toward each other, since it touches on virtually every facet of their political, social, economic, and cultural characteristics, and how these affect the relations between them. Canadian broadcasting policy is, in other words, and contrary to what one might at first surmise, a singularly suitable and apposite subject to be tackled in a collection of essays on Canada's perspectives on the United States of America.

The centrepiece of Canada's broadcast policy has always been an act of Parliament. The most recent version, that of 1968, as amended several times since, contains a description of what the Canadian broadcasting system should be. It states unequivocally that radio frequencies are public property and hence implies that they should be used in a manner promoting the public interest. The act nevertheless recognizes that Canadian broadcasting undertakings constitute one system, comprised of both public and private elements. This system, it is asserted, should be owned and controlled by Canadians, "so as to safeguard, enrich and strengthen the cultural, political, social and economic fabric of Canada." Another clause specifies that programming should use predominantly Canadian creative and other resources. The act also provides for two of the major actors on the broadcasting scene: a nationally-owned broadcasting corporation (the CBC) and "a single independent public authority" (the CRTC) which is to regulate and supervise the system according to the objectives enunciated in the act.

Underlying these and many other provisions is the assumption that broadcasting should not respond merely to the dictates of the market but that it should serve certain national interests, some of them related to the strengthening of a sense of Canadian nationality and identity. This concern with community goals rather than the profit motive (substantially at variance with the American pattern) is also reflected in the act's specifying that when a conflict emerges between the private and public elements, it shall be resolved in the public interest, "but paramount consideration shall be given to the objectives of the national broadcasting service."

The act accomplished three things: it set the goals of the Canadian broadcasting system (in greater detail than is suggested by my summary); it provided the objectives and mandate of the CBC; and it created a powerful regulatory agency independent of the government of the day.

Although the relative position of the CBC had been declining in English television since the creation of the private networks, the act reaffirmed its primary role in the system. It also charged it with special responsibilities in providing "for a continuing expression of Canadian identity." And it has certainly been the CBC which has played a key role in providing such Canadian drama as has been available. The private broadcasters for the most part tended to focus on producing news, public affairs, sports broadcasts, and some inexpensive light entertainment. In so far as television drama is concerned, they have relied virtually exclusively on the purchase of popular American shows, a programming policy which, to a lesser extent, even the CBC itself has had to emulate.

The reasons for the CBC's recourse to American drama and such programs as "Hockey Night in Canada" are instructive. As I have already noted, one way that Canadian broadcasters have used to attract audiences is to present popular American shows. Thus, for instance, "Dallas" is brought to us by our very own public corporation. Furthermore, only part of the CBC's income is derived from government subsidies. It must recover some of its expenses from advertising revenue.[5] This is said to have several advantages. First, it is an inescapable necessity in so far as the CBC's affiliates are concerned. These private stations, which operate in places where the public broadcaster does not own an outlet, depend for their survival on the sale of commercials. Secondly, advertising provides useful information and thus is seen by many business people and consumers as an essential service. Finally, income derived from sources other than parliamentary votes is considered to be some protection against possible political interference.

There are, of course, disadvantages. Advertising sometimes distressingly interrupts dramatic lines in a story and thus destroys its artistic effect. Many of the potentially most loyal CBC viewers were disgusted by the corporation's use of commercials during the showing of "The Jewel in the Crown" in 1984, and forsook the CBC for PBS, which had scheduled the series for a later showing without the maddening interruptions. The commitment to present lucrative sports events all too frequently compels the postponement of the "National" news and the "Journal" and thus appears to interfere with what some perceive to be a main part of the CBC's mandate. Some also argue that the advertising revenue adds little to the network's independence.

From the perspective of this essay, the most intriguing aspect of the CBC's and the private broadcasters' reliance on United States programming is that American cultural products are, in an important way, paradoxically used to diminish America's cultural influence.[6] Viewers display considerable loyalty to the station to which they are tuned. It is therefore argued that audiences attracted to Canadian stations by United States programs will continue being tuned to Canadian news, sports, and other programs which are offered by the CBC because of its policies, and by many private broadcasters because of the need to live up to the CRTC's Canadian content regulations.

The CBC has another excellent reason for purveying foreign shows, sports, and all manner of other programs. The Broadcasting Act enjoins it to provide "a balanced service of information, enlightenment and entertainment for people of different ages, interests and tastes covering the whole range of programming in fair proportion." This immensely broad mandate makes it imperative that the service cover a bewildering array of productions. When it is remembered that it must do this in both of our official languages, that it operates four superb radio networks, a northern service, and an international shortwave agency, and that it reports parliamentary debates via satellite, it becomes apparent that the CBC is among the world's largest and most active broadcasters.

Although like all big and aging structures the CBC has organizational problems and confronts formidable internal challenges, it has made and continues to make absolutely Herculean contributions to the broadcasting and cultural scene in this country. This is evident at two levels: the quality of its programs is, for the most part, extremely high; and its increasingly successful efforts are making Canadian programming available during the prime viewing hours. Compared to the record of the private broadcasters, its performance in this area is phenomenal.[7]

In addition, the program sales arm of the company, CBC Enterprises, is having increasing success in selling Canadian productions abroad, including the United States. The latter is particularly encouraging. American audiences, no doubt because of the timid and unventuresome habits of the commercial networks, have amazingly parochial tastes. Except for PBS viewers, who comprise only a very small proportion of the United States viewing public, Americans are not attracted to foreign shows. It is well known that some Canadian films and TV plays have had to have their Canadian features, such as place and street names or the presence of Canadian banknotes, Americanized before they became acceptable to United States buyers. The fact that such programs as "As It Happens," on radio, and "Seeing Things," "The Wayne and Shuster Show," "Empire, Inc.," as well as other CBC productions on television are being heard or viewed abroad indicates that the CBC may be able to benefit from the growing world television market. Still, realistically, one must recognize that the successes so far have been modest and that the costs of major Canadian drama productions are not likely to be recouped through exports. We shall have to continue to a very great extent finding domestic means of paying for our own television production.

If Parliament intended the CBC to be the principal player in our broadcasting bands, then the CRTC was to be the principal conductor. It has, as the act suggests, licensed broadcast undertakings and has supervised the overall system in an effort to ensure that the goals enunciated by Parliament are realized. Judgment of how successful it has been is by no means unanimous. Some see the regulatory agency as an overbearing ogre imposing élite tastes and unrealistic demands on a potentially enterprising but shackled industry. Others consider it to be a supine slave of the private broadcasters. On balance, it is probably fair to say that it has fought fairly tenaciously for Parliament's goal of a predominantly Canadian broadcasting system but that its efforts have often been blunted by some fundamental characteristics of the Canadian environment.

The CRTC has not been aggressive in ensuring the primacy of the CBC within the system and it has been rather lenient with respect to the Canadian content goals. Because of the staggering difficulty of defining the key terms, it has also largely avoided implementing the act's injunction that "the programming provided by each broadcaster should be of high standard."

Still, the CRTC's impact on what is available on the air has been very considerable and salutary. In the 1970s, the insistence, fiercely attacked by the broadcasters, that 30 per cent of the music played on AM radio be Canadian, created a Canadian record industry and poses no serious problems to the licensees. The benefits to Canadian musicians, and hence to their audiences, have been enormous.

Although Canadian content regulations on television are less successful, they have nevertheless made a considerable difference to the availability of Canadian programs on our stations, particularly private ones. In essence each broadcaster must, on the average, present Canadian programming during 60 per cent of the daily schedule and during at least half of the evening hours. The CBC is governed by more stringent requirements but has for some time exceeded these by a fairly wide margin. One result of the regulations has been that high quality news, public affairs, and sports are widely available on all Canadian stations. Variety, light entertainment, and drama, on the other hand—categories which are expensive to produce—have been woefully neglected by the private sector. With only rare exceptions, domestic children's shows have also been overlooked. To meet the Canadian content quotas, many stations have also resorted to inexpensive quiz shows and similar fillers, usually exhibited at low viewing times. This kind of programming and the allocation of inadequate resources to the rare production of Canadian drama have contributed to the low esteem enjoyed, by and large, by Canadian programs. Despite the indifferent reputation of domestic production in the minds of many, when good quality shows or mini-series are available, they attract very significant audiences.[8]

It is probably no exaggeration to say that the most powerful factor in the back of the CRTC's mind has been the need to protect the Canadian element in our broadcasting system. The presence of the United States is therefore of major importance in the evolution of Canadian broadcasting policy. Examples abound, but I shall mention only two. Knowing full well that Canadian broadcasters, particularly in the private domain, cannot produce Canadian programs unless their revenues are ensured, the Commission has defended the economic viability of its licensees whenever this was compatible with the terms of the Broadcasting Act. Thus rules were developed forcing cable systems to provide simultaneous program substitution when a United States and Canadian station carry the same show at the same time. Accordingly, a subscriber watching a program on an American station, which is available at the same time on a Canadian channel, would see the same material, including the advertisements, as one tuned to the Canadian source of that program. The purpose is, of course, to protect the advertising revenue of the Canadian broadcaster.

The other reason for the never absent awareness of the "United States factor" in Canadian broadcasting on the part of the Commission is that a majority of Canadians can, as we have noted, receive United States signals "off air," that is, without cable, and that to prevent Canadian cable systems from carrying United States stations is impossible in the current climate of opinion. Thus *too* stringent Canadian content regulations and other pre-scriptions giving our programming a distinctive flavour and quality could easily drive audiences into the arms of the American networks and out of reach of Canadian broadcasters and of the CRTC altogether. Thus the limits of what we can do in this country are set not only by ourselves but also in a very real sense by our neighbours. And when I say this, I mean not only the United States government but also private companies and individuals.

So far, in our survey of what has been done to give Canadians a choice between watching United States and indigenous television, we have caught a glimpse of the Broadcasting Act and its pivotal creatures: the CBC, private broadcasters, and the CRTC. But other instruments are required, farther removed from the parliamentary umbrella. The most remote, in this sense, is educational television. Under conditions laid down by the CRTC in re-sponse to a cabinet directive, educational television services were estab-lished in several provinces by agencies legally at an arm's length distance from the provincial government. Some of these, like the Knowledge Network in British Columbia, are devoted exclusively to instructional purposes but others, notably TV Ontario and Radio Québec, have defined their mandate very broadly. In some of their activities these networks resemble PBS, and they certainly cater in part to adult audiences. Although they carry a good deal of foreign programming, their schedules also provide considerable Canadian content. Substantially different from the commercial networks, they furnish viewing opportunities which are not otherwise available. Their children's services are excellent, but they do not add materially to the availability of Canadian dramatic shows for adults.

As we have seen, the Broadcasting Act focuses on the CBC, the private sector, and the CRTC as the chosen instruments for the realization of a successful policy. But the intractable nature of the problems, particularly in the light of technological innovation, has made it imperative that other agencies and measures come to the rescue. Some have been on the scene for a while, but others have emerged only as the result of growing difficulties. Among the former, the National Film Board (NFB) is a well-known and widely acclaimed producer of fine Canadian programs. For reasons which must be related to internecine rivalries, NFB programs have not been shown as frequently on Canadian television as they have, in recent years, on PBS. Neither the private broadcasters nor the CBC have utilized the rich store-house of Film Board footage to the extent possible, although at least one Quebec cable system does make effective use of it and the CBC has done much better than the private networks. Co-productions between the CBC and the NFB have become increasingly common lately and have resulted in some first-rate programs.

Beyond this, the federal government has developed a number of initiatives designed to strengthen Canadian program production and the general health of the television industry. Three deserve our special attention: the negotiation of international agreements facilitating co-productions between Canadian and foreign companies, the Canadian Broadcast Production Development Fund, and the famous (or infamous, depending on which side of the border you stand) Bill C-58. The first of these can be dispatched quickly. Ottawa has actively sought to enter into agreements with a number of governments, under the aegis of which Canadian and foreign partners would be able to benefit, in their production of films and television programs, from joint investments, in sharing larger markets, from access to their respective television outlets under preferred conditions, and from otherwise reinforcing one another's efforts to maintain a healthy domestic production industry. While many of the signatories are francophone countries, the scheme is by no means confined to them. The United States is, for obvious reasons, not included, and neither is Britain. In the latter case union agreements make such accords unacceptable.

The Canadian Broadcast Production Development Fund was announced by the then Minister of Communications, Francis Fox, when he launched his new broadcast policy in 1983. Its goal was to provide fairly substantial sums of money annually to private production companies and independent producers for assistance in the creation of drama, children's, and variety programs. A pump-priming feature required that for every dollar provided by the fund, the producer must raise at least two dollars elsewhere. Thirty-five million dollars were provided at the start, but the sum was to rise to $60 million by the fifth year. By that time, therefore, the fund was expected to inject $180 million for the production of programs in neglected categories.

Half of the monies available each year were to be allocated to productions intended for exhibition by private broadcasters and the other half by the CBC. The fund was to be administered by Telefilm Canada, the new name given to the Canadian Film Development Corporation. It was also announced that the cost of the project to the government was to be raised from the imposition of a 6 per cent tax on Canadian cable companies. Since the latter pay no royalties for the programs they deliver to their subscribers, this was deemed to be a fair arrangement, inducing the profitable cable industry to contribute to Canadian production. Canadians were to be given the opportunity to see indigenous programs meeting certain requirements by means of a redistributive arrangement drawing on funds collected from companies which derive their income to a large extent from distributing the services of the American networks.

This ingenious scheme got off to a good start and led to the commissioning of some promising Canadian programs. The CBC made ample use of the opportunity from the start; it committed about $23 million by commissioning new programs from independent producers. The private broadcasters, however, whose record in the production of Canadian drama, variety, and children's programming had for so long been generally shameful, still showed less interest, even with the new incentives, and put up only $10 million. The program is now in a state of crisis because cuts in the CBC budget announced by Marcel Masse, the new Minister of Communications, prevent the Corporation from making further use of the fund in the immediate future. The government is in the process of trying to revise the terms of the program so as to rescue it from oblivion.[9]

By far the most controversial initiative of the federal government in support of Canadian cultural development, including broadcasting, was its Bill C-58. This piece of legislation received extensive publicity, largely because of its impact on the Canadian editions of *Reader's Digest* and *Time*. President Carter personally intervened against the measure. The conversion of *Maclean's* into a weekly would not have been possible without it. But the Bill's most far-reaching impact on Canadian-American relations results from its effect on a small number of American television stations situated near the border.

Introduced in 1975, Bill C-58 sought to stop or reduce the hemorrhaging of Canadian advertising funds from Canada into the United States. Broadcasters to be protected were, for the most part, in the Toronto, Vancouver, and Montreal areas. American stations just across the border allegedly deprived the Canadian broadcasters of substantial revenue by accepting, and even aggressively soliciting, Canadian advertising beamed at Canadian viewers. Some stations were apparently established for the primary purpose of milking the Canadian market. The legislation, actually an amendment to the Income Tax Act, intended to put an end to this by no longer accepting the cost of TV commercials placed by Canadian advertisers on American stations as a tax-deductible business expense. It has been estimated that Canadians spent about $21.5 million on United States television advertising in 1975. This represented roughly 10 per cent of all Canadian television advertising. By 1978, as the result of the legislation, the revenue of American border broadcasters had dropped to $6.5 million.[10]

The American reaction could not have been fiercer. It is no exaggeration to say that the border broadcast dispute, which still festers on, has been the most threatening irritant in Canadian-American relations. It also illumines some significant differences between the two countries. The affected United States broadcasters lobbied as best they could to have the legislation rescinded, but without success. Since then, some heavy guns have become involved on both sides of the border. Henry Kissinger raised the matter with Alan MacEachen, then Secretary of State for External Affairs.[11] Congress retaliated by passing legislation which severely restricted income tax deductions allowed Americans who attended conventions in Canada. The revenge apparently cost Canada hundreds of millions of dollars in lost tourist income.

This measure was ultimately annulled, but matters did not stop there. It was proposed that punitive changes should be made to the United States–Canada automotive agreement if Bill C-58 was not rescinded. Legislation was introduced in Congress by Senator Barry Goldwater intended to prohibit foreign ownership of cable if no reciprocal rights are granted—a provision which would have hit several large Canadian companies with cable franchises in the United States. Presidents Carter and Reagan both urged Congress to pass legislation which would mirror Bill C-58. The most serious attempted retaliation was contained in an amendment to the 1982 Senate mirror bill, which would deny United States business tax deductions for the purchase of Telidon, Canada's videotext system. A successful move in this direction would seriously harm the future of Canada's high-tech industry, which is expected by some to play a pivotal role in the country's economy in the emerging information society.

Why has this dispute assumed such a virulent character? After all, a loss of some $15 million annually in revenue is trifling between countries whose trade exceeds $70 billion a year. As sometimes happens in the relations between states and neighbours, the controversy, though quite insignificant in many ways, encapsulates some extraordinarily sensitive issues which arise from fundamental assumptions and values central to both societies. It also reveals how political structures sometimes create problems as well as solve them.

The Canadian position grew out of a few central assumptions: Canadian cultural life was being threatened by the massive advantages that American cultural products derived from the huge scale of the American market. Measures needed to be devised to create an environment in which Canadian creativity could flourish and which would provide Canadians with their own cultural goods.

With respect to broadcasting, it was assumed that programming must be predominantly Canadian, and that for this to happen adequate resources must be available. A serious drain of such resources, particularly in the major markets, weakens the economic viability of the licensees and therefore their ability to live up to their commitments, particularly with respect to Canadian content. Something had to be done to protect them. Tax policy was seen as an acceptable means for achieving these ends.

Although economic measures were being used to promote national goals, the purposes of the enterprise, in so far as the government of Canada was concerned, were cultural and were related to the preservation of a distinct Canadian identity. It was of course also the case that Canadian broadcasters affected by the new measures would derive economic benefits from them.

Two major concerns animated the violent American reaction. The border broadcasters were outraged by what they saw as the unfairness of the Canadian action and they, and less immediately involved Americans, objected on the grounds that Canada was interfering with the free flow of information and with the salutary and efficient operation of the free market.

Canada's broadcasting system, so it was argued, benefited in no small measure from the free availability of American network programs. The

Canadian cable industry, in particular, sold subscriptions to the American channels without paying any compensation, and its rapid and vast growth rested on its ability to deliver these highly popular offerings. Canadian practices of commercial or signal substitution were seen as contributing to piracy. The ability to benefit from selling time to Canadian advertisers on the same footing as Canadian stations was therefore considered a fair compensation for the contribution made to Canada by the American stations.

It was further affirmed that the benefits of the Canadian tax provisions would not achieve their intended goal: Canadians would continue watching the American stations, and there was no assurance that the advertising revenue accruing to the Canadian companies would find its way into greater Canadian content. This train of thought was echoed in 1981 by Ted Rogers, one of Canada's leading cablecasters: "... there has never been a public accounting by the privileged few companies," he asserted, "who financially benefited from this ... legislation. There should be such a public accounting.... If the cash flow gain to these relatively few private companies is not going to produce enhanced Canadian programming—then the bill should be repealed."[12]

It is doubtful whether the cause of the border broadcasters would have received so much support in the United States, and for so long, had there not been a matter of deep-seated principle involved. A very large number of Americans, inspired in part by the First Amendment, have a passionate and absolute commitment to the free flow of information. No matter that this ideological position often miraculously coincides with crass self-serving economic interests and that, domestically, it is occasionally compromised by the mundane claims of competing interests; the free-speech rhetoric arouses ardent and genuine support among most Americans. To interfere with the transfer of information, as directed by the whims of the market, is to impose authoritarian and reprehensible restraints inimical to human freedom. It is this deeply ingrained terror of interference with freedom of speech which has led to the tragic misreading of the MacBride Report and of the New World Information Order and the related United States withdrawal from UNESCO, and which has also given the border broadcasters ideological support.[13]

There were other aspects of course. Senator Patrick Moynihan, in explaining his "strengthening amendment" linking the mirror legislation to the sales of Telidon, noted that "the Canadians have made the issue a major test of our will to protect United States service industries faced by unreasonable and unfair discrimination by a United States trading partner.... The border broadcast issue is indeed a test of our trade law."[14] So the problem is not seen merely as one of abstract principle but also as one possibly setting a precedent with respect to international trade and even property rights. But whatever the instrumental and egotistical motives for retaliation, and whatever the desire of certain politicians to cater to the interests of their constituents, the ideological drive and concern is not only genuine but also paramount.

What lessons can Canadians derive from this ongoing battle other than that, when the undefended border is concerned, a snowflake may grow into an avalanche? The first is that despite many similarities and affinities, profound disparities exist between our two countries. In so far as these relate to broadcasting, they have been admirably summarized by Theodore Hagelin and Hudson Janisch, on whose study of Bill C-58 I have drawn heavily in the foregoing discussion. Canadian and United States domestic communications policies, they say, "differ both in their ends and their means. Canadian policy seeks cultural development; United States policy seeks consumer choices. Canadian policy relies on program content regulation and a strong public broadcasting system to achieve its objectives. United States policy relies on structural, or industrial, regulation and a strong commercial broadcasting system to achieve its objectives."[15]

A major consequence of these differences is that when disagreements occur between the two countries, which is inevitable, both deep-seated ideological and mundane egotistical forces are likely to come into play. And, as the history of religious wars has so painfully taught us, disputes in which self-interest is bolstered by articles of faith are devilishly hard to resolve. Secondly, Americans, though in many ways among the most generous people in the world, can also be inordinately tough bargainers. In international relations and transnational dealings, they nearly always play hardball and rarely give 2.54 cm. Thirdly, because of the size of the country, its power and outlook, Americans are not always well informed about prevailing conditions and the philosophical preoccupations existing among others. Even the most enlightened find it hard to understand Canada's cultural nationalism. They cannot see why we would not wish to embrace joyously all manifestations of American civilization and why anyone should be afraid of it, or why it should pose any dangers. After all, they see it as benign, unassuming, and universally valid.

This lack of understanding is exacerbated at the official level by the complex and fragmented nature of the United States governmental structure. The imposition by the United States Constitution of the separation of powers has something to do with the highly differentiated character of Washington's organizations, but there are other reasons. The following bodies are involved in formulating international broadcasting policy: several "desks" in the State Department, the Federal Communications Commission, the National Telecommunications and Information Agency, the Office of the United States Trade Representative, various committees of each branch of Congress, and a special coordinator with ambassadorial rank attached to the Department of State. The proliferation of agencies leads to specialization, which may prevent the adoption of a holistic view on policy matters. It is, for instance, highly likely that the perception of Bill C-58 by officials involved in trade policy will completely ignore the cultural dimension of the legislation, and so fail to see its purpose and the importance attached to it by the Canadian government.

Finally, the absence of cabinet government bestows awesome powers on

Congress. Since party discipline there is relatively weak, it is not at all uncommon for various regional interests to cohere on policy packages serving specific local groups. Logrolling is rife, and the wishes of fairly small groups like those of the border broadcasters, for example, can be combined with others for the sake of forcing relatively unimportant or even unwanted policies on the nation. There is some evidence that not all the retaliatory motions against Canada introduced in the legislature had the support of the United States administration and that the latter does not favour the practice of linking one particular international issue to others which may be quite unrelated to it.

The insights obtained by our examination of the United States position on the border broadcasting dispute are instructive with respect to the theme of this essay—how to avoid cultural extinction in the face of the bubbling American presence next to and inside us.

At one level, the battle is obviously international and involves the usual armoury of weapons employed whenever our interests in Washington are at stake. A thorough knowledge of the American system and of American politics is required, as well as the willingness to engage in the power plays which determine American policy. There has been a change in this respect in recent years. Canadians no longer recoil from hiring lobbyists and from playing the game according to the local rules. The infinite subtleties and variations of American ideas, positions, and strategies must be fully understood and then utilized in the deployment of our plans. A Centre for American Studies can play a vital role in this context.

But although our problem is in a sense truly international or at least in the domain of transborder relations, its solutions are essentially domestic. No amount of pressure on Washington or even on American industry is going to sensibly diminish the inexorable American cultural influence. We need to review our attitudes to our country and its cultural traditions and opportunities. The quality of our cultural production must be enhanced so as to enable it to hold its own. This has implications for the educational system and for the organization of our economy. A review of broadcasting policy is in order in the light of current conditions. It appears that the government is gearing up to another attempt (the fourth since 1968) to produce a new Communications Act. Some of the matters touched upon in this essay must be borne in mind while this process takes place.

Public broadcasting needs to be strengthened rather than weakened, and its appropriate place and form reaffirmed. Likewise, the regulatory process awaits streamlining and adjustment to guide us effectively into the next century. Other governmental measures cry out for examination, as does a searching look at what must be done by the private sector if we are to maintain our national identity.

As in so many other areas, the prime ingredient in the escape from extinction is to recognize the problem realistically and then to have the will to act upon it. Ironically, whether we have these qualities, whether we can muster the force needed to defend ourselves effectively, depends in no

small measure on the extent to which we have already become Americanized. If we trust the market to pull us through, if we fail to pursue the public
interest through both public and private means, then, I fear, we are lost.

Notes

1. Pierre Juneau, "Public Broadcasting and the New Technological Environment: A Canadian
View," Speech given at Luxembourg, 16 July 1983, pp. 9-10 (Canadian Broadcasting Corporation).
2. Frank W. Peers, "Canada and the United States: Comparative Approaches to Broadcast Policy,"
in Canadian–U.S. Conference on Communications Policy, *Cultures in Collision: The Interaction of Canadian and U.S. Television Broadcast Policies* (New York: Praeger, 1984), p. 20.
3. *The Royal Commission on National Development in the Arts, Letters and Sciences* (Massey)
(Ottawa: Printer to the King's Most Excellent Majesty, 1951).
4. *The Royal Commission on Radio Broadcasting* (Aird, 1929); *The Royal Commission on
National Development in the Arts, Letters and Sciences* (Massey, 1951); *The Royal Commission on Broadcasting* (Fowler, 1957); *The Advisory Committee on Broadcasting* (Fowler,
1965); *The Federal Cultural Policy Review Committee* (Applebaum-Hébert, 1982); *The Task
Force on Broadcasting Policy* (Caplan-Sauvageau, due 1986).
5. In 1983–1984, the parliamentary appropriation was over $736 million and the advertising
revenue came to almost $180 million. Canadian Broadcasting Corporation, *Annual Report
1983–1984* (Ottawa), p. 50.
6. This holds for English Canada much more forcibly than for Quebec. Most of the argument
of this paper in fact applies to English broadcasting more than to French, but the general
tendencies visible in the former are also in evidence, albeit to a lesser degree, in the latter.
7. That this encomium is deserved does not diminish the need to examine the structure and
performance of the Corporation most carefully. There clearly are some serious problems
requiring solution.
8. See W.A. Johnson's, "Canadian Programming in Television. Do Canadians Want it?" Address
to the Broadcast Executive Society, Toronto, 19 February 1981, for compelling evidence on
this point.
9. Since this paper was delivered, new rules have been developed which have revived the
program. Private broadcasters have made more extensive use of the scheme since it has been
re-defined.
10. Arthur Donner and Fred Lazer, *An Examination of the Financial Aspects of Canada's
1976 Amendment to Section 19.1 of the Income Tax Act (Bill C-58) on U.S. and Canadian
TV Broadcasting,* (Ottawa: Department of Communications, 1979). Cited by Theodore Hagelin
and Hudson Janisch in "The Border Broadcast Dispute in Context" in *Cultures in Collision,
op cit.,* p. 62.
11. Hagelin and Janisch, *op cit.,* p. 52
12. Leslie R. Arries, Jr., "The Position of the Border Broadcasters," in *Cultures in Collision,
op cit.,* p. 147.
13. International Commission for the Study of Communications Problems, *Many Voices, One
World,* (Paris: UNESCO, 1980).
14. Hagelin and Janisch, *op cit.,* p. 54.
15. *Ibid.,* p. 56.

CHAPTER 12

Canada and the United States: Two Polities, One Society?

William D.H. Johnson

As Canadians stare at the United States and wonder how far they should go in making a free trade arrangement, it is fortunate that the current Canada–United States debate has been preceded by a Quebec-Canada debate. The Quiet Revolution and the 1980 referendum forced Québécois and, to a lesser extent all Canadians, to refine their political thought. The political rancour over a constitutional future provoked a clash of ideas and loyalties, a confrontation of mythologies, sometimes a demystification of ideologies, and an identification of dangers and opportunities. That exercise can be useful in approaching our relationship with the United States, because in both cases the very language we traditionally use tends to be mined and booby-trapped.

It is very difficult to escape a distortion in the debate on Canada–United States relations, because of a bias built in to our very vocabulary and the fundamental concepts that tend to be invoked. The concept of the tariff, and its opposite, free trade, have been given a special meaning in the Canadian consciousness because of the historical accident of 1866, when the United States repudiated the Reciprocity Treaty of 1854 between the two countries. There were several attempts, particularly on the Canadian side, to renegotiate the treaty; George Brown for one—the founder of *The Globe* and a father of Confederation—thought of protectionism as an American trait and of liberalism in trade as much more of a Canadian proclivity. But in 1879 John A. Macdonald brought in his National Policy, and Canadians soon made a virtue of rebuff, a foundation for Canadian nationhood, out of the tariff. The tariff became a high totem of our tribe, a sacred symbol of nation-building. To pay duty was elevated to the status of patriotic sacrifice, like bleeding for one's country. Anyone proposing to do away with paying customs tariffs became little better than a traitor or, at least, a person insensitive to the call of duty—what a later generation, echoing George Grant, would call a "continentalist."[1]

This special case of mystification exists with respect to the tariff barrier at the southern border. But the problem of seeing clearly as we look south is far more general. Our perception of the relationship with the United States is confused by the very tradition of the writing of history in the western world. There was a time when the writing of history was the chronicling of kings. But, with the ascendency of romanticism and of one of its variants, nationalism, historiography became the chronicling of a mystic entity called the nation. The nation was personalized. It became the collective existence of its citizens. The nation was born at a certain glorious moment in time and, thenceforth, though men and women may come and go, the nation goes on forever. The nation became the subject of history. It was the continuity through time, through war and peace, victory and defeat, glorious moments and periods of shame. The nation was the reference point of the consolidation of geography, the subject of the development of language and political institutions, agriculture, commerce and industry, and education and the arts. The history of the nation-state acquired a grand design to characterize it, for instance, from colony to nation. The achievement of national independence became a process of collective maturing— a process that must never be reversed. Can one imagine going from nation to colony? Or from independent state to semi-independent state? Even to consider federation with another nation could be viewed as a form of treason. The nation becomes a high ethical principle, with a claim on the lives and deaths of its citizens. The nation becomes the people writ large.

These general considerations affect more or less unconsciously the way we think about Canada and the United States. Canada, in reality, in substance, does not exist. What exists, in reality, is Canadians. "Canada" is a legal fiction, a mode of organizing aspects of twenty-six million people into a system. But, because of the conditioning of historiography, we think of Canada as a collective being that really exists, which has a more important existence than the transient humans who happen at any moment in time to make up its collective substance.

Through a process of misplaced concreteness, we not only make Canada exist as a real, transcendent being, we give it an identity, a personality. For instance, one of the contributors to this volume, Harold E. Wyatt, Vice-Chairman of the Royal Bank of Canada, has said:[2]

> The starting point for any research or any discussion about our transborder relationship must start with the premise that *we are not the same*. While we share many things in common, including much of our European ancestry, it is important for the United States to know that Canadians are most concerned about maintaining a separate identity. We want to be known as Canadians and not North Americans. Perhaps this is part of the problem, because we have not really defined what a Canadian is to ourselves, let alone others.

What is Wyatt implying when he says we are not the same? If he is saying, we are not the same because we are citizens of different states or different polities, then I agree with him. No, we are not the same, and one need not spend hours in thought trying to define the difference or make great efforts to "maintain a separate identity." All one has to do is pull out a Canadian passport, and the point is made with irrefutable clarity.

But Wyatt means more than that. He is discussing an elusive "identity" that is not legally defined. I am uneasy because he is entering the mode of mystical thinking, and that is why he can be so emphatic about the prime importance of "not being the same"—speaking of a distinct Canadian identity and yet being unable to define it. There are people, such as Seymour Martin Lipset, who have analyzed the differences between the United States and Canada as societies.[3] But Lipset is not talking about different identities, but of the somewhat different distribution of the same values in the two countries. The differences he finds are interesting, though not great. But, of course, they do not change the fact that the differences within each of the two countries are far greater than the mean differences between the countries. To put it another way, a university professor from Canada is more like a university professor from the United States than a Canadian university professor is like a fisherman from Newfoundland or an Alberta rancher. And, of course, the American professor is more like his Canadian counterpart than he is like a Hispanic share-cropper.

If this concept of national identity were used purely as a metaphor, one would have no quarrel. But such is not the case. Camille Laurin, the Quebec psychiatrist who was Minister of Cultural Affairs, wrote a series of essays in which he spoke of Quebec's *collective personality* requiring psychoanalysis.[4] He meant it literally. And, of course, if the collective is viewed as a personality, one becomes concerned that the personality be integrated, harmonized, unified. So Dr. Laurin saw English-speaking culture largely as an alien, unintegrated element in Quebec's collective psyche. The remedy, as he saw it, was to integrate the culture by making it practically all French, or isolating the discordant elements. This he began to do with Bill 101 and proposed to do further in the White Paper on Quebec's culture.

Is it only in Quebec that this abusive personalizing of a population occurs? Let me quote from John Meisel, who also has an essay in this volume:[5] "American popular culture, and particularly television, is thus an immense Trojan horse enabling foreign concerns and priorities to infiltrate our very minds and beings." That sentence speaks volumes. Its message is rather close to that of Dr. Laurin. Note the words "Trojan horse"—that means the enemy within the gates, a fifth column, a mortal danger unrecognized as such. A "Trojan horse enabling foreign concerns and priorities to infiltrate our very minds and beings." We are being mentally contaminated, brainwashed, injected with a false consciousness, with an alien and hostile presence in the very sanctuary of the nation: the channels of communication of the country. The enemy penetrates the country's homes, hearts, minds, and sensibilities, contaminating its very identity.

When one travels the path of identity as used or misused by the two authors I have quoted—and by so many others, in fact, by the vast majority of those who deal with the subject—one inevitably encounters the

Americans as the enemy. They are the ones who threaten our Canadian souls, our very identity. The implication is less clear in the case of Wyatt. But look at one of his metaphors:[6] "Although the United States is ten times the size of Canada in most things except land mass, in terms of influence our relationship is more like an association between an elephant and a flea." I have not made the precise comparison, but I would guess an elephant would have several billion times the mass and weight of a flea. That metaphor, in its absurd disproportion, is revealing of a fundamental distortion of perception. It suggests that Canadians are in constant and dire peril of being crushed, snuffed out in their very essence, in their identity, and in their existence as a nation. What greater enemies could we have than the Americans?

Prime Minister Pierre Trudeau was closer to true proportions, but still grotesquely far from life size, when he spoke of a mouse sleeping beside an elephant. Need I point out that no mating is possible, and precious little communication, between an elephant and a mouse. Surely the mouse's entire existential strategy, if it is caught in a state of co-existence, must imperiously lie in putting as much distance as possible between itself and the elephant.

With John Meisel, the latent state of hostility is more blatantly expressed. He has titled his essay, "Escaping Extinction: Cultural Defence of an Un-defended Border." Extinction is a strong word. It suggests the border should at all costs be defended, and strenuously, as a condition of our existence as an independent state. Meisel says, "The greatest threat to Canada lies in the possibility (some might even say probability) that, as the result of the strong presence of American influences, our cultural development may be stunted."[7] He ends his essay with this sentence: "If we trust the market to pull us through, if we fail to pursue the public interest through both public and private means, then, I fear, we are lost."[8] We are now at the heart of the pursuit. What does Meisel mean by "extinction"? What does he mean that "we are lost"? I do not think he means that Canada as a state will cease to exist, nor that Canadians will cease to exist. He means that Canadian culture, in a special and elusive sense, will cease to exist. That is, the *distinctiveness*, the *difference* of Canadian culture will cease to exist. And, clearly, for him, that would be a cataclysm. Meisel has a right to cherish the distinctiveness, the eccentricities of Canadian culture. (Of course we must continue to have an alphabet that goes from eh? to zed!). What is unacceptable to me is the ambiguity of his discourse, the loose use of words, the mystification involved in saying "we are lost," as though Canadians existed culturally only insofar as their culture is *different*. The contrary is true. Canadian culture is real and strong, but it exists only marginally by its distinctiveness.

I am reminded of Lise Payette saying once to Peter Gzowski: "You have no culture."[9] What she meant, of course, is that English-speaking Canadians have no different culture, no utterly distinct or unique culture. From her viewpoint and the Parti Québécois's understanding of the world, to have no *different* culture is the same as having no culture. By this yardstick, an isolated stone-age tribe discovered in the wilds of Indonesia has the most culture, while English-speaking Canadians have next to none.

This thinking, that Québécois culture was unique, original, not to be contaminated, underlay Quebec's White Paper on Culture. But though it had great appeal to intellectuals and artists—to the whole folk art and restored farm houses movement—most of the population was unimpressed. Their common sense told them that they spoke the language of Molière (even if it had a regional variation), that they worshipped at the Church of Rome, that they worked at General Motors, and after work dropped in for hamburgers at McDonald's. They were children of the Enlightenment, of the Industrial Revolution, and Anglo-French political culture. Despite the remarkable social cohesiveness of Quebec society, some 99 per cent of Québécois culture is shared; it is not unique. And they like it that way, even if it displeases some poets, politicians, and political scientists.

If that is true of French Canada, it is more true of English Canada in comparison with the United States. In my personal experience, I travelled a greater distance when I went from Montreal's St. Denis Street to Crescent Street than when I moved from Toronto to Washington! There is a vast difference between talking about Canadian culture, in the sense of the *real culture of Canadians*, and Canadian culture in the sense of the (marginal) difference between the culture of Canadians and the culture of Americans. To talk about Canadian culture in the first sense is to talk about Canadian culture as it is in itself, as it can be measured and defined. To talk about Canadian culture in the second sense—Canadian culture in so far as it is distinct, different, is not to talk about Canadian culture as it is in itself, but only as it is in comparison to some other culture. It is an extrinsic, relational concept. For instance, if some unexpected cataclysm were to kill all Americans at once tomorrow, Canadian culture in the second sense would go from being weak to being strong, that is, relatively distinct. Yet Canadian culture in itself, in its reality, would not have changed a whit, only the other pole of the comparison would have changed.

As a state, Canada has a legal identity. This state has a geographical location, a history, an accumulated body of literature. That distinct reference point of a unique state over time tends to create some common attitudes among a substantial number of its citizens. In that limited sense, there is a Canadian cultural identity, a distinct Canadian identity, and the *specificity* is important. But the mystification consists of pushing that identity, that difference too far, giving it more importance than it has, and drawing unwarranted conclusions for individual and collective goals.

The population of Canada is not wholly encompassed by Canadian nationhood. As a state, Canada is a critical reference point. As a cultural system, there is no reason except ideology, or romanticism, for making the precise boundaries of Canada the most significant point of reference for a cultural system. On the contrary, for many Canadians, Canada is too large or too small to fulfil that cultural role. For many Québécois, Quebec is a far more important cultural system of reference than Canada. Many westerners resent the domination of Toronto over the Canadian Broadcasting Corporation and feel more at home with American television than with the CBC. Many French Canadians outside Quebec cannot stand the affected accent and the inexorable intellectuality of the Radio-Canada luminaries, and they prefer to listen to local radio, where the announcer has the same despised accents as they have, rather than to the supposedly national Radio-Canada. And for many of us, Canada is too small to be our most significant cultural system of reference. Only a relatively small proportion of what we read and what we learn is specifically Canadian. Intellectually, we are citizens of a much larger community.

Canadian culture, purely in the sense of its distinctive aspect, may be frail as Meisel implied, though I do not believe it. It is becoming stronger over time and will continue to strengthen as we develop further our national journals and newspapers and our national audience for books. The natural focus for Canadian identity, in that sense of distinctive Canadian culture, is public affairs. And, in fact, Canadians do watch the national news and do write and read books that discuss Canadian public affairs. Look at the best-seller lists of *Maclean's* or the *Toronto Star*, and you will usually find that while foreign books dominate the fiction list, non-fiction has major Canadian contenders.

But we must recognize that what we are talking about in this sense is Canadian culture at the margin. The distinctiveness of Canadian culture is small Prince Edward Island potatoes compared to the massive cultural elements which are shared between Canada—particularly English-speaking Canada—and the United States. This is obvious when baldly stated. But the distinction has become lost in so much of public debate, and mystification takes over. John Meisel, when he said "we are lost," meant that the marginal (though still important) difference that characterizes Canadian culture could be diminished. But his formulation, evocative of ultimate catastrophe, was not fortuitous. It reflects the biases of nationalism, which is constantly summoning us once more into the breach to fight off the American invasion. Such mystifications do contaminate the national debate and do affect national policy.

Contrary to what Meisel suggests, Canadians have a culture which is strong, not frail. It is vibrant, in full expansion. It is not, as Margaret Atwood claimed, characterized by schizophrenia and paranoia.[10] It is not confused, fragmented, buckling under the assault of American culture. In a world of disrupted cultures—think, for instance, of Islamic civilization or African tribal cultures trying to cope with the modern state—Canada's culture is remarkably harmonious and serviceable.

But much of its character comes from a common European history shared with the United States, a common Western cultural tradition, and from the rapidity and ease with which Canadians absorb cultural pulses from the United States. For cultural purists, this is a cultural assault. But, if our analysis is to be true to reality, it must recognize that this permeability of our border has given Canadians a great enrichment to their cultural life, even if it has tended at the same time to reduce the distinctiveness or difference of Canadian culture. How many Canadians, for example, were introduced to feminism by Betty Friedan's *The Feminine Mystique*? Much of Canada's capacity to accommodate Quebec and pass the Official Languages Act was made possible by a process of thinking that originated in the American civil rights movement of the late 1950s and the 1960s. We were sufficiently inspired by what happened in the United States to see how we could be different.

Think of how many Canadians have studied in American graduate schools or have benefited from the rapid, cheap diffusion of new ideas and new techniques through books and magazines. How much more difficult, slow, and expensive it is to pick up American cultural products if you speak Afrikaans, or even French, Spanish, or Russian. Think of how many Canadians have listened on Saturday afternoons to the Metropolitan Opera.

Rather than have our perceptions distorted by nineteenth century ideologies which make the nation-state the measure of all things, we need to develop a vocabulary and a set of concepts to describe the reality of English-speaking North America. We are two distinct states and will remain so. But we are not two distinct cultures except at the margin. We are largely a single society. We need a language to express without ideological distortion the reality of two states that, both as states, societies and cultures, are so fully interpenetrated and in such close communion. One has only to travel a bit in the Soviet Union or in the Middle East to recognize just how shared are the fundamental spiritual values of Canadians and Americans. The language of our discussion must be able to consider this commonality as a strength and not just a threat.

We need to think not only of the well-being of Canadian institutions but of Canadians. For instance, it is part of the life experience of Canadians that a John Kenneth Galbraith could become a senior statesman of the United States, that Peter Jennings could be ABC's and perhaps American television's outstanding news anchorman, that Rich Little could perform at Ronald Reagan's inauguration, and that Norman Jewison's film "A Soldier's Story" could represent the United States in the official competition at the 1985 Moscow Film Festival. Sometimes we are tempted to consider these purely as examples of a brain drain. They are also part of the rich life-chances of Canadians. I would hope that my own son could have the experience at some time in his career of working in big American corporations. I look forward to the day when the American book market is fully open to Canadian publications. It seems to me that the openness of the two countries is precious and an objective to be pursued by the Canadian government. The burden of proof must lie on those who would promote exclusiveness, barriers, tariffs, immobilities, and rigidities between the two countries. They must be made to defend their proposals by clearly enunciating the values that are served by barriers and are threatened by removal of the barriers.

Appeal to atavisms is not enough. It is not enough to say, for example, that free trade would threaten Canadian values. What values are threatened must be specified, and the cost, the economic and cultural cost of preserving those values by protection must be computed and compared with the advantages foregone. Otherwise, we are in danger of continued mystification; we will engage in a dialogue of the deaf. Those who cry that the Canadian sky is falling will have great credence, and we could end up fighting hard to preserve what we think is Canadian distinctiveness, when all we are really preserving is mediocrity.

Notes

1. See George Grant, *Lament for a Nation: The Defeat of Canadian Nationalism* (Toronto: McClelland and Stewart, 1965).
2. Harold E. Wyatt, "A Business Perspective on the Canada–United States Relationship," p. 107.
3. See Seymour Martin Lipset, *The First New Nation: The United States in Historical and Comparative Perspective* (New York: Basic Books, 1963) and "Canada and the United States: The Cultural Dimension," in Charles F. Doran and John H. Sigler, eds., *Canada and the United States: Enduring Friendship, Persistent Stress* (Englewood Cliffs, N.J.: Prentice Hall, 1985).
4. Camille Laurin, *Témoignage de Camille Laurin: Pourquoi je suis Souverainiste?* (Montreal: Les Editions du Parti Québécois, 1972).
5. John Meisel, "Escaping Extinction: Cultural Defence of an Undefended Border," p. 156.
6. Wyatt, p. 107.
7. Meisel, p. 152-53.
8. Meisel, p. 168.
9. Lise Payette was a cabinet minister in the Quebec Government of René Lévesque, and opposed Quebec separation. Peter Gzowski is a journalist, author and broadcaster who currently hosts a popular C.B.C. radio show, "Morningside."
10. *The Journals of Susanna Moodie: Poems by Margaret Atwood* (Toronto: Oxford University Press, 1970), p. 62.

CHAPTER 13

Some Glosses on Johnson's "Canada and the United States"

John Meisel

It is almost *de rigueur* these days among a certain type of polemicist to accuse someone he disagrees with of "mystification." This is just what W.D.H. Johnson does in his comments directed in large part at my essay in this volume entitled "Escaping Extinction: Cultural Defence of an Undefended Border." I am not sure what he means by the word, although I certainly get the drift of his argument. My favourite lexicon—the *American* (!) *Heritage Dictionary*—defines "mystification" as the "act or an instance of mystifying," i.e., to perplex, bewilder or to make obscure or mysterious. My meaning was crystal clear, I believe, until it was distorted by Johnson. The mystification, if any, is therefore his, not mine.

It is not possible here to do more than offer a few glosses on his essay:

(1) William Johnson claims that Camille Laurin believes in the existence of a collective personality and then argues that "this abusive personalizing of a population" is not confined to Quebec. His evidence consists, inter alia, of citing one of my statements: "American popular culture, and particularly television, is thus an immense Trojan horse enabling foreign concerns and priorities to infiltrate our minds and beings." I see nothing in this phrase to imply that the influence is anything but one carried from a mass medium to individual members of audiences. The charge of "abusive personalizing" is therefore inapplicable.

(2) He argues that the image of the Trojan horse conveys the notion that Americans are an enemy. I admit that this would be a possible inference, were it not for the fact that I explicitly stated in the next sentence: "Lest that martial metaphor ... give rise to a misunderstanding, I hasten to add that the nationalist, pro-Canadian stance espoused here in no way reflects an anti-American sentiment."

It is possible, surely, to wish to ensure that conditions prevail favouring the *épanouissement* of a country's own cultures without being accused of hating the culture of others. My wife and I mercifully differ in numerous ways, a circumstance we both applaud, without considering each other as enemies.

(3) The differences between William Johnson and me stem from two central points: I believe that Canadian cultural expression is in danger of being thwarted to a great extent, particularly in the domain of popular culture and notably television drama. I showed why this is so and argued that certain measures needed to be taken as a consequence. He does not agree with these views, although his assertion that "Canadian culture . . . . will continue to strengthen as we develop further our national journals and newspapers and our national audience for books" suggests that even in his eyes there may have been and continues to be some weakness. I make the point in my essay that this strengthening requires an effort, the will (of many individuals) to bring about certain goals. I suggest that the existence of this will may be difficult to develop if our attitudes and values are unduly shaped by non-Canadian cultural experiences, particularly those provided by American television.

(4) The second basic difference is best approached through this assertion of Johnson's: "Canada, in reality, in substance, does not exist. What exists, in reality, is Canadians. 'Canada' is a legal fiction, a mode of organizing aspects of twenty-six million people into a system." I believe that Canadians as a distinct people may not continue to exist in the future, if the country is not seen as more than just a legal fiction but as a concrete historical, geographic, and cultural entity contributing to the developing of individual minds which share many common reference points and memories. To me, in short, Canada is more than a legal fiction, just as the United States, France, and Britain are.

Johnson detects what he calls my "latent state of hostility" in my title "Escaping Extinction . . . " and in the use of my argument that if certain things do not happen, we may be "lost." He wonders what I mean by that word and surmises that I do not mean that "Canada as a state will cease to exist." But that is precisely what I do mean. In the long run, if our cultural life fails to develop and maintain its own viable infrastructure and its own healthy institutions, the political will to preserve an autonomous state may also wane.

We shall be more true to ourselves, better world citizens, and more useful neighbours if we maintain and enhance our distinctiveness.

PART IV

American Urban
Issues

In conjuring up images of the United States, its peoples, its regions, and its history, few can deny the power and allure of its great cities. Nevertheless, there is obvious urban decay in the cities of the northeast; the golden cities of the west have been plagued with congestion and pollution; and the sunbelt cities cope with the impact of wealth in the midst of a boom and bust economy. Each one has a unique set of urban problems beyond the basic issues of housing, transit, education, social services, and crime that must be solved. For the 145 million Americans who live in cities of over 250 000, such solutions would be the expectation, yet we cannot help but feel that the majority of Americans would really prefer to be outside of the cities. "Old fashioned values" as President Reagan has observed, come from small town America.

This section presents the essays of two respected urban geographers who have had extensive experience in cities across North America. Their observations are timely, but more importantly the conclusions they reach will probably surprise and no doubt provoke challenge.

In Chapter 14, James Lemon begins his discussion by questioning why "social conditions are sharply different" between Canadian and American cities. With a keen eye on the literature, he takes up "the American urban experience" and approaches it from the perspectives of religion, property, class, and governing within the life and politics of the city. Lemon then intertwines what he sees as being two important contradictions which permeate American society, "freedom versus collectivism and the individual versus the community." Thus, he states, "Americans may be very reluctant collectivists when it comes to welfare" yet they are also very deferential, not to government, but to "major corporate symbols" and indeed "stand in awe and reverence of the successful." He paints a picture of the individual in search of community, and brings forth the proposition that "without the status of conveniently coloured minorities, other ethnics might not have risen so markedly nor allowed white Americans to perpetuate, even to strengthen, the myth of the classless society." Using the American city as his microcosm, Lemon ultimately concludes that "environment and people cannot be separated."

The theme in Chapter 15, as propounded by Michael Goldberg, revolves around what he calls the "American urban metaphor," one which has led to the development of "crisis-based urban policies." He asks whether the American urban model is applicable not only to other countries, but even to the United States itself. Like Lemon, Goldberg stresses the importance of the cultural context of the urban experience, namely the economic, political, and social cultures and the institutions associated with them. A brief review of the literature is supplied. He also is drawn into the individual/collectivist comparison between the two countries, referring to Canada as a "colonial economy" in its trading relations with the United States. He notes that economic forces do not wholly determine the form of cities, whether one takes a capitalist or a Marxist perspective. In fact, cultural factors seem to be far more important. Using a fascinating series of comparative statistics, Goldberg asserts that Canadian cities exhibit a more compact urban form than is the case with their American counterparts. Canada, he concludes, has vibrant cities even though no *national* urban policy exists, while the opposite is true in the United States. "This suggests that the United States should not really have a national urban policy either, because cities are local entities which require very different and locally specific policies and programs."

CHAPTER 14

Reflections on the American Urban Experience

James T. Lemon

The memorable title of one of Sam Warner's books is *The Urban Wilderness*. Other titles dealing with American cities suggest serious problems: *Urban Decline and the Future of American Cities; The Long Default: New York City and the Urban Fiscal Crisis; Urban America: From Downtown to No Town;* and *City and Suburb: The Political Fragmentation of Metropolitan America.*[1] On the front pages of American newspapers, we are told of vigilantes. The inside pages bemoan the crime, hordes of homeless bag ladies (and men), physical decay, and abandoned houses that characterize the inner city. Working-class industrial suburbs adjacent to empty factories are left stranded and poor. These perceptions have become widespread since about 1960 when Jane Jacobs published her *Death and Life of Great American Cities*, though the roots of this viewpoint can be traced more deeply into the past to Upton Sinclair's *The Jungle*, to Stephen Crane's *Maggie*, or back to Jefferson's anti-urban sentiments.[2] At the same time, there are those who view urban conditions in a more positive light. In *The Atlantic*, James Fallows has recently argued that urban decline and decay are simply part of America's changing economic landscape. He echoed with approval the 1980 Presidential Commission, *Urban America in the Eighties*, arguing that mobility of individuals is, as always, the solution to America's individual and collective problems, not least its urban problems.[3]

Nevertheless, the gulf between the poor run-down inner city and the affluent suburbs in most cities has been widely recognized, though awareness of suburban problems too has arisen. The disparities continue, despite the defenders of old inner mixed areas: Jane Jacobs of Greenwich Village; Herbert Gans of Boston's North End, who together with residents in the early 1960s slowed down redevelopment; Andrew Greeley praising Chicago neighbourhoods, a few persistent enclaves of the rich, and a modest trend toward gentrification.[4] Inner-city private poverty and public environmental squalor has intensified since 1975 and, with further cutbacks, even more since 1980. But the suburbs have not been without critics. The press daily informs us that suburbanites live stressful lives in stressful environments. Some now live behind locked gates with security guards and dogs on patrol. The 1950s suburbs, frequently treated then as the utopia for raising children, have aged too. Recently, many people have moved to small towns outside statistically defined metropolitan areas to find the quiet life, though many still commute to work in the city or its edges. The wave of decay spreads outward behind the expanding fringe.

Canadians commute too, and the suburbs are in many ways visually similar. But the social conditions are sharply different. Canadian inner cities, including the older pre–World War I suburbs, are largely clean, safe, neat, and orderly, at least in comparison with the United States. Americans notice these qualities: when asked for their impression of Toronto they say "clean." Or if they look more closely, they see people on the streets at night. In the 1970s, the American popular press heaped praise on Toronto as the future alternative urban environment. One writer even said he had seen civilization, and it worked.[5] Implied at home was savagery, or at least insecurity. This essay will examine the American urban experience and approach it from the perspectives of religion, property, class, and governing, since cities are major artifacts of American society.

Observers of America since Alexis de Tocqueville have pointed out the contradictory nature of American society.[6] Before considering the four more particular areas, let us mention two closely-related contradictions: freedom versus collectivism, and the individual versus the community. Freedom, expressed through such catch phrases as "Live Free or Die," as stamped on New Hampshire license plates, the "American Dream" or the "California dream," "new frontiers," "freedom of choice," or just plain "free enterprise," has long been the foundation of American society. With the political swing to the right, it has been stronger of late. No one has the right to stand in the way of entrepreneurs, since it is assumed that in the long run even laggards will benefit. Or better still, everyone should take up the cause of making money, then there would be no laggards. Everyone is free to succeed.

But on the other end of the spectrum is the strong tendency toward a collectivist society with the Pentagon at the top. A recent *Los Angeles Times* article even claims that it has a "stranglehold" on the economy through its central planning function and the parcelling out of contracts to General Dynamics and other large corporations.[7] Americans may be very reluctant collectivists when it comes to welfare; they still have no universal social programmes. But they are positively magnanimous when national security is invoked. The National Defense Education Act allowed scholars to teach summer school for upgrading high school teachers. Under the aegis of defence, the interstate highway system was built, most of it very quickly. Corporations benefit through orders for $300 claw hammers, $800 toilet seats, and $500 ash trays! Even Secretary of Defense, Caspar Weinberger, the arch proponent of increased military spending, has balked at such profligacy. But the beat continues: freedom for individuals is only possible with the utmost security. Freedom also depends on economic growth and development, which since 1940 has largely been based on military expenditures; under Reagan "military" Keynesianism has been even more pronounced. Americans as consumers rush into the bosoms of corporations. The first among fast-food equals, McDonald's, is very close to the consciousness of many middle- and working-class Americans. Perhaps it is not going too far to say that Americans are deferential to McDonald's and to other major corporate symbols. As European retailers in the United States have discovered, "stores have a very distinct national brand orientation because shoppers demand it."[8] Being free, Americans like to believe they are the *least* deferential of any people ever. I would suggest the opposite: as reflected in the popular press, many seem to stand in awe and reverence of the successful. They defer to the clever, entrepreneurial financiers of quick gain, such as T. Boone Pickens, or to the smooth entrepreneurial preachers of easy comfort, such as Orange County's Robert Schuller, as symbols of success.[9] Unlike a medieval lord, Pickens does not hold them in personal thrall, though Schuller may hold his congregation and television audience, and even McDonald's has to hustle to keep ahead. Individual and corporate celebrities come and go. And it is to the abstraction, success, that the knee is bowed. The code words "free enterprise," it can be said, provide the means of status identification for the masses who lack the energy or skill of free enterprisers themselves; they allow them to fantasize about power and success. As Alexis de Tocqueville noted, there is a strong pressure toward conformity: everyone has to believe he is free and so must act on his own behalf. One way to read this is by characterizing America as a business society: everyone should be pursuing success through making money. Freedom's other face is conformity.

Let us look at this issue of the individual and the collective from a slightly different perspective. The individual is praised, but the loss of community is sensed, creating uneasiness for many, even anguish for some. On the one hand, there is the independent male, the cowboy in Marlboro ads, riding alone. No others are present, no women, and no family, where pure macho prevails. Even God is macho: as a bumper sticker puts it, "God, guns and guts make America." Or, as a variation, we are to believe athletes: the "Lord" is their buddy when they survive an ordeal. But, on the other hand, the titles of books in recent times bespeak a desire for community: *The Eclipse of Community; The Search for Community;* or *In Quest of Community.* From these and other writings, it would seem that community should exist and maybe did exist at one time or another, as in Thornton Wilder's *Our Town*, put forward in the depressed 1930s, and in response, intended or not, to the scathing denial of community in the *Main Street* of Sinclair Lewis.[10]

If we look at recent studies of the colonial era, notably the biblical commonwealth of the Puritans, we can see a preoccupation with community. Rural towns of eastern Massachusetts and Connecticut are described as places of covenanted consensus—as closed, corporate, and utopian. Joyce Appleby has recently concluded that "America was not born free, rich, and modern.... Far from turning into modern entrepreneurs, Puritan men became rural patriarchs in towns remarkable for their cohesion and stability. They commanded their wives, controlled their adult sons and daughters, and kept out any deviants who might spoil the sweet harmony of their peaceable kingdoms."[11] Individualism was downplayed.

This belief that community and family values prevailed is a latter-day social version of an early twentieth-century economic definition of the "golden age of homespun."[12] In my view it is a romantic search for roots. John Locke is kept at bay by Appleby (as most scholars would prefer) until the late eighteenth-century or even later, when capitalism mysteriously appears on the scene. The latter-day Marxists are strong supporters of this sentiment since, if America was once upon a time not capitalist, then a revolution in the future will return the country to community and those halcyon days. Presumably the communities would be without patriarchs, but undoubtedly would have "keep out" signs displayed to repel ideological strangers.[13]

This strongly-held historical interpretation of a pre-capitalist early America neatly avoids evidence to the contrary. Most rural New Englanders did not live in nuclear villages—a spatial sign of social cohesion—as has been presumed by most historians. In fact, the General Court of Massachusetts had to retreat on legislation designed to keep farmsteads within a half mile of meeting houses as the settlers dispersed out onto their farmland, as was the case elsewhere in America. In their pursuit of the bucolic citizen, these scholars see cities like Boston as a totally commercialized "other." But Puritans, not just their Yankee descendants, hardly resisted commercial gain. Largely ignored too are padlocks on food storage bins to keep servants honest—or really dishonest. Ignored till recently has been the litigiousness of Essex county residents who took one another to court. A recent interpreter of that scene in fact goes so far as to say that the institution of the county court provided the most important institutional cement of community. Community was maintained not by consensus but by conflict.[14]

Returning to the present, the kind of community presumed lost and sought after by scholars reflecting a widespread belief is a deinstitutionalized, voluntary togetherness, face to face without the mediation of the languages of organizations, without the discipline of organizations, without law. But most Americans seem to adhere unwittingly to the language of national defence, of corporations, and of the courts as the languages of community. The language of unions has no place, as labour solidarity crumbles before the contradictory rhetoric of the "right to work." President Reagan, it seems, has successfully linked the macho image of male dominance to the cuddly feeling of belonging to the one big union, or rather, the one big family of America, trusting in God. But this combination results in a failure or an unwillingness to consider everyday social realities. These contradictions divide people and cities and so create urban wildernesses.

In hoping to bring us closer to an understanding of the urban reality, I will consider four further dimensions of American life, those of religion, property, class and governing, and then mold them together. The religious language of Protestant fundamentalism has been extremely influential, if not dominant, in secular life. While espousing the separation of church and society, Americans have not hesitated to link religion and culture closely.[15] Civil religion has taken up some cardinal notions: very explicitly, salvation; less clearly so, sin. As the individual is saved from sin, the world is in the process of being saved by the American way of life from backwardness and godless *isms*. Manifest destiny is the public counterpart to the individual guarantee of ultimate certainty or perhaps a heavenly though ill-defined New Jerusalem.

The fruit of salvation lies in the future, hence the present is denigrated. The New Jerusalem may shine in the distance, but the old Jerusalems lie in waste, wallowing in sin, like the wilderness found by the Puritans. Beginning in the depression, forays thrust into the old central cities under the campaign slogans of urban renewal and the war on poverty. It almost seemed that American cities—the fabric of roads, watermains, sewers, subways, and housing—had to degenerate to a point where religious enthusiasm could exercise the power of renewal, a form of secular salvation. Urban renewal became the watchword as long as federal funds were forthcoming.

But then a few critics observed that urban renewal made things worse, or at least noted that the deterioration continued. Between 1949 and 1968, 425 000 housing units were torn down but only 125 000 were rebuilt in their places. These critics blamed the federal bulldozer as the poor were forced to move without help.[16] The religious fervour of renewal petered out, largely because the public and private developers had their eye not on redeeming the old, but on building the new, the new that would bring a far bigger return in taxes and profit than public-housing high rise apartment blocks could deliver.

Americans with money pursue profit with a degree of religious enthusiasm not seen elsewhere. If renewal is the first key dimension, property is the second, and it is sacrosanct. More precisely, the right to use and exploit one's property is god-given, and indeed for those driven by the creed of the American way, it is one's obligation. While high technology and defence systems have been more conspicuous consumers of capital, the building and rebuilding of cities has been a central concern. In contrast to the urban development of the nineteenth-century—the great era of city building— postwar urban growth has exhibited not only fervency but has carried a tone of desperation. Since developers were unable to maintain the *relative* pace of nineteenth-century growth, the central government provided massive subsidies to pursue an ever-receding goal of more urban growth. It was ever-receding simply because most of the population had become urbanized. Replacement housing earns less than building brand new housing on newly urbanized land.

Postwar development has followed the dictates of the 1929 Regional Plan of New York.[17] While the professional planners may have been "dreaming the rational city," the business planners had their way.[18] The two main objectives were to suburbanize the population and to build offices in the centre, befitting New York's number one status as America's front office. Suburbanization was not a new phenomenon; with relatively fewer people to build for than in the nineteenth century, the solution was to supply more space, considerably more space per household than before. So aided by widespread car ownership and, after 1949, federal subsidies in tax concessions and loan guarantees, the golden age of homeownership, shopping centres and spacious single-floor factories was introduced. The "vital fringe" underscored the American way: making new urban land enhanced the sense of a new frontier and the reality of new returns.[19]

Following the New York plan, urban renewal was pushed in the inner city. Though the celebrated public housing schemes received more publicity, the major thrusts were primarily private: building office slabs and apartment towers for the affluent. Land that once carried middle- and lower-class housing was transformed also by the great public developers, such as Robert Moses, for opulent public structures such as the Triborough Bridge and the Lincoln Center. In Los Angeles, Dodger Stadium, for example, was placed in Chavez Ravine, reshaped for its vast parking lot.[20] The middle-class and the better-paid working-class moved willingly to suburbs celebrated for raising children. The poor were pushed out—a minority into high-rise blocks the critics saw as dreary, others into districts with increasingly deteriorating housing.

As early as 1952, David Rockefeller of Chase Manhattan Bank and an important advocate of the New York plan was admitting that the plan was working too well in suburbanizing people and activities.[21] The transit system, largely ignored in 1929, was deteriorating. Too many offices had actually followed the suburban exodus. Too few rich were living in the centre. What had happened was the creation of a vacuum: the older housing was either occupied by the increasing numbers of marginalized poor or was being abandoned. But planning measures stressing transit and upper-income housing came too late. Desperate measures, such as tax-free municipal bonds bought by the banks, only dragged New York down further eventually into the sink of a fiscal crisis.[22] Elsewhere the great industrial cities saw their turn-of-the-century industrial landscapes decay as the fringes of sun belt cities successfully gained the new technologies and new towns.

In most recent times, the central business districts of the financially-powerful cities, especially New York, have been captive to ever more office and luxury housing development, as the allure of prestige is the engine of growth. As in the late 1920s, superspeculation has, it would seem, set up cities for another crash. Cities without financial power have not seen their centres rebuilt. The Renaissance Center has not led to a renewal of central Detroit.

Property rights have been exercised. Politicians, financed by those with property, have been willing to subsidize the building of the "slab-spread" city and indeed build the infrastructure of expressways, water, and sewer lines.[23] The result is a distorted, even grotesque urban landscape of sharp differences. The rights of property were entrenched in actions in those early

New England villages. Today the poor survive on potentially valuable land waiting for the bulldozers of the developers. Mini-armageddons inflicted on the poor are hardly noticed

The third dimension is class. America, we have been told, is a classless society.[24] Another form of the statement is that America is a future-oriented society; that is, if disparities still persist they will disappear because Americans will work hard individually to overcome them. To be concerned with class is to be concerned with present conditions of the common life, and hence raise the problem of equality, something more than equality of opportunity or of access, more than Head Start programs, or the promotion of equal opportunity in President Johnson's War on Poverty.

Because of growth and the continued expectation of growth, class issues have been avoided in America much too easily. Hence, there is a strong tendency to ignore what does not fit the vision of classlessness. So inner-city conditions have been largely out of the line of vision since 1945, and in large measure because blacks have come to be the quintessential residents. For the few who notice, shadowy, nearly-redundant males, delinquent boys, and single mothers fill the picture in rundown houses or vast public housing projects. Only a few sterling athletes who succeed as tokens of black progress alter the scene. In the nineteenth and early twentieth centuries the burgeoning metropolises of the northeast and midwest developed their ethnic slums. But these were the first rung on the ladder for most ethnics. The metropolises were vehicles for upward mobility. European immigrants, or at least most of their children and grandchildren, worked their way up through the maze. By 1930, in Chicago at least, according to Thomas Philpott, the experiences of ghettos and slums were no longer a fact of life for most immigrants. The most ghettoized, the Poles, remained only 60 per cent concentrated.[25]

But at the same time 90 per cent of blacks were in ghettos in the relentlessly expanding black belt slums. The cost of escaping was great for many ethnics, but it has been far worse for blacks, fighting even to find a niche for survival in poverty. The creation of black neighbourhoods through "blockbusting" of white districts has continued since black Harlem was created in the early twentieth century. Today suburban residential segregation is still marked even for the modest number of professional blacks, as white, middle-class neighbourhoods continue to resist blacks. Despite the marches of the early 1960s and the subsequent riots, black gains are still token. The creation and maintenance of a largely black underclass allows the lower- and moderate-income whites—the "Archie Bunkers"—to puff up their egos. They can feel themselves to be permanently a cut above the blacks. So, after rising in the 1960s and 1970s, black incomes have fallen back to less than 60 per cent of whites.[26]

The dimension of governance is fourth. In his recent book, *Unheralded Triumph*, Jon Teaford has argued that those rapidly growing metropolises of the last century did cope in providing services. Most annexed the growing fringes to maintain the sense of one collective whole.[27] The triumph was unheralded, however, because no one could safely claim credit for the improvements—neither business reformers, large and small, nor other professionals, nor ward and city bosses. All contributed but they could not recognize a collective achievement in the midst of their warring politics. The pursuit of power based on division by class as defined by ethnicity and occupational status was too strong. Hence, the governing of cities was an uncertain task. Fragmented urban areas became the twentieth-century norm.

The arrival of the blacks in large numbers after 1900 and especially after 1914 seems to have destabilized the governing of cities further. Their migration coincided with the weakening impulse to run metropolises efficiently and to annex suburbs. Blacks were arriving when Henry Ford announced in 1912 that he would solve the problems of the city by moving the people out of the city. After 1912, socialism faded and with it a short period of working-class power in running cities. Suburbanization captures the imagination of the upwardly mobile. So-called race riots at the end of the war were followed by a mania of zoning and restrictive covenants intent on the exclusion of strangers, particularly blacks.[28] Since these measures only partially prevented blockbusting, as realtors ignored the rules, whites continued to move out to suburban enclaves. Again, property had its way. In the 1950s and 1960s the public developers, like Robert Moses, while building high-rise ghettos, showed little interest in questions of adequate incomes.[29] Then, the taxes collected in inner cities fell as suburban municipalities, state governments and the office-building owners failed to pay their share of maintaining services on the vast residential districts of the poor. "Deplanning" became frequent. Ultimately fiscal crises hit the cities, and the federal government had to step in to maintain a modicum of order, though the national leaders such as Richard Nixon and Gerald Ford were reluctant to help.[30]

Governing municipalities and states has not been an easy task in America since the beginning: local control by local elites has been strong. William Pynchon was the founder of the company town, Springfield, and one of the prominent adventurers who led the Puritans across the Atlantic away from centralized control. But he soon complained, too, about the influence of the General Court: "If the magistrates in N.E. (New England) should *ex officio* practice such power over men's properties, how long would Tyranny be kept out of our habitations?"[31] But escape to the new frontier, sanctioned by a piety that invoked providence for those saved from original sin and reflected in their property holdings, could hardly lay a firm basis for citizenship, nor for governing. In New England, some were warned out of the towns and so excluded from citizenship. In recent times, since the task of warning out has become insuperable, the saved move to escape as it were the sin of the inner cities. It seems the blacks carry the burden of sin today.

If there is any truth in Teaford's view that late nineteenth-century northern metropolises were a triumph of organizational ability, then, when electrified streetcars and especially the car arrived, those same cities turned their backs on the new minorities of Hispanics, but more especially blacks.[32]

This meant the abandonment of many areas of inner cities by whites. Further, without the status of conveniently coloured minorities, other ethnics might not have risen so markedly nor allowed white Americans to perpetuate, even to strengthen, the myth of the classless society. Racism—actually a case of forcing people into a nearly untouchable caste or class—fed by the property industries and the ideology of futuristic religion, created fragmentation and sharply separated the living environments of the rich from those of the poor, and the office concentrations of the corporations and the government from the ghettos around them.

The American city is a wilderness according to Sam Warner and others. The Puritan errand into the wilderness has turned in on itself: in the centre is the wilderness defined by unsafe, drug-driven streets, and the madness of financial institutions in the core.[33] Futuristic religion, property rights, a belief in classlessness, and an inability to govern have combined into a potent brew of self-destruction. The presence of visible minorities allows whites to reject universal social welfare schemes. There are no lynchings in the north, but in the nearly ungovernable cities, vigilantes take the law into their own hands. There is little late nineteenth-century talk of race superiority, but the practice remains. Blacks are far more frequently incarcerated and are more often the victims of violence than whites. The Puritans believed in original sin, and the notion seems very much alive in the America of today. In a society so strongly addicted to salvationism, even to armageddons, it is easier to transfer the burden to minorities than to bear the cross oneself, than to struggle through the agony of who is or is not saved, as did the first-generation Puritans.

I will sum up with this formula. To fend off sin, the American believes in future immortality for the individual. In its civic form, this promotes new frontiers, the American Dream, and such futuristic notions as the Strategic Defense Initiative ("Star Wars") to ensure America's status as the top power. Economic development is absolutely crucial; the system cannot be allowed to stagnate. Hence property rights are bolstered at any cost, investment seeks new possibilities, the business ethos is sanctioned, and those with money then are subsidized through supply-side giveaways. The successful in business are adulated because they have commanded the future. They do not look back. Left behind, even condemned, are those who would live in the present—many whites by choice or default and the disproportionate number of poor blacks who have no choice. Because they refuse to move, or cannot, they pay, by living in crumbling environments.

Environment and people cannot be separated. Fallows admits that the Urban America presidential commission's "'people, not places' policy must be built on an understanding of why 'place' matters to so many people."[34] Even though he recognizes the pain of those left in deindustrializing cities, or areas of cities, he cannot accept a view that places and environments, and hence the people living in them, have integrity. This is yet another expression of a society with not only a weak sense of collective goods but also with only a weak sense of geography, or worse a distorted sense. The only good of a fallen sinful environment is its availability for exploitation which is then abandoned when exhausted. Some latter-day wilderness areas in cities will probably be conquered once again by speculators. Where is the middle ground—the "middle landscape" of gardens and safe streets?[35] A recent call by the president of the National Geographic Society for more geography in American schools is a step in the right direction to create greater environmental awareness. But the glossy photos in his journal of far away places, if less romantic and more realistic than earlier, probably divert most readers from appreciating their more immediate living spaces.[36]

Let me underline the force of instability in American urban environments. A few years ago I showed the sights of Toronto to an historian of the United States visiting from China. Up in the CN Tower, we overheard two couples, obviously American, wondering how big Toronto was. Not being able to resist using my expertise on Toronto, I leaned over to inform that the census area was 3 million, Metropolitan Toronto 2.1 million, and the City of Toronto 600 000. Then I learned that they were holidaying from Detroit. Again not being able to resist, I observed that Detroit's population had thinned out considerably in recent decades. Instantaneously came the comment that blacks had driven the whites out of the city. This intrepid scholar of the American scene shot back: "Well that is *one* way to interpret what happened." End of debate, end of discourse. Enjoying a relaxed urban holiday depended upon forgetting their own environment.

Notes

1. Sam B. Warner, *The Urban Wilderness: A History of the American City* (New York: Harper and Row, 1972); Katherine L. Bradbury, Anthony Downs, and Kenneth A. Small, *Urban Decline and the Future of American Cities* (Washington D.C.: Brookings Institution, 1982); William K. Tabb, *The Long Default: New York City and the Urban Fiscal Crisis* (New York: Monthly Review Press, 1982); David R. Goldfield and Blaine Brownell, *Urban America: From Downtown to No Town* (Boston: Houghton Mifflin, 1979); Jon C. Teaford, *City and Suburb: The Political Fragmentation of Metropolitan America* (Baltimore: Johns Hopkins University Press, 1979).

2. Jane Jacobs, *Death and Life of Great American Cities*, rev. ed. (New York: Vintage, 1961); Upton Sinclair, *The Jungle*, rev. ed. (New York: Harper and Row, 1951); Stephen Crane, *Maggie: A Girl of the Streets* rev. ed. (New York: Fawcett, 1960).

3. James Fallows, "America's Changing Economic Landscape," *The Atlantic*, No. 255 (March, 1985) pp. 47-68; President's Commission for a National Agenda for the Eighties, *Urban America in the Eighties: Perspectives and Prospects for Metropolitan and Non-Metropolitan America* (Englewood Cliffs, N.J.: Prentice Hall, 1981).

4. Herbert Gans, *The Urban Villagers* (New York: Free Press, 1962); Andrew Greeley, *Neighborhood* (New York: Continuum Publishing Co., 1977).

5. Arthur Herschman, "Foreign Travel," *Science* 210 (14 November 1980), p. 763; James Lemon, "Introduction," *Toronto Since 1918: An Illustrated History* (Toronto: Lorimer, 1985); James Lemon, "Toronto Among North American Cities," in *Forging a Consensus: Historical Essays on Toronto*, Victor L. Russell, ed. (Toronto: University of Toronto Press, 1984). See also Michael A. Goldberg, "Comparisons of Canadian and American Cities," in this volume.

6. Alexis de Tocqueville, *Democracy in America* 1835–1840 2 vol. (New York: Vintage, 1945).

7. Rone Tempest, "Pentagon's Stranglehold on U.S.," *Los Angeles Times* as reprinted in the

Toronto Star, 10 July 1983; Richard Hallman, "Why U.S. Military Can't Rely on Weapons," *ibid*, 8 December 1985; "Defence Jobs Better Paid," *The Globe and Mail*, 23 November 1985; "Defence Firms Create Costly Problem for Pentagon," *ibid.*, 11 December 1985; "Feiffer,"*ibid.*, 13 January 1986.

8. "European Retailers Encounter Woe in their Ventures into the U.S. Market," *ibid.*, 21 January 1986. "Defence Firms Create Costly Problem for Pentagon," *ibid.*, 11 December 1985.

9. Richard Stengel, "The Apostle of Sunny Thoughts," *Time*, 125 (March, 1985), p. 66.

10. M.R. Stein, *The Eclipse of Community: An Interpretation of American Studies* (Princeton, N.J.: Princeton University Press, 1960); Edward Digby Baltzell, *The Search for Community in Modern America* (New York: Harper and Row, 1963); R. Jackson Wilson, *In Quest of Community: Social Philosophy in the United States, 1860–1920* (New York: John Wiley and Sons, 1968); Thornton Wilder, *Our Town: A Play in Three Acts* (New York: Harper and Row, 1938). See Donald W. Meinig, "Symbolic Landscapes: Some Idealizations of American Communities" in *The Interpretation of Ordinary Landscapes*, ed. Donald W. Meinig (New York: Oxford University Press, 1979), pp. 164-172; Sinclair Lewis, *Main Street* (New York: Harcourt, Brace and World, 1920).

11. Joyce Appleby, *Capitalism and a New Social Order: The Republican Vision of the 1790's* (New York: New York University Press, 1984), p. 7.

12. Percy W. Bidwell and John I. Falconer, *History of Agriculture in the Northern United States, 1620–1980* (Washington, D.C., The Carnegie Institute of Washington, 1925).

13. James T. Lemon, "Spatial Order: Households in Local Communities and Regions" in *Colonial British America: Essays in the New History of the Early Modern Era*, ed. Jack P. Greene and J.R. Pole (Baltimore: Johns Hopkins University Press, 1984), pp. 86-122.

14. Laurel Ulrich, "Food Theft and Domestic Conflict, 1661–1682" in *Foodways of the Northeast*, ed. Peter Benes and Jane Benes (Boston: Boston University Press, 1984); David Thomas Konig, *Law and Society in Puritan Massachusetts: Essex County, 1629–1692* (Chapel Hill: University of North Carolina Press, 1979).

15. Russell E. Richey and Donald G. Jones, eds., *American Civil Religion* (New York, Harper and Row, 1974).

16. Howard P. Chudacoff, *The Evolution of American Urban Society*, 2nd ed. (Englewood Cliffs, N.J.: Prentice-Hall, 1981), p. 288.

17. Robert Fitch, "Planning New York" in *The Fiscal Crisis of American Cities: Essays on the Political Economy of Urban America with Special Reference to New York*, ed. Roger E. Alcaly and David Mermelstein (New York: Vintage, 1977), pp. 246-284.

18. Christine Boyer, *Dreaming the Rational City: The Myth of American City Planning* (Cambridge: MIT Press, 1983).

19. Goldfield and Brownell, *Urban America*, Part IV.

20. Thomas H. Hines, "Housing, Baseball, and Creeping Socialism: The Battle of Chavez Ravine, Los Angeles, 1949–1959," *Journal of Urban History*, 8 (1982), pp. 123-143.

21. Fitch, "Planning New York," p. 279. *Cf.* Robert Caro, *The Power Broker: Robert Moses and the Fall of New York* (New York: Knopf, 1974; Vintage, 1975).

22. Alcaly and Mermelstein, *Fiscal Crisis*.

23. Fitch, "Planning New York."

24. Mary R. Jackman and Robert W. Jackman, *Class Awareness in the United States* (Berkeley: University of California Press, 1983).

25. Thomas Philpott, *The Slum and the Ghetto: Neighborhood Deterioration and Middle Class Reform, 1880–1930* (New York: Oxford University Press, 1978).

26. Gilbert Osofsky, *Harlem: The Making of a Ghetto: Negro New York, 1890–1930* (New York: Harper and Row, 1966); Andrew H. Malcolm, "New Generation of Poor Youth Emerges in America," *The New York Times*, 20 October 1985; "Racists Spoil Black Families' Dreams," *Toronto Star*, 24 November 1985; William Johnson, "Poor Have Got Poorer, Rich Richer under Reagan, U.S. Study Shows," *The Globe and Mail*, 16 August 1984.

27. Jon C. Teaford, *Unheralded Triumph: City Government in America, 1870–1900* (Baltimore: Johns Hopkins University Press, 1984).

28. Mel Scott, *American City Planning Since 1890* (Berkeley: University of California Press,

Comparisons of American and Canadian Cities

Michael A. Goldberg

1. Introduction

The questions addressed by this essay were raised originally as a result of a task force on housing, led by the then Minister of Transportation, who was responsible for urban affairs, Paul Hellyer. He concluded unequivocally in 1968 that Canada was on the brink of an urban crisis, and that the federal government had to move very quickly to stem the looming decay and destruction of the Canadian city.[1] This destruction or decay was not very much in evidence at the time. Two years later Harvey Lithwick also did a study for the federal government, and he concluded, once again, the crisis was still looming and that the federal government had to create new policy.[2] Since it was unconstitutional to set up a Federal Department of Urban Affairs under the British North America Act, the Ministry of State for Urban Affairs was created. While Federal departments have line and legislative respon-sibilities, ministries of state had no such responsibilities; they cut across departmental lines and programs. The Ministry of State for Urban Affairs was abolished in 1978, a demise not unrelated to the viability of Canadian central cities.

This inability to see an urban crisis in Canada's major cities sparked an interest in further research. Thus, when the American Planning Association had its annual meeting in Vancouver in 1975, I took part in writing a paper introducing Americans to Canadian cities.[3] The paper suggested that, while the cities may look similar, selling the same gasoline and toothpaste, they function very differently when you get behind the billboards. This caused me to ask some elemental questions about Canadian and American cities.

In 1978, John Mercer and I began working together. What follows is in essence an abstract of our book.[4] Our basic theme is that we have been so inundated by the American urban metaphor, that we have not taken time until very recently to ask if the metaphor is pertinent to the Canadian experience. Or even that of the United States. If it does not fit, then it is pointless for Canadians to borrow policies from the Americans. Moreover, if it does not fit in the United States, it is silly even for Americans to develop crisis-based urban policies.

Therefore we will be arguing first that cities are developed in a cultural context.[5] Cultures differ between Canada and the United States, and thus there is no reason to believe that cities should be the same in the two countries. Additionally, if Canadian cities are different from American cities, then this suggests that the whole corpus of urban research, which has been done in the United States and then taken as given around the Western world, is highly unlikely to be relevant in Canada. And, if we cannot adapt American research to the Canadian city, we are not going to make the American city travel very well across the oceans. This would clearly call into question the generality of the American urban model.

However, we also want to suggest that the American urban model might not even work well in the American context. To do all this, we argue against two interesting and opposing traditions. On the one hand is the traditional urban economic approach, which says that economic forces shape and drive the city. Once you accept this economic primacy and forget culture, it does not make any difference whether it is an American city or a European city, since the same basic forces and laws will be at work. This tradition says that cities are economically determined, and they can be comprehended by ascertaining basic economic relationships, most of which have been developed and tested in the United States.[6]

On the other hand there are the Marxists, who, ironically, also say that cities are economically determined, although they do not like the outcome. In a nutshell, the economic forces of capitalism drive cities, and thus cities should not differ, so long as they are products of advanced capitalist societies.[7] Suggesting that Canadian cities may be very different from American cities also indicates that both of these traditions may have to address some basic questions about their utility in explaining urban development, form, and function.

2. Contexts

First, we will examine briefly some of the differing cultural contexts of cities in Canada and the United States. Here, culture is used very broadly to include economic culture, political culture, social values, and their accompanying institutions. Next, having reviewed this "cultural" literature on the United States and Canada, we will look at our urban findings.

The institution of property requires preliminary comment, because it is so essentially different in the two countries and because it forms the basis for urban development. With respect to urban development we are clearly discussing property development. In the United States individuals can own land, and property rights are vested in the individual landowner. The fifth and fourteenth amendments to the United States Constitution explicitly guarantee such rights. In Canada, in a technical sense, no individual owns land. Her Majesty owns the land. We may own a fee simple interest in the land but not the land itself. This means that if Her Majesty wants her land back, she may take it. For example, under the Limited Access Highways Act, the province of British Columbia may not compensate landowners for up to 5 per cent of their property fronting on a limited access highway. The idea is that it is bestowing access, and therefore the gain to the property owner is offset by the property loss. Such an act would most likely be unconstitutional in the United States. It is also instructive to realise that the Canadian Charter of Rights and Freedoms granted a broad array of rights to Canadians. But property rights (partially as a result of the American experience) were explicitly excluded. Some constitutional scholars believe that when one has a constitution with enunciated rights, and there are classes of rights that are left unenunciated, those unenunciated rights have no force.[8] Thus the decision in Canada is to rank property rights at a much lower level than other civil liberties. These rather divergent traditions have very considerable consequences for the development of cities in Canada and the United States.

Within the cultural context, we ought first to look at social values. There are several areas to discuss, although I am not including reams of tables and supporting data within this essay.[9] Consider the mosaic versus melting-pot myths. The truth of each myth is less important than the fact that Canadians cling to the mosaic myth and Americans to the melting-pot. As most scholars of mythology tell us, the fact that a society clings to a myth is of vital importance. The Canadian mosaic myth has taken an interesting twist in the form of a federal Ministry of State for Multiculturalism. This contrasts with the notion of the "fellow Americans" whose support was frequently solicited by Lyndon Johnson. In urban areas the myth manifests itself in the very distinctive ways we view agglomerations of different ethnic groups. In Canada we call them ethnic neighbourhoods. The neighbourhood metaphor works; the American metaphor of the ghetto does not work. American ghettos are viewed as aberrations, since they have not melted, whereas in Canada these strongly ethnic neighbourhoods are viewed as essential elements in the urban cultural mosaic.

The second social value of importance to many economists and political scientists relates to the conflict between individualism and collectivism. Americans pride themselves on the rugged individualist frontier; while we, in Canada, for a number of reasons, have had to be a more collective society. When we look at an urban setting, this should manifest itself in much greater American reliance on private automobiles, on single family homes, and on private initiatives in general. In fact, this is the case in the United States.

There are notable differences such as race and respect for authority. One of the less persuasive books I have read was written in 1980 by Edgar Friedenberg, called *Deference to Authority*.[10] He imposed essentially American civil libertarian values on a Canadian social order. Friedenberg never bothered to ask the central question: are Canadians deferential because there is not much to protest about? In American cities, as I discovered in Boston, when the sign says "Don't Walk," one is evidently invited to rush across the street. This is a very perverse way of exercising one's constitutional rights. Alternatively, the extent to which Canadians defer to the authority of the red light is striking. Clearly we have a very different tradition. With the North West Mounted Police, law preceded development, as opposed to the American tradition of law following settlement. This has urban consequences as well in the lack of law and order in the American central city.

Finally, there is a very long tradition, going back to Jefferson and before, of Americans stating that they do not like cities.[11] A strong intellectual tradition in the United States is clearly anti-urban and it continues to evolve right up to the present time: planning literature is rife with such hostility, and certainly the post–1970 movement to non-metropolitan areas in the United States exhibits it. A fair amount of behavioural information suggests in contrast that Canadians really do like cities.[12]

Looking at economic values and institutions, the Canadian economy is really very different from the American economy, with significant urban implications. Canada is still very much a colonial economy, despite a high per capita income.[13] Indeed, the vaunted trade between Canada and the United States is very similar in kind to the trade the United States would have with Nigeria or other producers of natural products. Canada sells unfinished or semi-finished natural resource products and imports high-value-added manufactured goods. So despite the similar income levels between Canada and the United States and despite the similar degrees of urbanization, the economies themselves are really very different. Canada has come through the colonial era, in Wallace Clement's terms, a "comprador economy" used to servicing the colonial economy.[14] Finance institutions are an interesting result of that era; Canada has a disproportionate number of very large banks. They are large on a world scale, not just in a Canadian context. In the Canadian economy there is still a heavy reliance on taking natural resources, finishing them slightly, and exporting them. Servicing that export process with marketing, government, and financial institutions makes the Canadian economy very different.

One of the consequences for cities of differing economies is evidenced in the behaviour of income savers. Up to the mid–1970s in the United States and Canada, savings seemed to run very constantly between 4 and 6 per cent of earnings. This strange phenomenon was a kind of universal constant. Then in the mid–1970s, the rate of Canadian savings rose suddenly to double digits, and the American rate of savings fell to the 2 to 3 per cent level. That is not unrelated to financial institutions, and it is not unrelated to the fact that in Canada ironically, in the land of socialism, an unregulated financial market exists.[15] Paradoxically, the United States, which boasts about free enterprise, has a very tightly regulated savings sector, which greatly distorts the public's saving behaviour. As a result, most savings flow into investment and mortgage markets, which are the chief beneficiaries.

Mortgage debt is *the* debt in North America. The Canadian capacity to fund that debt through very high savings levels has allowed us to keep our cities reasonably healthy.

Another element under the heading of economic values and institutions is the fact that Canadians have not had any great aversion to public enterprise. In fact, Herschel Hardin, in a challenging book called *A Nation Unaware*, suggests the Canadian economic edge is achieved through public enterprise, where the American edge is clearly through private enterprise.[16] As a result, there is no revulsion in Canada against using governments to shape society. As a consequence, a whole host of crown corporations are actively involved in promoting varying aspects of the "public good."

In discussing the last of the contextual issues, political values and institutions, the focus will be on federalism.[17] The frequently stated fact that both countries are federal in nature is a very alluring but shallow similarity. American federalism bears no relationship to Canadian federalism, and it is somewhat of an irony, as Canadian Roger Gibbins points out in his book on regionalism in the United States. The whole notion of asking Americans about regional loyalty (e.g., are you more loyal to your region than to your nation?) would be so strange that Americans would not be able to answer.[18] In Canada, it is a perfectly legitimate question but, depending on where you ask it, you cannot be at all sure what the answer will be.[19]

A strange role reversal has occurred here. The United States was designed as a highly decentralized (or weak) system of loosely federated states meant to guarantee states' rights. All unenumerated (residual) rights and powers were not given to the federal government but to the states. The original Canadian constitutional document, the British North America Act (1867), was designed in reverse, with the Civil War being fresh in the minds of the Fathers of Confederation. There was to be a very strong central government, and all residual rights were allotted to the federal government. The provinces did have specific enumerated powers, but essentially the federal government was supposed to dominate. It turned out that the courts in both countries changed the original design. The Judicial Committee of the Privy Council in London remodelled Canadian federalism; the United States Supreme Court greatly expanded federal power. As well, some of the areas that were strictly for the provinces (property rights, cities, matters of a private and local nature, and education) have been growth industries in the last hundred years. The areas of jurisdiction for which the provinces were responsible grew very dramatically, and thus the provinces have a very important role in the Canadian federal system; this is very important when we look at cities. The demise of the Ministry of State for Urban Affairs is indicative of the way Canada has solved urban issues: we have let the "urbans" do it themselves. That is a dramatic and different approach from the United States. The provinces own the cities, and the cities themselves set their urban policy in concert with provincial priorities. Canada has repeatedly tried to forge a national urban policy, luckily with no marked success, and as a result the federal government plays a residual role in urban policy. Thus Canada can have local policies for local issues, which is very important because local property markets are just that; they are highly localized. Cities have highly individual problems which should be treated in highly localized ways.

The federal structure of the two countries is extremely important when we consider the two sets of cities. The United States federal government has a massive presence, through highways, educational expenditures, and direct spending on urban affairs. It also has the capacity to mandate the behaviour of local areas by restricting its largesse to cities. The Canadian federal government has no such capacity, and indeed when it tried to develop one during the 1970s, the provinces made it very clear that they would be happy to take money from the federal government and then give it to their cities as they chose. In sum, Canada has an urban-based, urban policy-making system.

To summarize, important differences between American and Canadian societies include the relatively greater collectivism in Canada versus the relatively greater individualism in the United States; much greater corresponding role for, and acceptance of, government action in Canada; and the differing institutions of property rights. Based on these contextual differences, we should expect cities in Canada to be different and indeed they are.

Our research to date has looked at a diversity of urban differences, including urban form and density (related to transportation), population characteristics, the urban private economy, and the urban public economy. These variables together identify a very distinctive set of cities called Canadian cities, and another set called American cities, with essentially no overlap.[20]

3. Urban Differences

Independently of our work, a colleague, Barry Edmonston of Cornell University was calculating density gradients. He measures the central population density in a city and sees how quickly it declines to the urban periphery. Edmonston made these calculations for American and Canadian metropolitan areas with a result that he could not explain. We had the explanation but we did not have the data.[21] Canadian central densities from 1940 onward have consistently been twice American central densities, while density gradients were at least as steep, all of which suggests a much more compact Canadian urban form. This is borne out by public urban transit patronage, per capita; there is 2.5 times as much use of such transit in Canada as in the United States. Turning to freeways, we needed a comparative measure so we reduced lane miles of freeway in metropolitan areas to a per capita base. There were 4.33 times as many of these lane miles per capita in the urban United States, as there were in urban Canada. Unfortunately, we did not receive data from California and Texas, so our result is obviously understated.

Finally, when you consider the way Canadians travel to work compared with Americans, 65 per cent of Canadians use private cars, whereas 85 per cent of Americans do so. Interestingly, 8 per cent of Canadians walk. All this suggests much denser Canadian urban areas, which are more reliant on public transportation than in the United States.

Looking at population characteristics, Canadian central cities have experienced much greater household change. Over the decade of the 1970s this averaged roughly 30 per cent: that is, a 30 per cent increase in households contained in central cities, compared with an 11.5 per cent increase in American central cities. If we review the ratio of central city incomes to metropolitan area incomes, using medians again, Canadian central city median income to the ratio of metropolitan income was 98 per cent, compared to 91 per cent in the United States. That is very significant statistically. If we consider the percentage of traditional families (husband, wife and children at home) for 1970, the traditional family made up 57 per cent of households in Canadian central cities. Only 40 per cent of American central city households were traditional family households. If you look at race, clearly a big difference, 17 per cent of residents were non-white in United States central cities, versus 2 per cent non-white in Canadian central cities. Interestingly, if we look at foreign born, there were 4 per cent foreign born in American central cities, and 16.5 per cent foreign born in Canadian central cities. Again, Canada is not totally out of touch by having a Minister of State for Multicultural Affairs.

In the urban private economy, once more there is a much greater concentration of activity in the Canadian central city. Looking at wholesaling establishments in the early 1970s, 77 per cent of all metropolitan area wholesaling establishments were in the Canadian central city, as opposed to 61 per cent in the United States. From the early 1970s, 76 per cent of all retail trade in the metro area was in the Canadian central city, compared with 60 per cent in the American central city. Finally, the figure for services is 82 per cent in Canada's central cities versus 66 per cent in American central cities. The picture that emerges is that the Canadian central urban economy is alive and well and shows no sign of diminution. American central areas do not fare as well on average.

Several things about the urban public economy are striking. John Mercer developed an index of municipal fragmentation: the number of governments in a metropolitan area per 100 000 people.[22] That measure was more than 2.5 times as great in the United States as the equivalent measure in Canada. We compared Seattle and Vancouver, which are roughly the same size. Seattle had 246 governments; Vancouver had 46 governments. Almost 20 of those 46 were a regional government in Vancouver that we broke up into 20 separate functions, so the figure for Vancouver is somewhat overstated.

The fiscal health of Canadian central cities also contrasts dramatically with American. All of the Canadian cities that had an American bond rating were rated higher than American central cities. Moreover, during the decade of the 1970s, Canadian central city bond ratings increased, while American central city bond ratings largely showed either decline or stability.[23]

Finally, the statistics on urban crime are rather interesting. For violent crime, crimes against people, Canadian central cities have one sixth as much violent crime as their American counterparts. Yet, for non-violent crime, crimes against urban property, the rates are essentially the same in the two countries. In short, you are just as likely to be the victim of a burglary in a Canadian central city, but much less likely to be mugged by the burglar.

Our last approach was to combine these numerous single variable differences into a rather complex statistical framework that looks at how these individual variables interact. Thus when we evaluated multi-variate measures, Canadian cities could be separated from American cities to a very high level of statistical reliability. In other words, the set of characteristics that describe and differentiate Canadian cities from those in the United States is well defined.

4. Concluding Comments

Canada and the United States are distinct. Not surprisingly Canadian and American cities are distinct. What this implies is that Canada and the United States must form their own distinct policy sets to deal with their urban areas. It further implies that the result of the transfer of urban policies from one country to the other is very unlikely to be successful. Moreover, one of the striking phenomena of our statistical measures is the fact that the dispersion (variation) within the American city set was enormous. Therefore we took central tendencies, or averages, for our comparisons. But when one looks at dispersion within the set of American cities, it was very large. There are numerous very healthy American cities that are still fiscally sound, but on average they tend to be dragged down by cities that face the more traditional crises. This suggests that the United States should not really have a national urban policy either, because cities are local entities which require very different and locally specific policies and programs. Our most probable conclusion is that, when all is said and done, policy-makers and researchers must be much more sensitive to local differences and much less inclined to making the broad generalities that academics are prone to do.

We have started to delineate these differences and hope other people will refine our work. We also strongly hope that policy makers will be somewhat more sensitive to local particulars than they have been in the past; and they should try to build on the needs, desires, and problems facing each urban area where policy is directed.

Notes

1. Canada, Task Force on Housing and Urban Development, *Report of the Federal Task Force on Housing and Urban Development* (Ottawa: Queen's Printer, January, 1969).

2. Canada, A Report Prepared by N.H. Lithwick for the Honourable R.K. Andras, Minister Responsible for Housing, *Urban Canada: Problems and Prospects* (Ottawa: Central Mortgage and Housing Corporation, January, 1970).

3. See Michael A. Goldberg and Michael Y. Seelig, "Canadian Cities: The Right Deed for the Wrong Reason," *Planning*, 41(3), 1975, pp. 8-13.

4. Michael A. Goldberg and John Mercer, *The Myth of the North American City: Continentalism Challenged* (Vancouver: University of British Columbia Press, 1986). The work discussed in this essay has been carried out over the past six or seven years with my colleague John Mercer of Syracuse University. We bring some very different, yet highly complementary views and skills to bear on the issues of cities in Canada and the United States.

5. This point is in fact the focus of a recent book by John Mercer and his colleagues. See John Agnew, John Mercer, and David Sopher, eds., *The City in a Cultural Context* (Boston: Allen and Unwin, 1984).

6. Goldberg and Mercer, *The Myth of the North American City*, Ch. 1.

7. *Ibid.*

8. William R. McKercher, "The United States Bill of Rights: Implications for Canada," and Douglas A. Schmeiser, "Entrenchment Revisited: The Effect of the Canadian Charter of Rights and Freedoms" in William R. McKercher, ed., *The U.S. Bill of Rights and the Canadian Charter of Rights and Freedoms* (Toronto: Ontario Economic Council, 1983).

9. Rather than going over the details of our analysis, I have just provided selected highlights of societal level differences between Canada and the United States. The details of these differences can be found in Goldberg and Mercer, *Myth of the North American City*, Ch. 2–5, and the implications of these differences for cities are in Ch. 6.

10. Edgar Z. Friedenberg, *Deference to Authority* (Montreal: Harvest House, 1980).

11. See Thomas Jefferson, *Notes on the State of Virginia* [1784], ed. William Peden (Chapel Hill: University of North Carolina Press, 1955), p. 13.

12. Two of the most complete surveys of American and Canadian attitudes toward cities are to be found in Office of Policy Development and Research, *A Survey of Citizen Views and Concerns About Urban Life* (Washington, D.C.: U.S. Department of Housing and Urban Development, HUD-PDR-306, May, 1978), and Canada Mortgage and Housing Corporation, *Public Priorities in Urban Canada: A Survey of Community Concerns* (Ottawa: C.M.H.C., 1979).

13. This argument is detailed in Goldberg and Mercer, *Myth of the North American City*, Ch. 4, along with other facets of the economic differences between the two countries.

14. See Wallace Clement, *Continental Corporate Power* (Toronto: McClelland and Stewart, 1977).

15. A compelling analysis of the differences in Canadian and American mortgage and capital markets, and the paradox of greater laissez faire in the Canadian mortgage market, can be found in George Gau and Lawrence D. Jones, "Canadian Experience with Interest Rate Risk and Rollover Mortgages," (Vancouver: Urban Land Economics Division, Faculty of Commerce, University of British Columbia, Working Paper # 22, 1982).

16. See Herschel Hardin, *A Nation Unaware* (Vancouver: J.J. Douglas, 1974).

17. For a more complete discussion of differences in the political system between Canada and the United States, and a fuller analysis of federalism in the two countries, see Goldberg and Mercer, *Myth of the North American City*, Ch. 5.

18. See Roger Gibbins, *Regionalism: Territorial Policies in Canada and the United States* (Toronto: Butterworths, 1982).

19. Strong regional ties in Canada were elicited in survey work reported in David J. Elkins and Richard Simeon, *Small Worlds: Provinces and Parties in Canadian Political Life* (Toronto: Methuen, 1980), Ch. 1.

20. The empirical analyses of urban differences are presented in Goldberg and Mercer, *Myth of the North American City*, Ch. 7–9. Ch. 7 examines differences across single dimensions such as density, race, etc., for Canadian and American cities, while Ch. 8 explores differences, again one variable at a time, for the urban public and private economies of the two countries. Finally, in Ch. 9 the multidimensional statistical analysis is carried out.

21. Differences in urban density are detailed in Barry Edmonston, Michael A. Goldberg, and John Mercer, "Urban Form in Canada and the United States: An Examination of Density Gradients," *Urban Studies*, 22 (3), 1985, pp. 209-217.

22. Goldberg and Mercer, *Myth of the North American City*, Ch. 8.

23. The fiscal health of Canadian and American central cities is examined in John Mercer and Michael A. Goldberg, "The Fiscal Condition of Canadian and American Cities," *Urban Studies*, 21, 1984, pp. 233-243.

Environmental and Resource Issues

Canadians have particular cause to be concerned with the environment and resources because these are the realities that form the historical and economic life-blood of a vast and largely unpopulated nation. Although the majority of Canadians live within 150 kilometres of the American border, the national character has been shaped by the hardships of the sea, the roughness of the pre-Cambrian Shield, the expanse of the prairies, the barrier of the Rockies, and the remoteness of the hostile and barren tundra to the north. In taking advantage of the bounty of the land, Canadians have come to rely upon the staples that this land provides—at one time primarily fur and fish, later lumber and minerals. In the future, we may rely on energy provided by hydro-electric power or even that most precious of resources, water. Canada is, in short, a resource-based economy whose resources are dependent upon a clean and healthy natural environment. This section deals with some of the issues that are of profound concern to Canadians, but for which we need Americans to help find the solutions.

In Chapter 16, dealing with the entire North American environment, Kenneth Hare examines our continental dependence. He begins with the assertion that "we have to be wholeheartedly uncompromising in defence of certain national environmental objectives." He describes how we have as much in common in these areas with the northern Europeans and the Soviet

Union as with the United States. Thus there are as many reasons to seek east-west links to these nations (a circumpolar perspective) as there are to concentrate on the transboundary issues which are at the heart of the Canadian-American relationship. In examining some of the important disputes between the two countries, he discusses in detail the causes of acid rain, and the problems associated with the regulation of water levels in the Great Lakes. In warning us of future problems, Hare maintains that the "big issue, the most visible issue, of the last decade has surely been acid deposition." Without casting blame, and accepting that more research on acid rain is needed, Hare urges us to deal with the problem through bilateral agreement as soon as possible. He describes the limitations of scientific research and "the very high level of scientific collaboration between the two countries" in the field, and in the end concludes that action is a matter of political will.

In Chapter 17, Donald Munton shows us how the desire of Canadians to reach a political solution on acid rain is complicated by economic cost/benefit realities and the intricacies of international diplomacy. "Conventional wisdom seems to be that environmental issues rank well down the national public agenda." Munton outlines two models or "sets of propositions or generalizations which give us some understanding as to the way the United States deals with its northern neighbour, and the methods by which Canadians try to come to grips with this very large and complex political system" to the south. The "partnership-interdependence" model and the "asymmetric dependence" model serve as useful explanatory tools in observing the relationship, with particular reference to the problem of acid rain. He concludes that the federal government can only lead on environmental issues when Congress and the president accept that they are pertinent to the health and welfare of the American people. He shows why this is so in his discussion of dependence between the two nations.

Constance Hunt, in Chapter 18, brings us to a topic which seems to have preoccupied the world since the early 1970s—energy. She uses Canada–United States energy trade as the intellectual vehicle to "explain the paucity of Canadian scholarship about American law." Although it is clear that the American legal tradition has to a degree affected Canadian law, most notably in the language of the Canadian Charter of Rights and Freedoms, Hunt argues that this is also true in the area of policy making. She concludes that at present "both private and public law mechanisms [in Canada] have succumbed somewhat to the pressures of the American marketplace, and attempts at Canadian independence have been largely abandoned." This is particularly true within the petroleum industry. In making her point Hunt examines the period from the late 1940s (with the discovery of oil in Alberta) to the present, to show how Canada has been forced to bow to the economic strength of the American market. In order to reverse or control these trends, "the public and private sectors in Canada might deal more effectively with American regulatory and commercial forces."

The North American Environment: Transboundary Issues

F. Kenneth Hare

In the course of my career I have had to cope with a number of transboundary obligations. Doing so has familiarized me with one aspect of Canada–United States relations, those that have to do with environmental questions and resource management, usually in a bilateral framework. Although I have been involved in similar endeavours in Europe as well, I have been far more concerned with disputes between Canada and the United States—in the kind of issues that are referred for settlement to the International Joint Commission.

Though I have been a citizen of Canada since 1951, I have had more dealings with Washington than I have with Ottawa. Until recently Ottawa seemed unaware of my existence, except for rare and infrequent consultancies for the Department of National Defence. But I have had many dealings with Washington, and close institutional links with many United States institutions. I have found this a very happy, friendly, useful relationship. More often than not I find myself agreeing with my American neighbours on important questions. So I have come almost to be a continentalist in environmental questions, and yet *not* to be a continentalist. In the long run we cannot say that environmental questions require only international solutions; there are times when we must assert our national claims. And so, though temperamentally given to compromise between nations, I think that we have to be wholeheartedly uncompromising in defence of certain national environmental objectives.

A few years ago, in a lecture to the Royal Society of Canada in London, Ontario, I challenged the frequently asserted position that the natural topographical grain of Canada leads Canadians to look southwards to the United States, or that there is something about our physical geography that predisposes us towards a link with the United States.[1] I did not want to overemphasize the point, because it is so patently true in many ways that Canadians are forever looking south. If one lives and works in Vancouver, the least demanding journey a person can take is south to San Francisco. Those living on the Prairies cannot fail to realize that their neighbours on the United States Great Plains are living much the same life as they are. The people of these regions have certain common interests. To those living in Toronto or Montreal, Florida is the nearest place with a decent southern climate. These links are so old and so well-established that we take them for granted. But perhaps we exaggerate them.

When it comes to environmental issues, there are, in contrast, other features that link us with our latitudinal neighbours in the Scandinavian countries. They are neighbours in a real sense, even though we are separated by the north Atlantic. The Soviet Union has also many things in common with us. If the world were organized simply on the basis of sheer experience, it would not really be with the Americans, I suspect, that we would have developed these links; it would have been with our northern European neighbours.

The fact is, of course, that today we are to a large extent an urban society; the common experience of the ordinary individual is with the urban environment. And the North American city is very much of a muchness. London and Toronto happen to be rather nicer places than the corresponding cities on the American side; we have in this country, by accident, created a better form of urban settlement. But, nevertheless, the common heritage with, for example, towns of the same size in New York state is obvious. Most of the everyday experience of most young Canadians in particular is related to the cities, and the points that I am about to make may seem strange to them, because the urban environment is where we share many things with the United States. Consequently in other than urban matters, a closer look is needed.

If we look at a topographical map of North America, we see that the grain does, to some extent, point southwards. The Western Cordillera unquestionably continue farther south, and the Americans have the experience of a montane west, just as we do. There is not the slightest doubt, when we travel south from British Columbia into Idaho or Washington, that we are still in the same geographical province, encountering people who have much the same economic experience as we do. Similarly we can see the Prairies continue southwards in the Great Plains. The Canadian Shield drops down into United States territory in Michigan as it does in the Adirondacks. But southern Ontario is, geologically and economically, analogous to the American Midwest. Maritime Canada is Appalachian in its affinities and links easily with New England. Hence there is still a good reason for looking south, even if we speak only about the physical geography of the continent.

Nevertheless there are powerful reasons for seeing our east–west links as equally important. The boreal forest formation and sub-Arctic ocean waters, for example, extend round the world in an irregular but more or less zonal fashion. The boreal forests of Canada and the U.S.S.R. are extraordinarily similar. There is a great deal of common economic experience, and even common folklore that refers to the realities of that forest.

This circumpolar perspective creates a different kind of linkage for us. If we enter a lichen woodland in the Labrador Peninsula and see a caribou, it may be surprising to know that such a landscape has a close parallel in Karelia on the Soviet-Finnish border on the Eurasian continent. Alaska has similar environments, as well as a bit of the Arctic; but for the most part, the United States does not have such topography. They do not share this with us. We share it with the European and Eurasian communities of the north.

Let us focus a little more on the border as a physical thing. In places it is marine, such as the entrance to the Straits of Juan de Fuca between Washington state and Vancouver Island. Some of the most significant disputes that have developed between Canada and the United States have had to do with that fact. The harbours of Seattle and Tacoma can be reached only through this entrance, which brings, of course, the stream of shipping originating from the United States close to the Canadian shore. We *do* claim these waters off the coastal entrance. The thought that big super-tankers, in imagination almost as wide as the Straits, should have to enter through this narrow and often stormy entrance was a cause célèbre between the nations. There are still numerous problems between the two countries related to fishing rights and the underwater course of the boundary between us. There is nothing quite like the Straits of Juan de Fuca elsewhere. It is not easy for us to bring in a body of precedent, to look for parallels elsewhere, or to introduce arguments that other people have thought about. We genuinely have to defend it on the basis of our own interests and experience.

Within the Western Cordillera, the Skagit Valley is another of the problem points between Canada and the United States. An American power company wanted to dam the valley to raise water levels in it. Part of the Canadian side would be flooded in order to increase the electrical supply to the city of Seattle. A legally binding agreement permitted them to do this. This was another bone of contention, a very ad hoc, very specific issue affecting the welfare of the Canadian environment.

Going still further east where the border crosses the Great Plains, even the road systems of states and provinces happen to join up. They run east–west and north–south. But in a satellite picture one can often see a northwest–southeast trending transgressive line, which is the line of a railway, carrying power lines and an aqueduct. Much of the penetration of the Canadian prairies came from the southeast. The linkages, when we did not have a transcontinental railway north of Lake Superior, tended to be with the southeast. It was from that direction, people thought, that the settlers would come. And so the odd thing about the Canadian prairies is these northwest–southeast lines that show up all over the place. Most of them are the ghosts of old, formerly busy links with the High Plains to the south.

In the Great Lakes–St. Lawrence sector, the boundary is largely within the water bodies themselves. The boundary does not exist in the atmosphere, nor does it exist within rivers, other than as a legal fiction. It is not a physical feature. In most areas it disregards not only the solid physical geography but provides no obstacle at all to the free movement of water and air. It is the transboundary migration of airborne things that has given us most trouble in recent years.

Bernhard Ulrich suggested several years ago that acid deposition, the deposition of sulphate and nitrate ions particularly, might damage forest ecosystems.[2] So far, on the part of the official agencies on both the Canadian and American sides, there has been little tendency to believe that this is true. Our own foresters were doubtful that the Ulrich effect was real. They have been little disposed to agree with the popular view that acid rain does indeed damage forests.

But now, for the first time, there is a growing agreement that stresses are indeed showing in the Canadian forest. We may be on the point of recognizing that terrestrial impacts are occurring from materials added to the atmosphere on *both* sides of the boundary. We have understood for some years the related impact of acid deposition on lakes and rivers and thereby on fish. For Canadians the terrestrial impact has now been added to this. In the next five years there may well be more emphasis upon the terrestrial problem than upon the aquatic.

Let us take another area in which there is an enormous amount of unfinished business between Canada and the United States, the care and maintenance of the Great Lakes system. The lakes are irretrievably binational, bilateral bodies. The international boundary runs through Lake Superior and Lake Huron, along the line of the Detroit and St. Clair rivers, through Lake St. Clair and Lake Erie, down the Niagara River, along Lake Ontario, and down the St. Lawrence to Lake St. Francis where it abruptly departs eastwards overland. The boundary is thus within the water bodies. Lake Superior is truly international. Lakes Huron and Michigan are a single water-body, since there is no difference of level between them other than short term ones produced by wind stress. Lake Erie, which has a much longer American shore than Canadian shore, is international. Lake Ontario is fully international. Lake Michigan is almost entirely within United States territory (*almost* entirely, because it is a moot point where precisely Lake Michigan ends and Lake Huron begins).

The point is that water finds its own level, and water levels are common to the two countries. There is absolutely no way in which you can regulate those levels without agreement. So, happily, the issue of Great Lakes water levels, though it has been a matter of bedevilment between the two countries, has also been most productive of useful institutions that try to solve the problems between us. The Boundary Waters Treaty of 1909 spawned the International Joint Commission. Ever since then it has been a body of common reference for the two federal governments in matters pertaining to the Great Lakes and other boundary waters. It has been extended by common consent to matters of air pollution and land use. Perhaps, at some future date, it may be extended still further into questions of a purely demographic and social kind. So the effort that we have had to make, because we have common bodies of water, has led us to create institutions of arbitration. This has been one of the very hopeful signs of common concern between our two countries.

The Great Lakes water levels are not unregulated but are still not *greatly* regulated. The water levels of Lake Superior are controlled a little, and so are those of Lake Ontario, by the Iroquois control dam. But basically this system is still little managed as far as discharge and water levels are concerned. In contrast, rivers like the Manicouagan or the Outarde, in Quebec, are fully managed. The original profiles of the rivers no longer exist. They are just a series of lakes with artificial spillways. And the La Grande on the old East Main slope of the James Bay power development has been similarly transformed. But the Great Lakes are still to a large extent unregulated and unregulatable, because of their giant size and the peculiarities of their geography.

There is a crude twenty-year rhythm in water levels, which are currently extremely high. We shall have a major problem on our hands if there is a significant storm in Lake Erie. With high water levels, storms do an enormous amount of damage. With high levels, of course, there is ample depth when a ship goes over the lock sills; the ships may stand rather high out of the water at their moorings but, basically, high levels are a problem for the shore itself rather than for shipping. And they are a problem when it comes to controlling ice. The big ice jam off Buffalo in 1985 is one of the characteristic features of a cold winter at times of high water levels. At other times, water levels may be so low that they create other hazards. A low water level leads to a loss of power at hydro-electric plants. It also creates a loss of navigation capacity, because the Upper Lakers fit into the locks like feet into old shoes, or hands into tight-fitting gloves. If you take water out, you reduce the capacity of those very significantly indeed, and nature often does just this. In the 1960s, for example, the water level was extraordinarily low.

There are now major anthropogenic threats to lake levels. The installation of thermal power stations, most of them on the American side, calls for lowering water levels extensively. Other diversions are visualized for the development of irrigated agriculture; for improved sewage facilities, which, oddly enough, do consume some water; and for increasing withdrawals for industrial and domestic purposes. These plans threaten to take discharge from the lakes down by about 9 per cent well before the middle of the next century. Climatic change is also threatening to put discharge down a further 21 per cent, so that we face a probable fall of the water levels, not by the metre or so that is typical of the annual range, and not by the bigger drop that is typical of the twenty-year rhythm, but by a major drop of the average level of the Lakes because of a 30 per cent drop in discharge.

It is clear that the control and management of lake water levels is going to be one of the major environmental challenges of the next half century. It will call for a renewed interest in diversions of water into the lakes. Thomas Kierans has recently revived his plan to divert James Bay water into the Lakes.[3] More people will listen now to what he has to say. But the threat will also mean that, whenever anyone tries to divert water out of the Lakes for any purpose whatever, the squawks will be even louder than they have been in the past; it is going to hurt that badly. This is the biggest environmental issue likely to arise between our two countries after the acid rain question has been settled, as indeed it must be sooner or later.

But what of more horrific, man-made problems? Does nuclear war bring nuclear winter? This is an international issue of a very special kind and a fringe dweller on the scientific scene; it is a contingency that might, possibly, happen. But it does involve the relations between our two countries. If there is a major nuclear war between the super powers, it is the usual view of the strategic community that it will probably lead mainly to a counter-force series of strikes. That is to say, the war will entail an exchange between the United States and the U.S.S.R. aimed in both cases at missile silos and their military targets. Since the strategic arsenals of those powers are in the order of 15 000 Mt of TNT equivalent, it might also be that a third or a half might be released in this phase. A 5 000 Mt or a 10 000 Mt exchange of a counter-force variety is at least worth thinking about (though it boggles the mind). Yet it is impossible to think about, because we have no possible way of visualizing a holocaust quite so devastating. The Nagasaki and Hiroshima bombs were in the kilotonne range, 12 kt and 22 kt. Here we are talking about thousands of megatonnes as the scale for this warfare.

On the other hand, there is another school of thought, represented notably by Carl Sagan, which thinks it very likely that there will also be a counter-value strike, perhaps on the same scale, aimed at the cities.[4] The cities contain a great deal of carbon in the form of asphalt, stored oil, wood, and plastics, that would burn with black smoke; and so do the forests into which, it is conceivable, misfired missiles might land. Out of this, the notion has come, since 1982, that vast amounts of smoke, in the order of one to five hundred million tonnes of carbon, might be released into the northern hemisphere and might cool the surface temperatures below the freezing point, producing the effect known as the nuclear winter.

Large natural forest fires add carbon to the atmosphere at a rate which has not yet been calculated, but which might be something like a million tonnes in the course of a single major outbreak. In terms of possible consequences, we have in this country a sort of natural laboratory, the great forest fires of late summer, in which one might look at this hypothesis.

Canada and the United States are irretrievably bound together in this question of nuclear war. Whether we are partners with American strategy or not, it is likely that if an attack is made upon the United States, then we shall be, at least partly, a target. We shall certainly receive the overspill in the form of radioactive fallout and also the probability of extensive fire in our environment.

So, at the gentlest edge of the relations between the two countries, they meet on environmental questions affecting the acidity of lakes, the water level in Lake Erie, whether to put an ice-boom in the Niagara river. At the other apocalyptic end, they meet over discussions of the nuclear winter.

We cannot afford to neglect the implications of the nuclear winter in our strategic arguments.

But the big issue, the most visible issue, of the last decade has surely been acid deposition. The facts are really not in dispute. Sulphur dioxide and oxides of nitrogen are produced largely in the industrial areas of North America. They come out of chimneys and exhaust pipes. They are carried by prevailing wind systems largely over the eastern United States, southern Ontario, and Quebec. Not far to the north are the vulnerable granitic terrains of the Canadian Shield, in which the soil cannot buffer the acids. The acidity of the falling precipitation averages out into a pattern which is unmistakably linked to industry. The result has been extensive visible damage to aquatic ecosystems in the granitic terrain, and allegations, with no firm proof, that there has been damage to the forests.[5]

In a very real sense, the acid rain issue epitomizes the kinds of environmental problems that arise between the two countries. In the first place, there is no question about the transboundary nature of the problem. Canada does indeed contribute to the acid burden of New England, New York state, and to a minor extent, the other parts of the United States. The United States undoubtedly does contribute to the acid burden of Ontario, Quebec, and the Maritime provinces. There is no real doubt about this. No rational person can doubt that the two countries do exchange air pollution.

In Europe there is not a single boundary but, of course, a patchwork of boundaries. There is no long-standing tradition of easy debate between any two countries. There is no International Joint Commission, and there is nothing equivalent to the ease of movement of ideas enabled by the common language in North America. But in Europe other elements are present: an even higher density of pollutant production, a much nastier airborne soup, a quieter atmosphere. And the result has been that it was the Europeans, and not we, who first identified the acid deposition threat, and who are now moving on to a realization that it is really the integrated pollution package that is damaging Europe's ecosystems, and not simply sulphates and nitrates, as they first alleged.

In dealing with the United States on this issue, we have been hamstrung by uncertainty, as always. It is very difficult to prove that a fish has died because it has been poisoned by sulphates from the American Midwest. They are not labelled. It is extremely difficult to resist the argument that we need more research, which is what the Reagan administration has consistently said. I would say, as an environmental scientist, that we most certainly do need more research. Most of the allegations that are made about the impact of acid pollution on the environment are still really speculation, and they are, to some extent, hearsay. They are repeated without being understood. The evidential basis for damage to ecosystems is not strong enough to avoid legal challenge; and, in particular, it has been the difficulty of proving terrestrial impact, as distinct from aquatic impact, that has made it possible for Mr. Reagan and his colleagues to hide behind the uncertainty.

I have no doubt at all that there is an impact on terrestrial ecosystems; that there is a cost, there is a burden; and that agreement between the two countries is a necessity, if we are to save ourselves a troubled future. But, unfortunately, I cannot prove that in a fashion which unmistakably puts any other argument out of court.

The two countries established Work Groups in 1980 under the 1979 Geneva Convention on Transboundary Air Pollution of the Economic Commission for Europe; oddly enough, it was a European instrument that we used for this purpose. The Work Groups met and agreed on almost everything, but they did not, really, agree on solutions.[6] And I think we made a mistake; we put too much weight upon sulphur dioxide, not as the only pollutant of importance, but as a sort of surrogate for the pollution package. We might have been wiser to deal with the oxides of nitrogen as well; and, furthermore, we might have insisted, as the Europeans now insist, that it is the complete oxidant package in the air that travels across the border that really matters. But we did not, and to date we have not succeeded in bringing the Americans to the point of decision on something that damages their environment almost as much as it damages ours. But the time will come, without doubt, because the process ultimately affects American interests.

Nonetheless, it is important to realize the very high level of scientific collaboration between the two countries in this field, and the high level of scientific understanding that is achieved, even though the evidential basis is weak. Internationally prepared inventories for the years 1978 and 1980 of sulphur dioxide emission by small divisions show obvious problems emanating from Sudbury; but emissions concentrate in the Ohio valley and are widespread over eastern North America.[7] The variable winds carry the emissions to targets that are also widespread and on the average shifted north-eastward by the prevailing winds. The patterns of average emission and average deposition are thus geometrically similar, though slightly eccentric.

That acidity of precipitation is a binational problem arising from sulphate and nitrate deposition of industrial origin is a conclusion thus depending on the resemblance of spatial patterns—and, of course, on qualitative understanding of the background chemistry. The case is strong enough to persuade most scientists; but it is still a case that can be challenged by clever lawyers almost indefinitely, because one cannot trace an individual particle through the system accurately; one cannot be precise about source/receptor relations.

That is what President Reagan means when he says we need more research. Without admiring President Reagan's policies, we can nevertheless agree with him when he says we need more research. To solve this problem we are going to have to develop effective means of identifying the relevant culprits for a given situation and a given location—who it is that produces the pollutants that affect a given area that is to be protected. And we need to know what is the economically effective strategy to follow to reduce the emissions without unduly burdening the emittor. If we unduly burden the emittor, we automatically make him absolutely determined not to help.

We need more research. And yet at the same time we need to press for action, because this is a threat that will not go away and must indeed be tackled. Hence the urgency with which we must promote the kind of research that will answer these questions and help to solve the problems.

The scientific community gives to the social scientist, the policy-makers, and the public at large a flawed kind of picture—flawed as to answers, flawed as to content, and in some ways even, flawed as to thinking. It is extremely difficult to think about anything as complicated as the environment in a rational way. Ecosystems are unbelievably complex, and full of numerous and varied control mechanisms that we know about in principle but cannot specify. Applied ecology is a very difficult field and so is applied meteorology. I do not get angry at my friends in politics, the social sciences, and government, who complain about this. The fact is that the messiness of the system, the complexity of nature, preclude the level of certainty that politicians, social scientists, and bureaucrats are entitled to expect from the scientist in other circumstances. That, plus the fact that it is genuinely impossible to do any experiments. One cannot, for example, experiment with the nuclear winter, nor in the acid rain field, except on a very small scale.

I apologize that the scientist is not able to deliver cut and dried answers for most of the transboundary problems that affect our two countries. Some are relatively easy to control if one chooses (for example, Great Lakes water levels in the technological sense). Others are massively difficult, and the control of acid deposition is one of those. Some are almost beyond the rational wit of mankind, like the control of the international strategic situation that brings the threat, after a nuclear war, of a nuclear winter. But in all these domains, whether one deals with the really tractable questions of water levels or the intractable question of international strategy, the element of scientific uncertainty remains to make it possible for the unwilling policy-makers to hide, if they so wish. We can only hope that they will not hide.

Notes

1. F. Kenneth Hare, "Does nature bind Canada together?" *Transactions of the Royal Society of Canada*, Series N, Vol. XVI (1978), pp. 27-37.
2. For an overview, see R. Mayer and B. Ulrich, "Input to soil, especially the influence of vegetation in intercepting and modifying inputs: A review" in *Effects of Acid Precipitation on Terrestrial Ecosystems*, edited by T.C. Hutchinson and M. Havas, (New York: Plenum Press, 1978), pp. 173-182.
3. Draft prospectus, The Grand Canal Company, dated 12 June 1985, issued by Thomas Kierans.
4. Carl Sagan, "Nuclear War and Climate Catastrophe: Some Policy Implications," *Foreign Affairs*, Vol. 62, No. 2. (1983–84), pp. 257-292.
5. United States and Canada, 1983: Work Group Report, *Memorandum of Intent on Transboundary Air Pollution*, Environment Canada, Ottawa, 4-42–4-51.
6. United States and Canada, 1983: *Memorandum of Intent on Transboundary Air Pollution*,

Canadian Perspectives on American Environmental Issues

Donald J. Munton

There is a convention—perhaps an apparent consensus—that environmental issues are secondary. Partly because of that, they are not only peripheral but also distinct. How else can we explain an American president thinking he could safely appoint, as Administrator of the Environmental Protection Agency, a person dedicated to dismantling that agency, and thus undermining its regulatory structure? How else can we explain a Canadian prime minister assuming he could appoint, as Minister of the Environment, a person not only without expertise in the House of Commons, but also without background and with little obvious interest in environmental issues, without incurring political damage? Indeed, how else can we explain politicians with so little understanding of environmental politics that they seemed surprised by the strong criticism that followed their respective efforts at budget cutting directed at that most sacred of environmental "cows," the Canadian Wildlife Service? The conventional wisdom seems to be that environmental issues rank at the lower end of the national public agenda.

Whether or not environmental issues generally are a secondary public priority in the United States or Canada, they are neither peripheral nor obscure *between* the United States and Canada. Nor are they entirely distinct or unique in political terms. Indeed, they fit very well into and are an important part of the broad pattern of Canada–United States relations. For the rest of this essay we will assume that most readers are more interested in looking at that broad pattern than in the physical chemistry of the emissions of sulphur dioxide or nitrogen oxides, the terrestial ecosystem impact of acid rain, the biological effects of phosphates in the Great Lakes, or the biochemistry of toxins.

What are the patterns in Canada–United States relations that appear dominant? Do they apply as well in the area of environmental issues? The arguments and assumptions of most environmental commentators follow one of two basic perspectives. One of these is dominant in the United States and more common than the other in Canada. The second remains undeveloped if not almost unknown in the United States.

It would be useful to outline these two perspectives, or as we might call them, two "models" of Canadian-American relations. These models are sets of propositions or generalizations that give us some understanding of how the United States deals with its northern neighbour, and of how Canadians try to come to grips with this very large and complex political system. One of these models, prevalent in Canadian minds, but certainly the one almost exclusively talked about in the United States, is what might be called the "partnership-interdependence" model. This model emphasizes a number of characteristics of the two countries—their similarity, their equality in some senses, their degree of economic and social interdependence, and other links between them. These and related factors lead, it is said, to an unusually close and responsive bilateral partnership and to a considerable degree of cooperation.

The second model, less commonly developed, even in Canada, but almost unknown in the United States, is what I would call the "asymmetric dependence" model.[1] Here the emphasis is on dissimilarities, in particular the differences in the national power or capabilities of the two countries, and on the degree to which Canada is consequently dependent on the United States. We hear from time to time, usually from predictable sources, about Canada's economic dependence, its cultural dependence, and sometimes its security dependence. The observation is made in most of these cases that the size of the American economy, the size of the American cultural market, the size of the American military, or whatever, is the key factor. What is seldom recognized is the extent to which in the environmental area there is a relationship of dependence as well.

Let us step back to the first of these models, and elaborate it sufficiently to see why it is unsatisfactory as an explanation for the policies toward Canada pursued by the United States. There is an emphasis in the partnership-interdependence model, and indeed in much of the common everyday rhetoric we hear about Canadian-American relations on neighbourliness, responsiveness, and cooperativeness. We heard this rhetoric in the early 1960s. There was a distinct down-playing through parts of the 1970s, but we are hearing it again, in crescendos, in the 1980s, and particularly before and during the Reagan-Mulroney summits.[2] A key assumption of this model is the fact that the interests of the two countries are close, if not essentially identical, in the political area, the economic area, and the social area. The mutuality of these interests arises out of the strong similarities between the two countries politically, economically, socially, and culturally, as well as from their geographic proximity. Thus, for example, they have a common interest in defending North America. It has even been said by commentators that the two countries have a common interest in preventing pollution of the Great Lakes. In one sense they do, of course. That, however, is not the interest that drives environmental policies concerning these lakes or elsewhere.

A second aspect of the partnership-interdependence model is what K.J. Holsti calls the common "diplomatic culture" between the two countries.[3] Here we refer not to broad social similarities, but common views, common approaches, and a common working technical language between diplomats and officials. Due in part to similar perspectives and to a very high level of exchange, Canadian and American officials tend to take a pragmatic approach to the problems at hand. Their interest is in solving the problems, rather than in making major issues out of them. There is also what Holsti calls a professional "diplomatic ethic"—a set of unofficial understandings or norms about the appropriate way to deal bilaterally with each other. In short, the argument is that commonalities, and especially a shared diplomatic culture, make the overall process of Canadian-American relations so unusual and so cooperative. And it is this diplomatic culture which largely explains what is assumed to be a lack of impact on the relationship of power disparities.

This argument could be debated at some length. Suffice it to say, the first model appears a rather limited one, and its perspective appears lacking in a number of respects. First, it emphasizes too much the element of process in Canadian-American relations. Second, it overlooks the impact of the structure of power and the background restraints which underly most issues in Canadian-American relations.

The process of bilateral discussion and negotiation undoubtedly facilitates a resolution of some Canada–United States disputes. It leads more often to agreements to disagree. In certain versions of the partnership-interdependence model this process gains credit not merely for resolving or managing differences but even for providing Canada with a significant advantage. Through a well-coordinated effort, it is said, Canada is able to use the diplomatic process to offset the superior power of the United States.[4] It is here that this model and its proponents overstate the potency of diplomacy. What is overlooked is the pervasive impact of superior U.S. power or capabilities on the issues comprising the bilateral agenda at any given time, on the processes of dealing with these issues, and on bargaining outcomes.

The asymmetric dependence model, it can be argued, provides a contrasting and more potent model, albeit complementary, of Canadian-American relations. It takes into account both the underlying structure and the process of Canadian-American relations. It explains much, not only about American actions toward Canada (and vice versa) but also a variety of phenomena that may at first seem surprising. The model provides answers to such questions as: Why is the United States generally slower to respond to environmental problems common to both countries? That is, why is it usually Canada that initiates discussion of these in the bilateral context? (Why, for example, did Canadians first raise the acid rain issue? They formed the Canadian Coalition on Acid Rain to lobby Washington, and since 1981 have put the issue on the agenda of both countries.) And why is it usually Canada that is pressing on matters of pollution in the Great Lakes?

In addition, why do environmental issues seem to create such conflict? Why is it that the differences seem so difficult to bury under bilateral summit rhetoric despite, in recent years, the slickest federal government public relations campaign ever seen in the history of Canadian-American relations? Related to this would be the question: Why is the level of formal cooperation between these two countries so low, despite the international treaties and agreements that exist in this area which are, by any international standard, extraordinarily strong?

And why are bilateral environmental problems so persistent and apparently so difficult to resolve? Pollution problems in the Great Lakes have been a bilateral issue since the early 1900s, and have been continually so since the 1950s. Acid rain, or to be more precise, the long-range transport of air pollution and acidic deposition, has been an issue since the mid-1970s. It still shows no sign of mutual action, let alone early resolution.

And finally, why do Canadian public attitudes on these issues differ so substantially from American public attitudes? Indeed, why do they differ from any reasonable interpretation under the partnership-cooperation perspective? Why, for example, is the Canadian public so much more aware of and concerned about the problem of acidic deposition than is the American public? Given the commonalities of media coverage and of social values in Canada and the United States, and given the lack of evidence that Canadians as a general rule are more environmentally conscious than their American counterparts, why would such marked divergences emerge in knowledge and attitudes on this specific issue? On a related point, why are Canadian environmental interest groups generally more deferential and less aggressive than their American counterparts? (This question emerges in other contributions to this volume, but can be addressed to some extent here.)

If a definition can be provided here of "environmental dependence," then answers to some of these questions can be given. The notion of dependence, at least in the current literature in international relations, refers to two different and distinct, but related characteristics.[5] The first is vulnerability. A country is vulnerable if it is influenced or affected by another. But vulnerability does not necessarily create dependence. Dependence exists when vulnerability is joined by a second characteristic—a lack of alternatives. If the supply of some goods important to a country is being affected by another, and there are alternative sources of those goods, then presumably those sources will be sought. The country would not then be in a position of dependence. If, however, there are no alternative sources, for whatever reason, then there is dependence. The characterization applies whether the other's influence is over sources of investment or over the environmental quality of a geographically proximate area. Dependence follows from vulnerability and a lack of alternatives. Just as much as Canada is dependent economically and militarily on the United States, it is dependent environmentally, in the sense that the quality of the Canadian environment in many areas depends on what occurs in the United States. Indeed, it often depends more on pollution emissions—and controls—in the United States than in Canada.

The United States, to be sure, is environmentally dependent on Canada, in some areas at least. The extent, however, is usually very small. Most of the pollution which crosses the border, either waterborne or airborne, comes from the American side. The simple reason is that most of the industry and human population in North America is located in the United States. In the case of transboundary air pollution, the pattern is compounded by the prevailing southwest to northeast winds. That means, generally speaking, that Canada is more dependent environmentally on the United States than vice versa.

It follows, and with respect to the first question posed above, that transboundary environmental issues tend to exhibit a pattern of Canada as *demander*. It is Canadian politicians and officials who attempt to put these problems on the bilateral agenda, and try to influence their American counterparts to establish more rigorous pollution controls. This is because environmental dependence is generally felt more broadly and keenly on the Canadian side of the border. Environmental dependence also explains why Americans often find themselves confronted with Canadian environment ministers urging new or stronger international agreements on air or water quality. It is extremely important for Canada to have American cooperation in reducing emissions, so as to maintain and perhaps, someday, to restore the Canadian environment. Even if Canadian sources of pollution were entirely shut down, there would still be damage in Canada from transboundary pollution. United States environmental regulatory action often benefits Canada. International environmental agreements, therefore, even those that only call for weak controls, are better than no agreements at all, if those agreements encourage any American pollution control action which otherwise would not take place. On the other hand, given the relatively little transboundary pollution flowing from Canada to the United States, Canadian regulatory actions offer little benefit to Americans and consequently are of less interest to Americans.

This same factor of environmental dependence is thus crucial to an understanding of Canadian perspectives on the United States in the environmental arena. It is crucial also in setting the agenda and influencing the political processes between the two countries. And its impact is also felt on outcomes, in the sense that any bilateral agreement usually involves Canada ultimately accepting as strong a United States commitment as Canadians practically, pragmatically, and reasonably think can be extracted. The American position, understandably, is usually one of undertaking no more additional pollution control commitments than absolutely necessary to reach an agreement.

American officials, moreover, tend to be aware of the weaknesses in the Canadian position in these negotiations. The evidence in United States documents on Great Lakes Water Quality Agreement negotiations in the 1970s is clear. While not articulating the notion of environmental dependence, nor explaining why Canada does not have the options, American officials recognized that if they stood firm, the Canadians would probably drop their "unreasonable" demands and accept weaker United States commitments than Canada had originally proposed.[6]. We need not infer from this any sort of malicious intent on the part of American officials. The simple fact is that with a large population and a large industrial base, and thus more emission sources and more pollution, the costs involved in implementing United States environmental policies are many times what they are in Canada, and usually more than the ten-to-one ratio of the respective populations. Thus, there are strong domestic political constraints that American officials tend to accept as given. They assume their Canadian counterparts do, or ought to do, likewise.

Furthermore, from the American perspective, there is little to be gained from bilateral cooperation beyond good relations. Why sign an international environmental agreement with Canada, when the benefits of that agreement accrue largely to Canada, and perhaps the costs of United States pollution controls are not matched with significant benefits to American constituents? Sooner or later, in most negotiations, some official or agency on the United States side raises this point. It is particularly difficult to convince the strategically placed Office of Management and Budget that the United States government needs to spend considerably more money, for example, for trunk sewers or sulphur dioxide controls. Politically, the point is a very telling one. The costs of certain pollution controls in a heavily industrialized, but large country like the United States often seem greater than the benefits. When many of the benefits of expensive controls are not felt by American voters and taxpayers, it is understandably even harder to justify the costs. And when governmental action is thus doubly constrained, the problems are even less likely to be addressed squarely, and solutions are unlikely to emerge quickly.

Canada's position of environmental dependence can also explain, at least in part, the different orientation and operating style of Canadian environmental interest groups. American groups, it is often observed, are more active and more aggressive in their lobbying. Given the nature of the problems they are concerned with, and the well-accepted rule that aggressive lobbying is almost required in order merely to be heard in the rough-and-tumble of American politics, the style is appropriate. For U.S. environmental activists, the aim—securing government action, usually federal, to deal with a pollution problem—is clear. In Canada, however, not only does the political machinery operate in a less adversarial fashion, but also the nature of the problem differs and thus so do the objectives. Put simply, Canadian environmental groups, implicitly recognizing their country's position of dependence, view the Canadian government less as part of the environmental problem, and more as key to its solution, given the need to pressure the United States into action.

One might draw conclusions as to what Canada can do politically to raise the priority of environmental issues, to lessen this environmental dependence, and to improve the outcome of United States–Canada environmental politics. Transboundary lobbying, such as that now carried out by the

Canadian Coalition on Acid Rain, is one step. The conclusions here, though, should relate more to a Canadian appreciation of American dilemmas. It is surely not treasonous to have some empathy with the difficulties faced by American environmental officials and politicians, particularly in an era of low economic growth and unprecedented budget and balance of trade deficits.[7] Nor is it fair to forget or overlook those specific areas where American pollution standards exceed Canadian ones.

At the same time, Canadians ought not to anticipate firm or imminent American action against transboundary pollution, nor expect that the mere existence of principles such as "thou shalt not pollute thy neighbour," nor even their acceptance as valid principles, will alone move political obstacles to United States policy action. Nor should Canadians have any illusions about what might be expected from summit meetings and the rhetoric of "partnership."

All that having been said, the Canadian perspective should not be characterized by resignation, hopelessness, and despair. Shedding illusions ought instead to be the beginning of a realistic understanding of living, environmentally and otherwise, with the United States.

Notes

1. These two models are developed more fully in Donald J. Munton, "Dependence and Interdependence in Transboundary Environmental Relations," *International Journal*, Vol. xxxvi, No. 1 (Winter 1980-81), pp. 139-184. The concept of "environmental dependence," suggested there has been adopted, for example, by Stephen Clarkson, *Canada and the Reagan Challenge* (Toronto: James Lorimer & Co., 1982), Ch. 8.

2. [Ed. note] In the "Shamrock Summit" of 17 March 1985, Prime Minister Mulroney and President Reagan agreed to appoint "special envoys" in a joint effort to find solutions to the acid rain problem. Former Ontario Premier, William Davis, and former U.S. Transportation Secretary, Drew Lewis, were chosen for the task. Their *Joint Report of the Special Envoys on Acid Rain* was released on 8 January 1986. The *Report* and its recommendations (one being a U.S. $5 billion contribution to developing technology to burn coal more cleanly) were accepted in principle by President Reagan on 19 March 1986, during the second summit in Washington.

3. K.J. Holsti, "Canada and the United States" in K. Waltz and S. Spiegel, eds., *Conflict in World Politics* (Cambridge, Mass: Winthrop, 1971), pp. 375-396.

4. See, for example, Gilbert R. Winham, "Choice and Strategy in Continental Relations," in A. Axline, et al., eds., *Continental Community? Independence and Integration in North America* (Toronto: McClelland and Stewart, 1974), pp. 228-239; and Joseph S. Nye, "Transnational Relations and Interstate Conflicts: An Empirical Analysis," *International Organization*, Vol. 28, No. 4 (Autumn 1974).

5. See James Caporaso, "Dependence, Dependency and Power in the Global System: A Structural and Behavioral Analysis," *International Organization*, Vol. 32, No. 1 (Winter 1978), pp. 13-44.

6. These documents have been obtained by the author under the U.S. Freedom of Information Act.

7. This is not to imply that anyone ought to accept the sorts of exaggerated claims made in recent years by some U.S. groups and individuals about the extent of negative economic effects

Canada–United States Energy Trade: Canadian Law and Policy

Constance D. Hunt

1. Introduction: A Canadian View of American Law

Given the overall thrust of this volume, it may be appropriate to offer a few preliminary remarks about how Canadian lawyers view the United States, or about how Canadian legal scholars perceive the American legal system. Although many Canadian lawyers study in the United States, they often use the experience to enhance their understanding of *Canadian* law. For example, while I was a graduate student at Harvard Law School some ten years ago, my Canadian colleagues tended to write theses about Canadian legal topics. We were exposed to American law in the classroom but seemed reluctant to embark upon in-depth critiques of American law and institutions.

What are the reasons for this reluctance? Canadian and American law have the same roots, namely, the English common law. However, American law diverged from these roots both earlier and more radically than did Canadian law. Moreover, the American system has been affected dramatically by the United States Constitution and the Bill of Rights, two factors that have distinguished it from the Canadian system. Thus, a Canadian studying American law experiences feelings of strangeness on the one hand, and familiarity on the other. This alone, however, does not adequately explain the paucity of Canadian scholarship about American law.

A better explanation may lie in the fact that Canadian legal scholarship is, in many respects, still in its infancy. This was one of the conclusions of a 1983 report, *Law and Learning*, which studied the state of Canadian legal research.[1] The report also pointed out that there has been remarkably little study, by English-Canadian common law scholars, of Canada's "other" legal system—the civil law system of Quebec. The same point emerged with regard to studies of the common law system by French-Canadian lawyers. If we spend so little time understanding the law and institutions of our own country, perhaps it is not surprising that we have found even less to examine the American system.

It is not that Canadian legal scholars have not scrutinized American law. However, they have tended to do so from a comparative, as opposed to critical, framework. Their enquiries have usually been based on the notion that legal problems in the United States will also emerge in Canada, and that, therefore, American legal solutions ought to be studied with a view to their possible application in Canada.

It is interesting to speculate about future possibilities for Canadian scholarship about American law— scholarship that would focus not on solutions that American law offers to Canada, but rather on questions such as: "How does American law look from a Canadian perspective?"; or "What impact does American law have upon Canada?"; and "What can Canadian legal experiences offer by way of solutions to American problems?" Two examples may help to point out the richness of the possibilities.

First, the new Canadian Charter of Rights and Freedoms has adopted some of its language from the United States Bill of Rights. Canadian lawyers have become eager to study American jurisprudence and interpretation and to use it in arguing cases under the Canadian Charter.[2] As the Canadian jurisprudence develops and grows, perhaps this process can also occur in reverse, with American lawyers and judges learning from the Canadian application and interpretation of words and phrases similar to those found in the United States Bill of Rights.

Second, as a result of the 1982 *Ocean Ranger* disaster, Canadian lawyers have been exposed to the vagaries of American civil litigation.[3] For many, this experience has been a great shock. The control that American lawyers exercise over the direction of law suits, through arrangements for contingency fees, is repugnant to many Canadian-trained lawyers. The complexity inherent in the United States' dual (federal-state) court system is mystifying. The resulting delays are grossly inefficient both in time and financial terms. Indian lawyers are doubtless now experiencing similar reactions, as a result of the gas leak in Bhopal and the ensuing litigation. Given our common language and largely common value systems, perhaps Canadian lawyers are uniquely well-placed to offer Americans a useful perspective on the legal fall-out from such controversies.

The topic of this essay, however, is not American law and policy. Rather, it is Canadian law and policy in the context of the petroleum industry and attempts by American law and policy to influence it. The thesis is that in the early days of Canadian petroleum development, before our resources were integrated with the energy needs of the American state, Canadian law was resistant to American influence. As Canadian energy resources began to feed American appetites, our public law institutions continued their attempts to be independent of American legal and regulatory influence. Private law arrangements, however, were less resistant. In the more recent era, it appears that both private and public law mechanisms have succumbed somewhat to the pressures of the American marketplace, and attempts at

Canadian independence have been largely abandoned. What this may mean for the future is, of course, a matter for speculation.

The period of time canvassed in this essay is relatively short, being less than four decades. The first era (from the late 1940s to the early 1970s) saw the early exploration and development of petroleum resources in western Canada. During this stage, the influence of the law was felt primarily in the context of private arrangements, as the courts were called upon to interpret and apply individual petroleum contracts.

The second era extended from the early 1970s to the early 1980s. It was characterized by the perceived energy crisis and by the rise of Canadian nationalism. By then, networks of natural gas pipelines had been built from Canada to the United States, and natural gas trade had become well established. During this period, Canadian policy-makers were under some pressure to respond to American consumption needs and pricing perceptions but tried to resist such forces. In contrast, private contractual arrangements (as exemplified by the TOPGAS Agreement) were altered to accommodate the reality of the American marketplace.

The third era, the current one, is characterized by a free market philosophy on both sides of the border. American policy has very much influenced the direction recently taken by Canadian decision-makers in regard to natural gas trade, and American protectionism has contributed to a massive reordering of private contractual relationships. Thus, the public and private law mechanisms that govern natural gas exports to the United States are presently in considerable harmony, both having been substantially re-shaped by American market forces.

2. Era One: Petroleum Exploration and Development

Although natural gas was discovered at Turner Valley in the 1920s, it was not until the major oil discovery at Leduc in the late 1940s that the petroleum industry started to become an important part of the western Canadian economy.[4] Since American multinationals dominated early exploration efforts, it is not surprising that the basic legal document pursuant to which wells were drilled in this development period, the freehold oil and gas lease, was modelled largely upon a document that had been used widely in Oklahoma, Kansas, and Texas.[5]

This lease form, the Producers 88, had been designed for situations where lessees (typically oil companies) had obtained rights to more oil and gas exploration areas than they could reasonably explore in the time available. In order to avoid obligations to make rental payments when lessees chose to forgo these rights, the lease form was set up so that, upon failure to pay, the lease automatically terminated.

In Canada, however, freehold leases were procured by oil companies in many areas where lessees wished to retain rights, even though, through inadvertence, payments were missed or the strict terms of the leases were otherwise abrogated. As a result, by the late 1950s, Canadian courts were being called upon to interpret and apply leases which were derived from the American Producers 88. Given the origin of these documents, one might have expected the Canadian courts to be heavily influenced by the established American jurisprudence.

In general, however, this temptation was resisted, particularly by the Supreme Court of Canada. For example, in *Canada Cities Service Petroleum Corp.* v. *Kinninmouht*,[6] the lessee relied upon several American authorities to support its position that the lease in question had not terminated, despite the fact that no well had been drilled within the time required by the lease terms. In refusing to follow the American authorities, Mr. Justice Martland observed: "However, irrespective of what construction may have been placed by courts upon other leases, the essential task in the present case is to construe the terms of the lease which is in question ... (I)n my opinion, the lease terminated ... ."[7]

Canadian courts have followed their own path in interpreting oil and gas contracts in other ways. For example, American courts have been willing to read into petroleum leases certain "implied covenants," an approach that has also been largely resisted in Canada.[8] Furthermore, Canadian courts, unlike their American counterparts, have refused to grant property status to many types of royalties commonly created in petroleum contracts.[9]

The result of this judicial restraint in following American legal precedent has been that Canadian lawyers have had to redraft the earlier American petroleum contracts, taking into consideration the views of Canadian judges as to their interpretation. In this way, both Canadian petroleum law and, to some degree, Canadian petroleum contractual practices have diverged from those of the United States. Arguably, this has led to the development of Canadian oil and gas law and practices that reflect local circumstances and conditions.

At the same time as the Canadian courts were responding to private law problems engendered by the establishment of the petroleum industry, Canadian energy resources were being integrated with American needs.[10] In 1957, Westcoast Transmission Company began deliveries of natural gas to the border at Sumas, Washington. In 1961, California received its first Canadian gas, which originated from the Alberta and Southern Gas Co. Ltd. system in Canada. Some eastern American markets began to receive Canadian gas through a spur line from the TransCanada Pipeline system.

The latter project proved extremely controversial.[11] As a direct result of this pipeline debate, the National Energy Board (NEB) was established.[12] It became the body responsible for certifying oil and gas pipelines of an interprovincial or international nature, and for overseeing the export from Canada of energy resources such as oil and natural gas. The construction of the TransCanada Pipeline also involved some participation by the United States Federal Power Commission, since proponents of the project wished to import United States gas into eastern Canada (in order to develop markets) in advance of the pipeline's completion. They also wished to build a spur line into Minnesota and Wisconsin in order to realize early revenues that would help finance the eastern Canadian part of the line. Regulatory delays in the United States on these proposals further complicated a project whose scope and size had already created heated debate in Canada. Thus, by the early 1960s, the influence of public law and regulatory bodies in regard to energy trade was being felt on both sides of the border.

3. Era Two: Energy Crisis and Canadian Nationalism

During the 1960s, large quantities of western Canadian gas were committed to American markets pursuant to long-term private contracts entered into by Canadian producers.[13] These exports were licensed by the NEB, but the prices were set primarily by market forces. By the early 1970s, this relatively open-ended situation had been altered in two ways. First, in 1970 the Board developed a formula for determining if and when gas proposed for export could be considered to be surplus to Canadian needs.[14] This test, known as the 25A$_4$ Formula, was designed to protect Canada's reasonably foreseeable natural gas needs. Over time its application resulted in some curtailment of gas exports to the United States. This test was replaced in 1979 with a new three part surplus test.

Secondly, by the early 1970s concerns began to develop about the low price at which Canadian natural gas was being sold to the United States. This marked the beginning of a temporary halt to gas export pricing by private agreement.[15] In 1975, the NEB held a hearing on gas export pricing and thereafter recommended border price increases to Cabinet. In 1976, the NEB proposed further price increases, which were strongly opposed by the United States government. Increases were implemented, but ultimately they were applied uniformly to all export gas, as requested by the United States government, and not on the differentiated basis recommended by the National Energy Board. In 1977, Canada began to use the concept of "substitution value." Under this method, the gas export price was tied to the cost of alternative fuels. Since energy costs were escalating, this resulted in six border price increases in the period between 1977 and 1981—from Can$1.94 to U.S.$4.94 per MMBtu. The United States government questioned an increase proposed in January 1980 (from U.S.$3.45 to U.S.$4.47 per MMBtu). As a result of letters exchanged between the Canadian Minister of Energy and his American counterpart, export gas continued to be priced on the substitution value concept, but alterations to the price would be made only when a change of more than U.S.$0.15 was indicated by application of the formula. Under this formula, one increase occurred in April, 1981.

The gradual tightening of Canadian regulatory control over gas exports in the 1970s, both as to quantity and price, reflected public perception and reality both in Canada and the United States. The energy crisis of 1973 raised serious concerns in Canada about its own future self-sufficiency. In the United States, on the other hand, gas shortages sent pipeline companies and others scurrying to find new sources of supply in other countries and in such frontier areas as the Arctic. The Alaska oil discoveries generated several controversial proposals for energy pipelines traversing Canada from the Arctic. The energy crisis also resulted in dramatic increases in energy prices and gave rise to concerns that Canadian export resources were grossly underpriced. Canadian regulators acted to protect their view of the Canadian public interest. They were somewhat responsive to American complaints on certain issues but retained a relatively independent stance in their pursuit of policy objectives.

As the 1970s drew to a close, however, the situation began to change, especially with regard to natural gas. Rather than the shortages experienced earlier, and still anticipated, American markets became flooded with cheap natural gas. In 1982, after a substantial period of criticism, the NEB relaxed its surplus test for gas exports. By then, however, American demand had slackened considerably. Nevertheless, border prices remained tied to the substitution value concept and were relatively high compared to the price at which other gas had become available to American purchasers.

As indicated earlier, Canadian producers had committed their gas to purchasers under long-term contracts. A large amount of this gas (for example, some of that sold to carriers such as Alberta and Southern, and TransCanada) was destined for the United States market. Although the price of such export gas could not be negotiated between sellers and buyers, since it was regulated by the NEB, most such contracts contained "take-or-pay" clauses. These provide that the purchaser must either buy, or pay for, annually committed amounts of gas. If gas was paid for, but not taken, the purchaser would attempt, in the future, to recover the gas. Such clauses are intended to protect the producer from bearing all the market risk and to assure the producer a minimum level of cash flow.

In the early 1980s, as a result of some of the factors described above, certain American gas purchasers refused to honour their contractual obligations.[16] Various legal arguments have been put forward to support their positions, and in some cases the disputes are still before the United States courts. These actions reverberated through the entire natural gas industry and eventually affected Canadian pipeline companies shipping to the United States. On the one hand, their purchasers refused to take contractual volumes. On the other hand, Canadian pipeline companies were bound to Canadian producers by virtue of take-or-pay clauses.

A reduction in the export price of gas might have aided the situation, but Canadian regulators were slow to respond. Instead, major shippers of export gas negotiated arrangements with Canadian producers to reduce the extent of take-or-pay obligations. In the case of TransCanada Pipelines, the result was a comprehensive agreement involving itself, a consortium of bankers, and most of TransCanada's purchasers.[17] This 1982 TOPGAS Agreement (and a subsequent amendment to it) modified some 2 400 gas purchase contracts in Canada, and, in some cases, resulted in a reduction to TransCanada's take-or-pay obligations by as much as 50 per cent. The arrangement enabled Canadian shippers to avoid protracted litigation with purchasers in the United States. At the same time, however, Canadian producers experienced a severe dilution of their strict contractual rights. In 1983, the Canadian government introduced a reduction in the border price of natural gas from U.S.$4.94 per MMBtu to U.S.$4.40. It then implemented a system of discounting the price of gas sold in large volumes (the Volume-Related Incentive Pricing program or VRIP). These regulatory changes, however, came some time after the type of private reordering exemplified by the TOPGAS Agreement had already taken place. It is an illustration of the fact that, even though during this era Canadian public law mechanisms were slow to respond to a changing American marketplace, private contracting parties found ingenious ways to deal with the newly created circumstances.

4. Era Three: Let the Market Govern

Throughout the difficult period of the early 1980s, American and Canadian regulators and the natural gas industry strained to come to grips with the reality of a gas glut in the United States market. One result was that, late in 1982, the United States and Canadian governments commenced informal discussions on the natural gas trade.[18] The United States–Canadian Energy Consultative Mechanism (ECM), a forum established in 1979 for periodic exchanges on bilateral energy issues, was also reactivated.[19]

At the same time the United States undertook a review of its policy on gas imports. Section 3 of the Natural Gas Act of 1978 required the American government to authorize the import of natural gas, unless "the proposed importation will not be consistent with the public interest." Since Congress did not define the "public interest" in this context, it was left to the Economic Regulatory Administration of the Department of Energy to do so.[20] This occurred in February, 1984.[21]

The cornerstone of the new U.S. policy on gas imports is competition. Buyers and sellers are free to negotiate their own import contracts, but such contracts will not receive regulatory approval unless they meet the new guidelines. Although the guidelines do not apply to already-approved imports, they do apply to renewal applications. Thus their effect on Canadian exports is massive. One important point of these guidelines is that the gas purchase contract must provide a supply of gas that the importer can market competitively over the term of the contract: "The contract arrangement must be sufficiently flexible to permit pricing and volume adjustments, as required by market conditions and available competing fuels, including domestic natural gas."[22] Following this, the Federal Energy Regulatory Commission (FERC) issued its Order No. 380, which severely weakened take-or-pay clauses in export/import contracts.[23]

Canadian regulators perceived that, in view of the new American import policy, changes in Canadian regulatory approaches were almost mandatory: the access of Canadian sellers to American markets would be severely curtailed, unless Canadian sellers were permitted to strike deals with the United

States buyers that would satisfy the new American policy. Thus, in July 1984, the Canadian minister responsible for energy announced changes in gas export pricing policy effective 1 November 1984. Under the new policy, gas sellers may apply to the NEB to amend existing gas export licences.[24] The export price in such contracts may differ from the government-imposed border price, so long as certain conditions are met. The export price must not be less than the price of gas at the Toronto city gate and must at least equal the price of major competing sources in the United States market area. Most importantly, the new Canadian policy effectively tracks the United States policy by requiring that such contracts contain provisions which permit adjustments to reflect changing market conditions over the life of the contract. Somewhat ironically, in view of the recent history of broken take-or-pay obligations, the exporter must also show that there is a reasonable assurance that volumes contracted will be taken. Immediately, when the new policy came into effect, contract amendments, embracing price reductions, were approved in regard to six major Canadian gas shippers to the United States.[25] These contracts govern nearly 80 per cent of Canada's gas exports.

That the new Canadian policy was directly responsive to the American policy is made evident by the remarks of Geoffrey Edge, chairman of the National Energy Board: "The Board's procedures provided for an expedited review of such contracts in order to try and facilitate their approval by 1 November 1984, otherwise Canada could have lost millions of dollars in gas sales. FERC Order No. 380 would have caused a dramatic reduction in sales in 1984/85 under the Volume-Related Incentive Pricing Scheme, whereas the new Canadian policy was designed to regain sales volumes lost in previous years."[26]

Thus, in the current era, competition is the order of the day. The "free market" environment, which has permeated the thinking of American gas regulators, has been greeted in kind by Canadian regulators. It has also been embraced by private parties through their contract renegotiations. It is somewhat ironical, perhaps, that, despite this rapid adjustment by Canadians to American thinking, some American gas producers are now complaining that Canadian exports are priced *too* competitively, and that Canadian producers are engaged in what has been termed "predatory pricing practices."[27] Nevertheless, in the view of at least one American writer, Canadians have something special to offer: "There is another factor which works against the entry of Canadians into a debilitating price war with American gas producers. For want of a better word I would call this factor the 'gentlemanliness' of gas men in Canada (there are few women). Canadians are possessed of a reasonableness and care that have no match in the U.S.A. There is a basic, genuine and attractive quality about Canadians that makes them good long term trade partners."[28]

5. Conclusion

Over the past four decades there has been a noticeable shift away from Canadian efforts to be independent of American law and policy in the energy field. In the developing days of the petroleum industry, Canadian courts were reluctant to rely upon American jurisprudence to interpret contractual terms in documents that had originated in the United States. This judicial independence, however, had no major economic implications. During the energy crisis era, Canadian regulators imposed restrictions both on the quantity and price of natural gas being exported to the United States. To a considerable degree, this was done without major influence applied by the American government. Near the end of this period, however, American market forces began to intercede. Canadian regulatory mechanisms were slow to respond, particularly with regard to gas pricing, but private arrangements nevertheless underwent massive reordering to accommodate the new circumstances. More recently, American protectionist moves vis-à-vis gas imports have led to major United States government policy changes. Canadian regulators have been quick to amend their gas export policies, thus permitting private contractual arrangements to complement American policy.

It is probably too soon to say exactly what this trend implies for Canadians. It may mean that, over the long term, American commercial forces are too strong to be resisted by either the private or public sectors in Canada. It might suggest that, despite the efforts of the Canadian nationalists in the 1970s, a North American energy policy is inevitable. Perhaps Canadians are too possessed of "gentlemanliness" and "reasonableness" to assess the difference between their own short-term and long-term interests. Whatever the trend bodes for the future, it seems obvious that both the private and public sectors in Canada might deal more effectively with American regulatory and commercial forces, if they were able to develop a more uniquely Canadian view of how such forces operate and what propels them.

Notes

1. *Law and Learning. Report to the Social Sciences and Humanities Research Council of Canada by the Consultative Group on Research and Education in Law* (Ottawa: Minister of Supply and Services Canada, 1983).
2. An example of this approach in the resources law field is D. Estrin and H. Dahme, "Regulatory Hearing Reform—Legal Principles of 'Fairness,' Timely Access to Information and a Constitutional Right to Funding of Public Participation," in *Facility Siting and Routing '84 Energy and Environment*, 15-18 April 1984, Banff, Alta., Proceedings, Vol. 2, p. 507 (Ottawa: Minister of Supply and Services Canada 1984).
3. The accident occurred on 14 February 1982, off the coast of Newfoundland. It involved the total loss of crew of eighty-four men, as well as the rig itself.
4. For a general discussion of the history of petroleum development in Canada, see Earle Gray, *Impact of Oil* (Toronto: McGraw-Hill Ryerson Limited/MacLean Hunter Ltd. 1969).

5. See generally, John Bishop Ballem, *The Oil and Gas Lease in Canada* (Toronto: University of Toronto Press, 1973).

6. [1964] S.C.R. 439.

7. *Idem* at 447.

8. See D. Lewis and A.R. Thompson, *Canadian Oil and Gas Law* (Toronto: Butterworths, 1971), p. 121.

9. See W.H. Ellis, "Property Status of Royalties in Canadian Oil and Gas Law." (1984) 22 Alta. L. Rev. 1.

10. See Arlon R. Tussing and Connie C. Barlow, *The Natural Gas Industry: Evolution, Structure and Economics* (Cambridge, Mass.: Ballinger Publishing Company, 1984), pp. 51*ff*.

11. *Ibid.*, p. 54.

12. See generally, William Kilbourne, *Pipeline* (Toronto: Clarke, Irwin and Company, Ltd., 1970).

13. Some statistics about these contracts are contained in Phillip Sykes, *Sellout. The Giveaway of Canada's Energy Resources* (Edmonton: Hurtig Publishers, 1973), pp. 83*ff*.

14. The history and development of the surplus test is outlined in Constance D. Hunt and Alastair R. Lucas, *Canada Energy Law Service* (Toronto: Richard DeBoo Publishers, 1983), I, 10-1553*ff*.

15. For a more detailed description of pricing changes see *ibid.*, I, 10-1557*ff*, and *Federal Register*, 22 February 1984, Part VII, Department of Energy, "Natural Gas Imports; Policy Guidelines and Delegation Orders; Procedural Orders."

16. Tussing and Barlow, *The National Gas Industry*, *op. cit.*, p. 174.

17. The TOPGAS Agreement and its amendment are reviewed in detail in J. Jay Park, "Developments in Natural Gas Purchase Contracts," (1984) 22 Alta. L. Rev. 43.

18. *Federal Register*, 22 February 1984, Part VII, p. 6686.

19. The ECM is described more fully in C. Geoffrey Edge, "United States-Canada Energy Trade," (1984) 6 *Geopolitics of Energy* 1 at 3.

20. *Federal Register*, 22 February 1984, Part VII, p. 6687.

21. *Ibid.*

22. *Ibid.*, p. 6688.

23. C. Geoffrey Edge, "Observations on the Renegotiated Contracts for the Export of Canadian Natural Gas," a speech presented to the Natural Resources Section of the Canadian Bar Association, 11 April 1985, Calgary, Alta., p. 2.

24. National Energy Board, Memorandum to gas export licence holders, NEB File 537-1, 2 October 1984.

25. National Energy Board, News Release, 2 November 1984, "Important Negotiated Gas Export Prices and Contract Amendments Approved."

26. Edge, *op. cit.*, "Observations on the Renegotiated Contracts for the Export of Canadian Natural Gas," p. 3.

27. "Canadian gas pricing is not predatory," *Oilweek*, 25 March 1985, p. 7.

28. "Freeing up oil and gas markets," *Oilweek*, 13 May 1985, p. 3, quoting the American writer, Jerry Brady.

Bibliography

The books listed here are a broad sample of those that form a core of Canadian writing on the United States. They are, as one might expect, of a predominantly comparative nature. Many of them, especially the more recent, provide extensive bibliographies that could be of great assistance to those wishing to pursue further study.

H.G.J. Aitken, *American Capital and Canadian Resources* (Cambridge: Harvard University Press, 1961).

Willis C. Armstrong, Louise S. Armstrong, and Francis C. Wilcox, *Canada and the United States: Dependence and Divergence* (Cambridge Mass.: Ballinger, 1982).

W.A. Axline, J. Hyndman, P. Lyon, and M.A. Molot, *Continental Community: Independence and Integration in North America* (Toronto: McClelland and Stewart, 1974).

Carl E. Beigie, *The Canada-U.S. Automotive Agreement* (Montreal and Washington: Canadian-American Committee, 1970)).

Richard P. Bowles, James L. Hanley, Bruce W. Hodgins, and George A. Rawlyk, eds., *Canada and the U.S.: Continental Partners or Wary Neighbours?* (Scarborough, Ont.: Prentice-Hall, 1973).

John E. Carroll, *Acid Rain: An Issue in Canadian-American Relations* (Washington and Montreal: Canadian-American Committee, 1982).

————, *Environmental Diplomacy* (Ann Arbor: University of Michigan Press, 1983).

Stephen Clarkson, *Canada and the Reagan Challenge: Crisis and Adjustment 1981–1985*, rev. ed. (Toronto: James Lorimer and Co., 1985).

————, ed., *An Independent Foreign Policy for Canada?* (Toronto: McClelland and Stewart, 1968).

Wallace Clement, *Continental Corporate Power: Economic Elite Images Between Canada and the United States* (Toronto: McClelland and Stewart, 1977).

Ramsay Cook, *The Maple Leaf Forever: Essays on Nationalism and Politics in Canada* (Toronto: Macmillan, 1971).

233

Percy E. Corbett, *The Settlement of Canadian-American Disputes: A Critical Study of Methods and Results* (New Haven, Conn.: Yale University Press, 1937).

Ralph K. Cowan, ed., *The North American Automobile Industry: Shaping a Dynamic Global Posture*, Proceedings of the 25th Annual Seminar on Canadian-American Relations (Windsor, Ont.: Institute for Canadian-American Studies, 1983).

Gerald M. Craig, *The United States and Canada* (Cambridge, Mass.: Harvard University Press, 1968).

Robert D. Cuff, *The War Industries Board; Business Government Relations during World War I* (Baltimore: Johns Hopkins University Press, 1973).

———— and J.L. Granatstein, *Ties that Bind: Canadian-American Relations in Wartime. From the Great War to the Cold War*, 2nd ed. (Toronto: Samuel Stevens, Hakkert and Co., 1977).

Kenneth M. Curtis and John E. Carroll, *Canadian-American Relations: The Promise and the Challenge* (Lexington, Mass.: Lexington Books, 1983).

Charles F. Doran, *Economic Interdependence, Autonomy, and Canadian/American Relations* (Montreal: Institute for Research on Public Policy, 1983).

————, *Forgotten Partnership: U.S.–Canada Relations Today* (Baltimore and London: Johns Hopkins University Press, 1984).

———— and John H. Sigler, eds., *Canada and the United States: Enduring Friendship, Persistent Stress* (Englewood Cliffs, N.J.: Prentice-Hall, 1985).

D.R. Deener, ed., *Canada–United States Treaty Relations* (Duke University Commonwealth Studies Center: Duke University Press, 1963).

John Sloan Dickey, ed., *The United States and Canada* (Englewood Cliffs, N.J.: Prentice-Hall, 1964).

O.P. Dwivedi, ed., *Resources and the Environment: Policy Perspectives for Canada* (Toronto: McClelland and Stewart, 1980).

H. Edward English, ed., *Canada–United States Relations*, (New York: Proceedings of the Academy of Political Science, 1976).

————, Bruce W. Wilkinson, and H.C. Eastman, *Canada in a Wider Economic Community* (Toronto: University of Toronto Press, 1972).

Elliot J. Feldman and Neil Nevitte, eds., *The Future of North America: Canada, The United States and Quebec Nationalism* (Cambridge, Mass.: Center for International Affairs, Harvard University; Montreal: Institute for Research on Public Policy, 1979).

J.L. Finlay, *Canada in the North Atlantic Triangle* (Toronto: Oxford University Press, 1975).

Annette Baker Fox, *The Politics of Attraction* (New York: Columbia University Press, 1977).

————, Alfred O. Hero Jr., and Joseph Nye, *Canada and the United States Transnational and Transgovernmental Relations* (New York: Columbia University Press, 1976).

Earl H. Fry and Lee H. Radebaugh, eds., *Regulation of Foreign Direct Investment in Canada and the United States* (Provo, Utah: Brigham Young University, 1983).

Steven Globerman, *Cultural Regulation in Canada* (Montreal: Institute for Research on Public Policy, 1983).

————, *U.S. Ownership of Firms in Canada* (Montreal, C.D. Howe Institute, 1979).

Walter L. Gordon, *What is Happening to Canada* (Toronto: McClelland and Stewart, 1978).

Allan E. Gotlieb, *Disarmament and International Law: A Study of the Role of Law in the Disarmament Process* (Toronto: Canadian Institute of International Affairs, 1965).

J.L. Granatstein, ed., *Canadian Foreign Policy Since 1945: Middle Power or Satellite* (Toronto: Copp Clark, 1969).

———— and R.D. Cuff, eds., *War and Society in North America* (Toronto: T. Nelson, 1971).

George Grant, *Lament for a Nation: The Defeat of Canadian Nationalism* (Toronto: McClelland and Stewart, 1965).

Rodney de C. Grey, *Trade Policy in the 1980s: An Agenda for Canadian–U.S. Relations* (Montreal: C.D. Howe Institute, 1981).

————, *United States Trade Policy Legislation: A Canadian View* (Montreal: Institute for Research on Public Policy, 1982).

Richard Gwyn, *The 49th Paradox: Canada in North America* (Toronto: McClelland and Stewart, 1985)

Craig Heron, ed., *Imperialism, Nationalism and Canada* (Toronto: New Hogtown Press, 1977).

J.M. Hitsman, *Safeguarding Canada, 1763–1871* (Toronto: University of Toronto Press, 1968).

John W. Holmes, *Life with Uncle* (Toronto: University of Toronto Press, 1981).

John Hutcheson, *Dominance and Dependancy: Liberalism and National Politics in the North Atlantic Triangle* (Toronto: McClelland and Stewart, 1978).

Hugh L. Keenleyside and Gerald S. Brown, *Canada and the United States: Some Aspects of their Historical Relations*, rev. ed. (New York: Knopf, 1952).

Robert Keohane and Joseph Nye, *Power and Interdependence* (Boston: Little, Brown, 1977).

James Laxer, *Rethinking the Economy*, (Toronto: New Canadian Publications, 1984).

Robert M. Laxer, ed., *(Canada) Ltd.,: The Political Economy of Dependency* (Toronto: McClelland and Stewart, 1973).

Fred Lazar, *The New Protectionism: Non-Tariff Barriers and their Effects for Canada* (Toronto: J. Lorimer, 1981).

James T. Lemon, *The Best Poor Man's Country: A Geographical Study of Early Southeastern Pennsylvania* (Baltimore: Johns Hopkins University Press, 1972).

K. Levitt, *Silent Surrender: The Multinational Corporation in Canada* (Toronto: Macmillan of Canada, 1970).

David Leyton-Brown, *Weathering the Storm: Canadian-American Relations 1980–83* (Washington, D.C. and Toronto: Canadian-American Committee, 1985).

Richard G. Lipsey and Murray G. Smith, *Taking the Initiative: Canada's Trade Options in a Turbulent World* (Toronto: C.D. Howe Institute, 1985).

I. Litvak, C. Maule, and R.D. Robinson, *Dual Loyalty: Canadian–U.S. Business Arrangements* (Toronto, New York: McGraw-Hill, 1971).

Ian Lumsden, ed., *Close the 49th Parallel: The Americanization of Canada* (Toronto: University of Toronto Press, 1970).

Peyton V. Lyon, *Canada-United States Free Trade and Canadian Independence* (Ottawa: Economic Council of Canada, 1975).

Helen G. MacDonald, *Canadian Public Opinion of the American Civil War* (New York: Columbia University Press, 1926).

Edelgard E. Mahant and Graeme S. Mount, *An Introduction to Canadian-American Relations* (Toronto: Methuen, 1984).

William R. McKercher, ed., *The U.S. Bill of Rights and The Canadian Charter of Rights and Freedoms* (Toronto: Ontario Economic Council, 1983).

Livingston T. Merchant, ed., *Neighbours Taken for Granted: Canada and the United States* (New York: Praeger, 1966).

S.E. Moffett, *The Americanization of Canada* (Toronto: University of Toronto Press, 1972).

Janet Morchain, *Sharing a Continent* (Toronto: McGraw-Hill Ryerson, 1973).

Peter Morici, *The Global Competitive Struggle: Challenges to the United States and Canada* (Washington D.C. and Toronto: Canadian-American Committee, 1984).

Janice Murray, ed., *Canadian Cultural Nationalism* (New York: New York University Press, 1977).

Caroline Pestieau, *The Sector Approach to Trade Negotiations: Canadian and U.S. Relations* (Montreal: C.D. Howe Institute, 1976).

R.A. Preston, ed., *The Influence of the United States on Canadian Development* (Durham, N.C.: Duke University Press, 1972).

John Quinn and Philip Slayton, eds., *Non-Tariff Barriers After the Tokyo Round* (Montreal: Institute for Research on Public Policy, 1982).

Stephen J. Randall, *The Diplomacy of Modernization: Columbian American Politics* (Toronto: University of Toronto Press, 1977).

John Redekop, ed., *The Star Spangled Beaver* (Toronto: Peter Martin Associates, 1971).

A. Rotstein and G. Lax, eds., *Independence: The Canadian Challenge* (Toronto: Committee for an Independent Canada, 1972).

Royal Commission on the Economic Union and Development Prospects for Canada. *Report.* 73 vols. (Toronto: University of Toronto Press, 1985).

Peter H. Russell, ed., *Nationalism in Canada* (Toronto: McGraw-Hill, 1966).

Richard J. Schultz, *Federalism and the Regulatory Process* (Montreal: Institute for Research on Public Policy, 1979).

E. Shaffer, *Canada's Oil and the American Empire* (Edmonton: Hurtig Publishers Ltd., 1983).

Robert Spencer, John Kirton, and Kim Richard Nossal, eds., *The International Joint Commission Seventy Years On* (Toronto: Centre for International Studies, 1981).

Denis Stairs, *The Diplomacy of Constraint: Canada, the Korean War and the United States* (Toronto: University of Toronto Press, 1974).

Frank Stone, *Canada, the GATT and the International Trade System* (Montreal: Institute for Research on Public Policy, 1984).

Roger Frank Swanson, *Canadian-American Summit Diplomacy, 1923–1973* (Toronto: McClelland and Stewart, 1975).

Richard S. Thoman, *The United States and Canada* (Columbus: Merrill, 1978).

Allen Tupper and G. Bruce Doern, eds., *Public Corporations and Public Policy in Canada* (Montreal: Institute for Research on Public Policy, 1981).

James R.Warren, *Wartime Economic Co-operation* (Toronto: Ryerson Press, 1949).

Roger N.Williams, *The New Exiles* (New York: Liveright Publishers, 1971).

Robert W. Winks, *Canada and the United States: The Civil War Years* (Baltimore: Johns Hopkins Press, 1960).

R.J. Wonnacott, *Canada/United States Free Trade: Problems and Opportunities* (Toronto: Ontario Economic Council, 1985).

———and Paul Wonnacott, *Free Trade Between the United States and Canada, the Potential Economic Effects* (Cambridge: Harvard University Press, 1967).

Contributors

RUSSELL S. BOYER is Professor of Economics at the University of Western Ontario. He has held visiting professorships at the London School of Economics and Carnegie-Mellon University. He has published numerous articles in professional journals.

PETER BUITENHUIS is Professor of English at Simon Fraser University. He is author of *The Grasping Imagination: The American Writings of Henry James* (1970).

DAVID H. FLAHERTY is Professor of History and Law at the University of Western Ontario and Director of its Centre for American Studies. He is the author of *Protecting Privacy in Two-Way Electronic Services* (1985).

MICHAEL A. GOLDBERG is the Herbert R. Fullerton Professor of Urban Land Policy and Associate Dean, Faculty of Commerce, University of British Columbia. With John Mercer, he has written *The Myth of the North American City: Continentalism Challenged* (1985).

ALLAN GOTLIEB, O.C., has been Canadian Ambassador to the United States of America since 1981. He was educated at the University of California, Harvard Law School, and Oxford University. He joined the Department of External Affairs in 1957, and was Under-Secretary of State for External Affairs, 1977–81. He is author of *Human Rights, Federalism and Minorities* (1970).

F. KENNETH HARE, O.C., is Provost of Trinity College and University Professor Emeritus in Geography at the University of Toronto. He chaired the Royal Society of Canada committee that produced *Nuclear Winter and Associated Effects: A Canadian Appraisal of the Environmental Impact of Nuclear War* (1985).

CONSTANCE D. HUNT is Executive Director of the Canadian Institute of Resources Law, and Professor of Law at the University of Calgary. She is co-author of *Canada Energy Law Service* (1981).

WILLIAM D.H. JOHNSON has been Washington correspondent for *The Globe and*

Mail since 1984. From 1978 to 1984, he was national correspondent in Quebec for the same newspaper.

JOHN J. KIRTON is Associate Professor of Political Science, University of Toronto, and Associate Director of Research, the Canadian Institute of International Affairs. He is co-author of *Canada as a Principal Power: A Study in Foreign Policy and International Relations* (1983).

JAMES T. LEMON is Professor of Geography at the University of Toronto. He is the author of *Toronto Since 1918: An Illustrated History* (1985).

DAVID LEYTON-BROWN is Associate Professor of Political Science at York University and Acting Director of its Research Programme in Strategic Studies. He is the author of *Weathering the Storm: Canadian-American Relations, 1980–83* (1985).

WILLIAM R. McKERCHER is Assistant Professor of Political Science at King's College, University of Western Ontario. He is editor of *The U.S. Bill of Rights and the Canadian Charter of Rights and Freedoms* (1983).

JOHN MEISEL is the Sir Edward Peacock Professor of Political Science at Queen's University, and former Chairman of the Canadian Radio-television and Telecommunications Commission.

DONALD J. MUNTON is currently in the Political Science Department at the University of British Columbia. From 1981 to 1985, he was the Director of Research at the Canadian Institute of International Affairs and a Senior Fellow at Trinity College in Toronto. He is writing a book on Canada–United States relations focused particularly on environment issues.

DENIS SMITH is Dean of the Faculty of Social Science and Professor of Political Science at the University of Western Ontario. He is the author of *Gentle Patriot* (1973).

STUART L. SMITH, M.D., is Chairman of the Science Council of Canada. He was formerly leader of the Liberal Party of Ontario.

JOHN WHALLEY is Professor of Economics at the University of Western Ontario, and Director of its Centre for the Study of International Economic Relations. He is the author of *Trade Liberalization Among Major World Trading Areas* (1985).

BRUCE WILKINSON is Professor of Economics at the University of Alberta. He is the author of *Canada in the Changing World Economy* (1980).

HAROLD E. WYATT is Vice-Chairman of The Royal Bank of Canada, based in Calgary. Until 1985, he was co-chairman of the Committee on Canada–United States Relations of the Canadian and American Chambers of Commerce.

Index